TEXAS FORGOTTEN PORTS

VOL. II

Books by the Author

Texas Forgotten Ports, Vol. I

Texas Forgotten Ports, Vol. II

Texas Forgotten Ports, Vol. III
(Publication Summer, 1994)

The Legend of Chipita

History of San Patricio County

River Ports on Red, Brazos, and Rio Grande Rivers
Landings on Caddo Lake, Ports of Jefferson, Houston, and Galveston
Buffalo Bayou Landings, San Luis, Freebooters

TEXAS FORGOTTEN PORTS

VOL. II

By Keith Guthrie

Illustrated by Iris Guthrie

EAKIN PRESS ★ Austin, Texas

FIRST EDITION

Published in the United States of America
By Eakin Press, P.O. Drawer 90159, Austin, TX 78709

A Division of Sunbelt Media, Inc.

ISBN 0-89015-878-9

Library of Congress Cataloging-in-Publication Data
(Revised for vol. 2 and 3)

Guthrie, Keith.
Texas forgotten ports.

Includes bibliographical references and indexes.
Contents: v. 1. Mid Gulf coast ports from Corpus Christi to Matagorda Bay – v. 2. River ports on Red, Brazos, and Rio Grande rivers; landings on Caddo Lake, Ports of Jefferson, Houston, and Galveston; Buffalo Bayou landings, San Luis, Freebooters – v. 3. River ports on Trinity, Neches, Angelina, and Sabine rivers; ports of Beaumont, Orange, Port Arthur, Port Neches, and Sabine Pass.
1. Gulf Region (Tex.) – History. 2. Texas – History, Local. 3. Harbors – Texas – Gulf Region – History. I. Title.
F392.G9G87 1988
976.4'1 88-16504
CIP

ISBN 0-89015-661-1 (v. 1)
ISBN 0-89015-666-1 (invalid)
ISBN 0-89015-878-9 (v. 2)
ISBN 0-89015-898-3 (v. 3)

Dedication

Proofreaders are the oil that keeps writers operating at their best. There are times when writers would like to banish them forever when they chop out a line of "deathless prose," but in the end they win out because they are right – usually. My proofreader was a navy nurse when she said, "I do." I'm sure she didn't have proofreading in mind as a second career. But she cleaned endless galleys of newspaper proofs before tackling book pages. Don't blame her for any errors: The computer did it.

Contents

Preface

Doing research for a new book is a rewarding experience because of the many interesting people you meet. Historians and librarians are a breed apart and are usually helpful in sharing material or in helping you meet people who can answer questions.

I started out to write a sequel to *Texas Forgotten Ports,* which was published in 1989 and covered the old ports from Matagorda Bay to Corpus Christi Bay. It was not long until it became apparent that the available material for a sequel would fill two volumes.

Visiting on the Red River was a new experience. On many trips that have taken us north, we have passed over the Red River, noting only that it was really red in color. Once years ago we did cross over on a ferry at New Boston, and that was an experience for our kids and us.

Images of riverboats do not necessarily come to mind as you speed over the Red River, but a stop at Clarksville will change everything. We headquartered in the public library and visited with Annette Lovett, Red River County Historical Commission chairman, and Anne Evetts, lover of history and owner of a treasure trove of information about early history of the Red River which was saved by her grandfather, E. W. Bowers, historian and former district clerk for twenty-four years. Bowers wrote extensively about the history of Red River ports and collected numerous papers pertaining to early days on the river. Mary Housler, county clerk, and Mary Kate Hale, a descendant of early river merchants, were good sources of information.

We visited in Grayson, Fannin, and Lamar counties to add to our knowledge of the Red River. The Austin College Library at Sherman was a pleasant place to research.

We stopped at the Harrison County Historical Museum in Marshall and had a profitable visit with Inez Hughes, director. Mrs. Opal Ketchum knew who to call at what time to get best results. We were fortunate in being able to talk to Franklin Jones, an attorney who loves history. He furnished us with priceless tapes dealing with rivermen in the area. Nearby, in Jefferson, the Carnegie Library was a good source of materials, as was Mrs. Katherine Wise of the Marion County Historical Society. She led us to vertical file information about the activities of rivermen on Caddo Lake, and at Monterey and Jefferson.

The Brazoria County Historical Museum in Angleton is a depository of a great deal of information about the Brazos River. Margaret Kelly and Linda Wood were eager to open their files for us, and it was through them that we became acquainted with Marie Beth Jones, newspaper writer, author, and an authority on Brazos River information. The museum is well equipped to assist in research. At the public library we made contact with an old friend, Sarah Kelso, who not only invited us to her home but loaned me her copy of the *History of Brazoria County*.

Up the river at Richmond, George Memorial Library and Michael Moore of Fort Bend Historical Museum provided guidance and a lot of help. We visited in the Hempstead Public Library. At the Navasota Public Library, Louise Keelan, assistant librarian, gave us Pam Puryear's phone number and we were able to visit with this young co-author of *Sandbars and Paddlewheelers.* She not only is a walking history book but lives in an ancestral home that dates back before the turn of the century. Ellen Murray of the Washington-on-the-Brazos State Park and Star of Republic Museum stopped her work long enough to give our research a new direction. While steamboats never visited Independence, we enjoyed a stop at the Texas Baptist Historical Museum and listened to the story about how Baptists got their start in Texas.

The Nancy Carol Roberts Memorial Library in Brenham was a good reference source. In the Bryan Public Library, Alice Nixon, reference librarian, filled our requests and visited with us about her parents in Bayside (near our hometown of Taft).

The Houston Public Library staff assisted us with a number of original papers.

We spent several days in the Rosenberg Library in Galveston. Casey Green, director of the historical room, was a big help in pointing us in the right direction. While researching in Galveston, we met Dr. Margaret S. Henson, writer and teacher, who told us about the research center in Wallisville.

The Rio Grande Valley has always been a favorite spot for us, and we enjoyed a drive from Rio Grande City to the Gulf of Mexico. You see different things when you visit libraries and museums.

Donna Hutchins, Taft librarian, handled our countless requests for books from the Texas Inter-Library Loan program. If you have not had occasion to use this program, you are missing a rare opportunity to have most of the books in Texas at your disposal. This service is invaluable in historical research, as it allows you to pore over the books at your own pace rather than having to scan rapidly on out-of-town library visits. Margaret Rose, director of local history at the Corpus Christi Public Library, always found time to help locate material for us.

If you want to meet a lot of interesting people, write a book that requires local museum and library research anywhere in Texas. You'll enjoy the trip as much as we did.

Red River

The Red River is a big part of Texas history. Its muddy waters stood in the way of the great cattle drives, just as it served as a hurdle for thousands of early Texans who forded the frothy water with their meager worldly goods. Indians who hunted and fished along its winding course were friend and foe. The river held out promise as a great waterway for trade but effectively blocked all early attempts at navigation. It was a force to be reckoned with by pioneers.

Four rivers join at different locations to finally make up the Red River: the North Fork, the Elm Fork, the Prairie Dog Town Fork, and the Salt Fork.

The North Fork rises in eastern Carson County and makes its way across Gray and Wheeler counties before plunging into Oklahoma. The Prairie Dog Town Fork is formed by a junction of Palo Duro and Tierra Blanca creeks in Randall County. As it flows southeastward through Palo Duro Canyon, it crosses Armstrong and Briscoe counties and continues eastward through Hall and Childress counties. When it crosses the 100th meridian, the river's south bank becomes the state boundary between Texas and Oklahoma and the northern line of Hardeman and Wilbarger counties to a point about twelve miles north of Vernon. There the North Fork of the Red joins the Prairie Dog Fork to officially form the Red River.

The Elm Fork rises in Wheeler County, flows southeastward through Collingsworth County and into Oklahoma, and finally joins the North Fork of the Red. The Salt Fork of the Red River rises in southwestern Carson County and heads southeast across Armstrong, Donley, and Collingsworth counties before it enters Oklahoma. It continues to the southeast and finally joins the Prairie Dog Town Fork at the extreme northern point of Wilbarger County, about sixteen miles north-northwest of Vernon.

With all four branches furnishing water, the Red forms the north boundary of Wilbarger, Wichita, Clay, Montague, Cooke, Grayson, Fannin, Lamar, Red River, and Bowie counties to the Oklahoma-Arkansas state line. At this point the river becomes the boundary between Arkansas and Texas until it runs out of Texas and turns in a general south-by-southeast direction, finally joining the mighty Mississippi River.

The Red River stretches out over 1,360 miles, with 640 miles in Texas or along its borders, draining some 30,700 square miles in Texas. One of the largest man-made lakes in the United States was formed when a dam was built in 1944 that created Lake Texoma. The river has had many names through the years, with most referring to its red color: Rio Roho, Rio Roxo, Red River of Natchitoches, or Red River of Cadodacho. Legends abound that feature its Indian experiences as well as influences from French and Spanish culture.

After the Louisiana Purchase, the Red River was considered the boundary line between the Spanish to the south and the United States to the north. Indian trading posts were established on the Red River, especially where old game and Indian trails crossed. These later formed the seeds from which communities grew. For instance, a road known as the Central National Road of the Republic of Texas crossed the Red River at Travis Wright's landing, which was six miles above Jonesboro. This was considered the head of navigation on the Red for some time, until a steamboat captain rode a freshet even farther up the river. Other crossings became famous during the days of the cattle drives, such as Doan's Crossing (north of Vernon in Wilbarger County on the Dodge or Western Trail), Ringgold Crossing (Montague County), and Red River Station (crossing for Chisholm Trail in Montague County).[1]

The Red River of the South was a river of dreams. Shippers and plantation owners alike dreamed about using the Big Red as a means of transportation, but very few boats made it past the Great Raft in the early periods when the frontier was developing. The *R. T. Bryarly* made headlines when pulling away from the landing in Shreveport in September of 1859 because the boat was so heavily loaded with cotton that its decks were barely clear of the muddy red water. A few days later, it was greeted in New Orleans as a prophet of things to come. The *Choctaw* and *Woodsman* were part of Robert Jones' dream as he sought to bring riverboats to the upper Red. Capt. Henry Miller Shreve piloted the *Enterprise* in 1815 into unchartered snags, and that venture was followed by the *Newport* in 1819 and a year later by the *Yankee, Beaver, Alexandria, Governor Shelby, Neptune,* and *Arkansas.* These boats only ran from New Orleans, Baton Rouge, and Alexandria, with rare trips into Natchitoches. The snag boats *Helipolis* and *Belvidere* did some early work at the mouth of the Red River on the Mississippi to improve steamboat access to the river. But these were only small problems. The Great Raft was the thing that discouraged all except the very daring captains.

The *Pearl, Laurel,* and *Helipolis* were the snag boats that Shreve used in his work in 1833. In 1834 some 42,500 bales of cotton arrived in New Orleans, brought from the Red River on the steamboats *Beaver, Planter, Lioness, Bravo,* and *Caspian.* By 1840 no fewer than thirty-six steamboats were working the river out of Shreveport, including the *Hunter, Creole, Black Hawk, Revenue, Col. A. P. Kouns, R. T. Bryarly, La Belle, Texas, Lorts 3, Belle Rowland, O. H. Durfee, W. J. Behan,* and *Ashland.* During the Civil War, the Confederate ram the *Webb* was one of the last steamboats on the river. The *Webb* was scuttled by its crew when it appeared the boat might fall into Yankee hands. The same fate perhaps was also suffered by the *Trenton, General Beauregard, Eras No. 4, 6, 7, Doubloon, Countess,* and *General Quitman.* These boats all sought shelter in Shreveport but were unaccounted for once the war was over.

Immediately after the Civil War, some of the old boats were pressed into service as showboats, running up and down the river with minstrel shows. Boats engaged in these pursuits were the *Cotton Blossom, River Maid,* and *Water Queen.* Some of these old boats served up only the cheapest of shows, and some were just barges towed up and down the river with gas boats. The *French Sensation* burned below Shreveport when tied up at the Elmwood Plantation.[2]

Navigation on the Red River was hampered for many years by the Great Raft, an accumulation of uprooted trees and driftwood that blocked the channel for as much as seventy-five miles. This raft had been in place long enough for islands of land to be formed where vegetation and trees grew. In the vicinity of the raft the water sought ways to go downstream. As a result, new riverbeds were carved out as the water flooded bayous and creeks in the area. This massive logjam that backed water up in the sloughs, bayous, and creeks opened a steamboat route that would penetrate all the way inland and make a great river port out of Jefferson, Texas.

Removal of the raft was too large a task for individual ports, cities, or states. It was something that had to be done by the federal government with congressional action. Andrew H. Sevier, a congressman from Arkansas, took the lead in the project and presented a detailed report to Congress concerning the problem. Joseph Paxton, Mount Prairie, Arkansas, a long-time resident of Arkansas and a trained scientist, provided the material necessary. In one of his letters he outlined the problem:

> Opening the raft, then, would reclaim at least three-fourths of the land at present occupied, and rendered entirely useless by it [the water], and thus would place at the immediate disposal of the United States, property in its present situation of no value, but which would then be worth the enormous sum of seven hundred thousand dollars . . . . The raft is eighty miles long, and will average twenty in width. This section . . . would be more completely reclaimed, and when reclaimed, would be better, inasmuch as it would be more free from inundation, than the bottoms of this river generally; and the numerous lakes in this valley that formed by the river so frequently cutting across the necks of its bends, are filled up . . . . These circumstances, together with its advantageous situation in other respects, would render it equal, if not superior, in intrinsic value, to any section of its size whatever.[3]

Paxton and others pointed out that the raft was not static but was growing yearly, "spreading desolation over a most lovely country." The cost in destruction of value of timber and land was placed at $100,000 yearly. Benefits to be derived by removing the raft were listed as: easier transport of supplies headed for the army base at Fort Towson; greater control over Indians; lumber along the Red River would be available once the raft was removed; and the increased value of the land once the backwater was drained in the proper way. Proponents also pointed out that the government would actually make money, since the Red River would be open so that settlers could reach new areas with greater ease and increase the government's tax base. On more than one occasion, the backers of the raft removal reminded the government of the high cost of supplying their forts on the Red River and how this cost would be greatly reduced when the river was open to navigation all the way to Fort Towson during favorable river levels.[4]

The first money provided by the federal government for raft removal was $25,000, made on May 23, 1828. Capt. Henry Miller Shreve of the Army Corps of Engineers was appointed to direct the work. The army's chief engineer, Brig. Gen. Charles Gratiot, finally authorized the work to start on February 8,

REMOVING RAFT from the Red River in 1872. After years of talking, the Army Corps of Engineers finally used the steamer Aid *and lots of nitroglycerin to break the Great Raft that had kept steamboats out of the Upper Red River.* (Source: U.S. Corps of Engineers and Institute of Texan Cultures)

1833. Snag boats named the *Archimedes,* the *Souvenir,* the *Java,* and the *Pearl* were assigned to the project.

For the next several years, Shreve labored at the project. Still, by 1839, more than $200,000 had been expended and the raft continued to grow. Congress was unimpressed with requests for more funds. Finally, in 1841, an additional $75,000 was appropriated, and the job was turned over to Col. Stephen Harriman Long. Private contractors were also brought into the project, with Thomas T. Williamson awarded a contract for work amounting to $15,000. The attempt to use private contractors was deemed a failure and was abandoned. Work on removal of the raft ceased in the late 1850s, when Congress refused to put up any additional funds.[5]

It was 1872 before Congress again turned its attention to the problem of the Red River raft. An appropriation of $150,000 was approved. Little was done in 1872, but in 1873 Capt. C. W. Howell, engineer in charge, wrote this report:

> In breaking the jams and cutting off snags, nitro-glycerine had been found indispensible, from 60 to 75 pounds being used in a day, generally in from 2 to 5 pound charges. For instance, the 31st [of October] was almost entirely spent in an unsuccessful attempt to remove a snag under water, which stopped all drift pulled [from floating downstream]: the last attempt for the day was made with a 7½ inch premium line led to the large steam-capstan of the *Aid* [one of the snag boats]. The capstan was "stalled." The next morning a 5-pound charge of nitro-glycerine removed the obstruction . . . . Cans, containing from 10 to 20 pounds of nitro-glycerine, were sunk as near the bottom of the river as possible and exploded, with the effect of breaking the long logs and a general loosening of the mass in the immediate proximity. Small charges were also used in cutting long logs and stumps too far beneath the surface of the water to be operated on by other means.[6]

Nitroglycerin had been the key to solving a problem that had plagued rivermen for over sixty years as they sought to run steamboats up the river. The removal of the raft was a signal for more and more people to move into the Red River Valley. Trade continued on the Red River for quite a few years, until the railroads finally beached most of the riverboats.

Grayson County

Grayson County was created out of Fannin County in 1846 and named for Peter W. Grayson, who was attorney general in President David G. Burnet's cabinet. Sherman was named as the county seat. The area was inhabited by several tribes of the Caddo confederation when the first Anglo settlers began to move into the area. Daniel Dugan was among the first to arrive in 1836, settling near Abel Warren's trading post, just across the border in Fannin County. Early settlers seemed to gather in a community that became known as Pilot Grove, named for a ranch owned by James P. Dumas. It was located about twenty-five miles from Sherman on the stage line from Bonham to McKinney and was sometimes called "Lick Skillet."

Settlers were also in the Preston Bend area. One of them, John Hart, may have been in the area as early as 1822. Holland Coffee established a trading post in 1837 on the south bank of the Red River in what is now Grayson County.

The first of three courthouses was built in old Sherman in 1847 but was torn down in 1858 to settle a bet as to whether or not a gray goose was nesting under the building. It is not known who won the bet, or if a goose was actually nesting under the building. The second courthouse, built in new Sherman, was burned in 1930 by a mob in an ugly race riot. The present courthouse was built in 1846.[1]

Grayson County's first representative in the legislature was Col. T. J. Shannon, who secured permission to move the county seat from old Sherman to new Sherman. He also donated $100 for the purchase of forty acres for the site of the new town. The first term of court in new Sherman was held under a large pecan tree on the southeast corner of the present public square. The courthouse in old Sherman was bought by George Dugan and moved to new Sherman as part of a residence on North Travis Street. J. G. Thompson was the first chief justice of the county.

The old pecan tree was something of a community center. The court met there, and on Sunday worshipers held services under the tree and stacked their guns nearby in case of an Indian attack. Weekdays the tree also served as a post office and bank. An old coat has hung on the tree and letters were deposited in the pockets. Traders in the area would come to the county seat to transact business and hang their saddlebags loaded with gold over the limbs of the tree. No one made unauthorized withdrawals from the pecan tree bank.[2]

A description of the county seat in 1852 was given by an old-timer: "The real town of Sherman consisted of a row of clapboard business houses along the east side of the public square. A long house on the northeast corner was used as a saloon and a double log house on the north side was the Sherman Hotel run by John R. Bean."[3]

In 1840 the Texas Republic established mail route No. 8 that ran from the "seat of justice of Fannin County to Coffee's Station, via Warren." Port Caddo to Coffee's Station was operated from January 26, 1839, to December 13, 1839. A post office was established in Sherman in 1847.[4]

The first commercial transportation to Grayson County was by the Red River – during periods of high water. The mail packet *Era* made its first trip to Grayson County in 1856. The captain was John Kouns. The *Era* was built especially for the Red River trade and ran whenever the water would permit. When empty, the boat drew twelve inches of water, and with 700 bales of cotton it would run in three feet of water. By 1858 the Butterfield Overland Mail Route was coming through Sherman and at that time seven other post offices were created in the county. Freight came to Grayson County by ox wagon from Jefferson or from the Red River, with paddlewheelers coming in at Preston or Shawneeton. Actually, three steamboats were named *Era*: No. 1, No. 2, and No. 3. The first two were built as light as possible, but *Era* No. 3 had commodious cabins for passengers. Once when Captain Kouns came into Preston with a full load of watermelons, someone asked him why he brought a cargo of watermelons up the river. His answer: "I was afraid the river would go down and I'd need them to float my boat."

Buffalo hides were shipped out of Sherman in huge quantities. It was not uncommon for a wagon train with as many as 80,000 green buffalo hides to arrive for shipment, provided the water was at the right level. Old-timers tell stories about wagon trains loaded with green hides that could be smelled miles away.

Sherman depended on the ports of Preston and Rocky Ford as an outlet for the trade that merchants generated. During the period just before the Civil War, Thomas M. Arnett, James Crooks, and Capt. Benj. F. Savage were partners in a

HAULING COTTON to market was hard on men and wagons. If a wagon wheel broke during a trip to market with a load of cotton, it was usually left beside the trail to pick up when a spare wheel could be found. Cotton frequently was hauled overland from the upper Red River plantations by wagons to Jefferson.

steamboat company specializing in upper Red River trade. As many as fourteen boats were engaged in the trade during this period. It was not uncommon to see one or more boats tied up waiting for a favorable rise in the river.[5]

Preston Bend/Preston Landing/Coffee's Bend

These three names were interchangeable and usually refer to the same spot on the map. Preston Bend refers to a huge, horseshoe-like bend open on the south side. The name used probably identifies a period of time in the early 1830s to 1850s.

John Hart was possibly the first to use the landing. He was a trapper and Indian trader, probably as early as 1822, who had operated posts at Jonesboro before moving to Preston Bend. In about 1837 he and James S. and William R. Baker settled at the mouth of the Washita River, where they cleared land and built three cabins. The partnership seems to have dissolved in 1839, with Hart receiving the land. However, he settled at Warren and was elected as the first sheriff of Fannin County. This was before the formation of Grayson County in 1846.

While Hart was absent from his property at Preston Bend, Holland Coffee occupied the premises without formality. A brouhaha involving Coffee, Hart, Basil Cason, and Daniel Montague ensued. It was ended when Coffee's business partner, Silas Colville, murdered Hart in 1840 or 1841.

Coffee, like Hart, was well known in the area, having been in the trading business at Cross Timbers as early as 1833. His arrival at Preston Bend seems to fall between 1836 and 1837. Coffee and his reputation must have been well known, as the second Congress of the Republic considered suppressing his trading house. But he also had friends, as he was elected to the third Congress in 1838.

The exploits of Coffee and his wife, Sophia, would make good tabloid reading even today. If Sophia was a lady of the night, however, she was also able to hold her own in the raw trading post frequented by Indians. Coffee's post had a tradition of hospitality, even though he was evidently a quarrelsome man. The Clarksville *Northern Standard* reported that Coffee was fired upon by assassins in August of 1842. The ball passed through both breasts of Coffee's coat and pierced the sleeve at the shoulder.

Coffee's stature as a trader can be seen by the wealth that he gathered in a short time. In 1845–46 he built a house near the fort and called it Glen Eden. Massive white chimneys on either end of the two-story double log house, with a central dog trot and brick ell containing kitchen and dining room, were indicators of a man with wealth.

Preston had a post office as early as 1852 and possibly earlier. Fort Preston was built in 1840, taking its name from the first commanding officer. The landing became an important shipping point during the days of the Texas Republic. When Sherman became a major shipping point, it took on an even greater role. In the Grayson County commissioners court session of January 11, 1847, the following order was issued: "Roads ordered laid out: From the public landing at Preston by the nearest and best way to the town of Sherman." This road became known as the "Texas Road," and thousands of settlers crossed the Red River here and headed toward their new homes. By this time the village of Preston was listed as being about one-half mile north of the mouth of Little Mineral Creek on the bank of the Red River. Probably Preston shifted with the changing of the river's course. By the spring of 1845, enough people were living at Preston that a townsite was laid off and several buildings were built. Several mercantile firms that had been doing business at Fort Washita moved to Preston. The editor of the Clarksville *Northern Standard* dropped items into his newspaper about the lack of a dependable steamboat schedule. He noted: "Red River down – out of printing paper and can't help ourselves until the river rises." At times the editor ordered paper delivered to Jefferson and brought overland, just in case.[6]

Since Preston was near the limits of early steamboats, and because of the large volume of trade generated at the post, almost every boat that ran the upper Red went as far as Preston. The ferry took travelers into Indian Territory, so a great number of traders made their way through this old port.

Denison: A Port City

Actually, Denison doesn't qualify as one of the early-day ports on the Red River. However, since it was served by a paddlewheeler, it deserves a place along with the rest of the old ports.

Conceived by the Denison Chamber of Commerce, the *Annie P.* was envisioned as a way to dramatize the idea of the Red River being navigable in the early 1900s. A deal was struck with a shipyard in Shreveport to build the paddlewheeler for $2,000. Payment was to be made when the boat was delivered in Denison. The boat, backed by William Porter, was supposed to have been named for William's wife, Anne Porter, but the sign painter ran out of space and the boat ended up being christened *Annie P.*

When completed, the *Annie P.* was loaded with all sorts of goods and started upriver. Everything went fine until they reached a point where a bridge was too low to allow passage of the smokestacks. Everything was put on hold until a blacksmith cut the smokestacks off and put them on hinges so that they could be lowered to go under bridges. North of Bonham, a snag put a hole in the boat. This was repaired temporarily, and they made it to Denison on April 21, 1905. The whole town turned out for the celebration.

A second voyage was made that summer, but business did not support the ship and the *Annie P.* was subsequently sold. She came to an ignoble end while operating on the Ouachita River near Monroe, Louisiana. A railroad bridge blocked her passage, and to settle the controversy the railroad bought the ship and allowed her to rot at her moorings.[7]

Shawneetown

The Shawnee Indians had a village on the Red River on the upriver side of Coffee's Trading Post, near Denison. The site was purchased by Col. Wm. C. Young in 1850. Evidently, the Indians started a ferry at their village to have communications with part of the tribe on the Oklahoma side of the river. This probably grew into a steamboat landing, either run by the Indians or by someone unnamed. Merchants in Sherman depended upon the landings of Shawneetown and Preston for their supplies.[8]

Grayson County Ferries

Mitchell's Ferry: The importance of this ferry was emphasized by the commissioners court of Grayson County in 1847 when they ordered a "road laid out from Mitchell's Ferry to the county seat site [Sherman]."[9]

Colbert's Ferry: This ferry was established by Benjamin F. Colbert, who gained a bit of national recognition when he was restrained by the Supreme Court from building a ferry at Preston. The problem was that he was in competition with one that had been in operation there by George N. Butts for several years. Colbert then decided on a site some eight miles below Preston. The Butterfield Overland Mail route used his ferry from 1858 to 1861. John Malcolm was the ferryman for several years following 1870. Previously, he had worked at Rocky Bluff Ferry. A ferry operated at this spot until 1931, when it was replaced by a bridge. The Centennial Commission erected a marker at the site in 1936.[10]

Rocky Bluff Ferry: This ferry not only served as a means to ferry people from one side of the river to the other, but it was also an important steamboat landing and a major crossing for big cattle drives. A letter written by John Malcolm offers an insight into life at Rocky Bluff during a big cattle drive:

> One morning two men rode down, and looked the place over; told me they had a herd of 1800 or more to cross; asked me to take everything out of the way as they were going to stampede the cattle and run them across. Soon we heard them shooting and whooping, then heard the roar of the cattle coming down the road, horns and hoofs a'pounding, and into the water they went, nearly damming the river. They did not lose a one, but it sure was a sight to see that many cattle on a wild run.[11]

Doan's Crossing

Doan's Crossing was not a river port or landing. It was probably one of the most famous crossings on the Red River, as the river drops from the High Plains with a rush that cuts slashes in the earth's surface that are similar to Palo Duro Canyon. When the Red breaks out of the Texas Panhandle its character changes, but it is remembered as a swift, terror-filled river by the thousands upon thousands of cowboys who herded literally millions of cattle up the Western Cattle Trail. Two other crossings were also famous: the Chisholm Trail, which forded at the old town near Ringgold in Montague County, and the Shawnee Trail, which forded near Preston in Grayson County, now covered by Lake Texoma.

For drovers who started deep in South Texas, the Red was the most feared river. They made their way across the Nueces, Guadalupe, San Antonio, Colorado, and Brazos rivers and a host of smaller creeks, but the Big Red merited most of their yarns.

Doan's Crossing is just a few miles north of Vernon, Texas, in Wilbarger County. A historical marker tells the story of an estimated six million cattle that crossed the river at this spot. A trading post was established on the south side of the river in 1878 by C. F. Doan and his uncle Jonathan Doan. They had decided to establish the post at the urging of Indians whom the Doans had befriended at Fort Sill. The Kiowas and Comanches wanted a trading post south of the Red River in their territory.

At the height of the trail drives, the little community on the banks of the Red had grown to a town of about twenty to twenty-five people. The community boasted a hotel, the Bat's Cave, twelve houses, and a wagon yard. A post office was granted in 1879 and stayed in business until 1919.

One of Doan's favorite stories was handed down by his

grandson, Tip Doan. Shortly after the family had settled in their rude log hovel, with a buffalo skin for a door, they received a warning from the U.S. Cavalry that Indians from the Oklahoma Territory were raiding and killing. The pioneer quickly packed his wife and two small daughters up and hid in a cave on the river bluff for three days until the Indians had left.

Often more than one large herd would be forced to wait for the Red River to go down, as the rises meant even swifter than normal water.[12]

Chisholm Trail

This trail was named after the famous Indian trader Jesse Chisholm, whose wagon tracks were followed northward in 1866 by Capt. Henry Spekes with a herd of cattle. Other herds followed until they had beaten a path through Texas to Wichita, Kansas.

Like many old trails and roads, the Chisholm has many branches and crossings. It depended mainly where the herd started and where it was convenient to join the main track. The trail crossed the Red River at Sivell's Bend, Spanish Fort, Rock Bluff, or Red River Station. The latter was the favored crossing. Monument Hill, near Addington, Oklahoma, was a landmark that most herds headed for before moving north to the railheads. Quarantines also had a lot to do with where the trail would finally head. Dodge City became known in song and story as the end of the fabled Chisholm Trail.

Chisholm was a plainsman, Indian trader, guide, and interpreter. His services as a guide and interpreter, as well as his ability to speak in fourteen Indian dialects, placed him at many council and treaty meetings. During the Civil War he lived in Wichita, Kansas, on Chisholm Creek. At the close of the war he and James R. Mead loaded a train of wagons at Fort Leavenworth and established a trading post at Council Grove on the North Canadian near present Oklahoma City. His route was followed by friends, and soon the trail was known by his name.[13]

Sam A. Vaughan of Kentuckytown once accompanied a drive through Sherman, crossing the Red at Rocky Ford. He made these comments:

> Preston road and the crossing at Rock Bluff saw the passing of many thousands of cattle to the northern markets. This bluff was considered ideal for getting the cattle into the river

and preventing their milling before consenting to swim. They were driven into this natural "chute" and were in the water and swimming before they could stop and hesitate about going in. I helped drive 1,500 steers over the Chisholm Trail, starting from the San Marcos River. I went as far as Fort Gibson in Indian Territory, but I had chills and fever so bad, I came back home. This was the last big herd that came through Sherman and crossed Red River at Rock Bluff.[14]

Shawnee Trail

Holland Coffee's trading post and plantation on the south side of the Red River was the meeting place for a lot of cattle drives out of East and Central Texas before the Civil War, and again in 1866-67. The drives crossed at one of three fords in the area – Preston, Colbert's, or Rock Crossing – all a few miles from the mouth of the Washita River. A Shawnee Indian village was nearby and no doubt furnished the trail's name.

The present Missouri, Kansas, and Texas Railroad follows rather closely the old route of the Shawnee Trail through Oklahoma. The main branch crossed the Arkansas River at Three Forks, just north of present Muskogee, Oklahoma. Sometimes above this point the trail was referred to as the Sedalia Cattle Route.

Trouble broke out in 1866, when people began to settle in eastern Oklahoma. Some men chose to put their cattle on the closest rail head, while others swung to the west to take their cattle herds on to Abilene. This trail became known as the West Shawnee Trail.[15]

Fannin County

In 1836 Daniel Rowlett formed the first permanent settlement at Tulip on the Red River in what was to become Fannin County. At that time Carter Clifft, the first Anglo settler, Charles Quillan, and Stephen Westbrook were already living in the area. The county, created in December of 1837, was named for James W. Fannin, Jr., the hero of the Battle of Goliad, in the spring of 1838. Tulip, or Lexington, was the first seat of justice, but the people of old Warren built a log courthouse in 1840, perhaps thinking that they would get the county seat. They were right. To further confuse matters the settlement of Bois d'Arc was named county seat in 1843, at which time the name was changed to Bonham. It appears that Fort Inglish was near the settlement of Bois d'Arc and in the center of a growing area. A post office was granted to Bonham in 1846.[1]

Tulip Landing

The first landing to be started in the county was at the mouth of Bois d'Arc Bayou near the western edge of the county, where Carter Clifft had settled about 1817. Four families from four states of the Old South were the yeast that got the new community off to a good start. They were Richard Locke, of Somersville, Tennessee; Dr. Daniel Rowlett, Wadesboro, Kentucky; Daniel Slack, Mississippi; and Edward and John Stephens of Lamar County, Alabama. The families of Jabez Fitzgerald and Mark Roberts came overland from Tennessee through Arkansas and Cherokee country to the Fort Towson Landing, where they crossed the Red River to join the group at Jonesboro. The original families came aboard the steamer *Rover,* which they boarded in Memphis, Tennessee, for a trip down the Mississippi to New Orleans and then up the Red River to their new home. The party was organized in the autumn of 1835, but it was not until March 1, 1836, that they arrived at their destination. After the group arrived at Jonesboro, they traveled overland to Carter P. Clifft's residence on Bois d'Arc Bayou, arriving about April 1, 1836. The men left the women, children, and slaves while they went farther up the river to prospect for new home sites. On this expedition several men drowned while making a river crossing.

Slack selected a location on the east side of the Bois d'Arc Bayou, while Rowlett picked his land on the Red River in Tulip

Bend. He built several cabins on Pepper Creek, about a hundred yards below its junction with the Red River. Evidently, the Locke, Roberts, and Fitzgerald families selected land in the area and joined in the formation of the Tulip Settlement. The settlement was originally called Lexington, probably because Locke was from Lexington, Kentucky. John and Edward Stephens located on the Red River between the mouth of the Bois d'Arc Bayou and Blue Bluff, which was upriver from Lexington.

On May 10 the men belonging to the river settlement formed a militia company and immediately went on a scouting trip that took them to the headwaters of the Trinity River. Upon returning and getting their families settled, Rowlett, Richard Locke, Daniel Slack, and John Seymore departed for South Texas to take part in the War for Independence. All of these men served from July 18 until October 20, 1836.

Rowlett, a doctor and lawyer as well as a planter, was recognized as the leader of the group and was instrumental in the organization of Fannin County. He was the owner of a large number of slaves. Since he and all of his neighbors were farmers, they built a steamboat landing at the mouth of Bois d'Arc Bayou. He was an active Mason and served in a number of county jobs, as well as being a member of the House of Representatives in the Fourth and Eighth Congress. Two days after he arrived at the capital, he presented a petition from sundry citizens asking for the creation of a new county west of Bois d'Arc Bayou. Before the session ended, Fannin County had been separated from Red River County as the petition had requested.

Rowlett's plantation was located where Pepper Mill Creek joined the Red River. The landing at this point was called Pepper Creek for a short time and later was known as Tulip. Since the men in the area had large plantations, probably at least one or more steamers managed to make it to this landing when the water level was high enough. In dry years, planters had to take their cotton all the way to Jefferson, which was roughly 150 miles away. When the weather was wet the roads were almost impassable. Even in good weather it was a long, hard haul for men and oxen.[2]

Bois d'Arc Landing

This landing was more or less the saga of Carter P. Clifft and John Emberson, both frontiersmen, both adventurers. Emberson, with three or four fellow Tennesseans, packed into the Red River country in the winter and spring of 1815–16 and ran a string of traps on Emberson's Lake, near present-day Sumner in Lamar County. The wilderness of the Red River apparently made an impression on him, because after marrying he returned to Texas in 1823 or 1824 and settled within a few miles of his old hunting camp. Clifft is credited with being the first white man to settle in Fannin County. He and his wife, Abigail, lived comfortably in a log cabin near Rocky Ford which was immediately below the mouth of the Bois d'Arc Bayou. Clifft's wife was supposed to have inherited a considerable amount of wealth when her first husband, James Garland, died.

Since a number of the early citizens picked out land on the Bois d'Arc Bayou, it follows that a large amount of cotton and

CABIN ON THE RIVER – When the first settlers moved into the Red River Valley, the first order of business was constructing a house. Heavy stands of hard woods were found in a plentiful supply along the banks of the river and creeks that provided the timber. Roofs were made by splitting the logs into rough shingles. Early windows were boarded over, and fireplaces were made out of native stone or some type of river clay bricks.

corn was grown in the area. It is likely that the cotton was put on flatboats, or keelboats, in Bois d'Arc Bayou and brought down to the Red River. It could have been held there until it was determined whether the water would be high enough to cover Rocky Ford and allow steamboats to get into Fannin County. It was possible to get a keelboat or a flatboat over Rocky Ford, so in dry years probably most cotton went down the river rather than make the long overland trip to Jefferson.[3]

Inglish Fort

When John Bailey Inglish and other families settled in the Bois d'Arc Bayou area, they felt the need for protection. In 1839 a blockhouse was built near, or as a part of, Inglish's residence, as a place for settlers to stay in case of an Indian attack. The blockhouse was sixteen feet square with a twenty-four-foot-square story above projecting four feet on each side. The name of the community was changed to Bonham in 1843, at which time it was made the county seat of Fannin County.[4]

Warren

Known as the ultimate head of navigation on the Red River, Warren was located in the northwestern part of Fannin County about a mile south of the mouth of Choctaw Creek. Eighty-eight first-class land grants were issued in the area before 1838.[5] The old site is about a mile northeast of Ambrose in Grayson County, but boats were known to have traveled as high as Fort Preston in Grayson County. For a short time Warren was the county seat in 1840. During the 1830s, John Jouitt had a store in the old port. John Hart also operated a store there in 1837,[6] as did James S. and William R. Baker. William was the nephew of James S. Baker, a Presbyterian minister. Other Red River settlers during 1836 were John and Thomas Jouitt, Joseph Murphy, Joseph Swagerty, Richard R. Beal, Jacob Black, Hilary B. Bush, Joseph Sowell, John R. Garnett, and Joseph P. Spence. Daniel Montague, of Louisiana, came to Texas too late to take part in the Battle of San Jacinto. However, liking Texas, he returned to Louisiana and sold his interests so that he could move his family to Texas and settle in Warren. He entered into a partnership with William Henderson, and they established a general merchandise store. He was the first surveyor of the Fannin Land District, and by the customary practice of accepting fees in land, he accumulated a vast estate. He fought in the Mexican War and the Civil War. Montague County is named for him.[7]

Abel Warren moved to the Red River in 1836 and built an Indian trading post, which became the focal point of the community that grew up in the area. He built a fort and stockade, which has been described as follows:

> The post was surrounded by a strong, heavy picket of logs planted in the ground, about fifteen feet high, with a two story log tower (i.e., blockhouse) at each corner, with portholes for shooting through, covering the approaches. The log towers were about twelve feet square and furnished with sleeping bunks for the men and a dozen muskets for short range work. On two sides of the enclosure were strong gates for the admission of stock and wagon trains. Sheds and warehouses were on the inside of the walls and a corral for stock on the prairie outside.

In 1837 Warren moved his trading post to present Love County, Oklahoma, in order to be closer to the Indians who were his customers. He moved his post for the second time, and in 1848 he left the business in charge of a partner and returned to Massachusetts to marry his boyhood sweetheart. When he returned to Texas he discovered that the partner had sold his business and departed. He died in Fort Smith, Arkansas, in 1882.[8]

During these early years, quite a number of permanent settlers came into the territory, giving rise to the possibility of making Warren a port to serve the area. This did not come to pass since Warren was accessible to steamers only during seasons of high water. In dry seasons it was impossible to get a boat to Warren.

While the new port city failed to fulfill the hopes of its businessmen, the community did gain strength from 1838 through 1841. During that time different military units used the Warren Stockade as a base for their operations against hostile Indians south and west of the new port. The Fourth Militia Brigade made the fort its headquarters for several years. Lt. Col. Daniel Montague was in charge of most of the brigade's activities until 1840. The companies under Robert Sloan, Jesse Stiff, John Emberson, Nathaniel T. Journey, Mark R. Roberts, and

Joseph Sowell were part of this brigade. Several were mustered out of the service in Warren after fulfilling their objectives.

The Fourth Brigade's aggressive raids against the Indians in the summer of 1841 more or less ended organized Indian resistance. It is possible that the fort and stockade stayed in good repair during these years. With the transfer of the county seat to Bonham, the use of Warren as a fort or port was limited.[9]

A post office was established in Warren in 1847 and operated until 1876.[10]

Sowell's Bluff

This community was founded by Joseph Sowell. He was a captain of a militia company connected with the Fourth Militia Brigade, which was charged with putting down Indian trouble along the Red River. His company was mustered out of service at Camp Warren on August 31, 1839. A ferry operated across the Red River at this point.[11]

Coffee Station/Preston Landing

Holland Coffee established this trading post in 1837 on the north and south Indian trail on the south bank of the Red River in what is now Grayson County. The village of Preston grew up around the trading post, and it was here that steamboats landed during periods of high water. A few steamboats traveled as high as Preston. The site is now covered by Lake Texoma.[12]

Raleigh's

John G. Jouitt founded this landing in the late 1830s and named it after his hometown of Raleigh, North Carolina. It was incorporated on January 4, 1839, and the following year a post office was granted.[13]

Fannin County Ferries

Bryant's Crossing: This crossing was made famous by Philip Nolan in 1797. He built rafts and crossed the Red River, calling the place Blue Bluffs because of the blue shale exposed in the bluff of the river. He camped here for several months and traded with the Indians. In 1867 George Grubbs owned and operated a ferry nearby after a change in the course of the river. In 1870 an Indian raid hit the site, and in 1895 a cable ferry was operated here by the Bryants, Darlings, and Dil Darling until 1926 and 1927, when the Bryant-Fannin Bridge was built.[14]

Rocky Ford: In January 1839 John Stephens, Joseph Swagerty, George Dameron, and Daniel Montague were appointed to build the Rocky Ford toll bridge, which they completed in 1840.

Thomas Jouitt Ferry: A petition was submitted in 1841 by Jouitt for a ferry at nearby Rocky Ford.[15]

Colbart Ferry: This ferry belonged to the Choctaws and was the crossing of the Butterfield Stage route. The franchise reads: "... as long as grass grows and water flows ..."[16]

Lamar County

Lamar County was formed in 1840 out of Red River County. Like Bowie and Red River counties, it lies in between the Red and Sulphur rivers. This was an excellent location for pioneer settlers looking for fertile land and an abundance of water, plus good drainage.

George Wright, a native of Tennessee, floated down the Ohio and Mississippi as a seven-year-old and poled up the Red River in a keelboat with his family to then Red River County on September 5, 1816. He was elected to represent Red River County in the First and Third Congress of the Republic of Texas and as a member of the Senate in the Ninth Congress. He was also a member of the Convention of 1845 and the Secession Convention of 1861. His brother, Travis Wright, was a scout for United States troops who found and liberated white captives held by the Osages. While boundaries were fluid in North Texas, Travis was elected to the Arkansas legislature from Miller County, Arkansas. Ironically, George and Travis were both living in the same house when George was serving in the Texas legislature and Travis in Arkansas.

George was a businessman and trader and at one time operated a store at Jonesboro. He purchased several thousand acres of land in the western part of Red River County and used his influence in the Texas legislature to have Lamar County formed, which included his land. The first county seat was

Lafayette. The county seat was then moved to Mount Vernon, where the court met in the Mount Vernon Tavern. About a year later, the county seat was moved to Paris, where Wright had given fifty acres. The first Lamar County courthouse was torn down after being judged unsafe. The second, an ornate granite structure, burned in the great fire of March 21, 1916. The granite structure that was built as a replacement still stands in 1993.

Lamar County delegates to the Secession Convention voted against secession from the Union. Later, in a vote of the people, the count was 553 for secession and 663 against.[1]

Franklin

Samuel Moore Fulton was born in Norfolk, Virginia, in 1800. By 1818 he was established as a trader with the Indians on the Red River. He received a league and a labor of land in what is today Lamar County. He named the Red River community that he established Franklin. Before a post office was granted in 1842, it was also called U.S. Factory. Fulton was the

COTTON provided the bulk of income for farmers along Texas rivers. Usually the bottomland was rich and produced bumper crops. Cotton was one of the main cash crops on the Red River, with some going down the river to market and the remainder taken overland to Jefferson.

postmaster. He built a landing and a trading post at the port, where he carried on a trade with the Indians across the river.[2]

Fulton was an official in the Ohio, Red River, and Mississippi Packet Company. In addition to being associated with this company, Fulton owned his own steamboat, the *Fulton,* which made regular trips up the Red River. In late May of 1848, the *Fulton, Duck River, Monterey,* and the *Shaw* arrived in the upper part of the Red. After discharging their incoming cargoes, two of the ships, *Duck River* and *Monterey,* went on up to Fulton and took on a load of cotton. The *Fulton* and the *Shaw* went upriver to Towson Landing, took on a load of cotton, and departed downriver. Fulton was active in business and community affairs. While on a business trip to New Orleans he died of yellow fever in 1853.[3]

In 1854 the Clarksville *Northern Standard* reported that the river had experienced a ten-foot rise overnight, allowing the steamers *Wm. C. Young, R. M. Jones,* and *Runaway* to take advantage of high water to make a run up the river. The *Young* went as high as Fulton.

Arthur City

Arthur City, a small town that grew up about a mile east, and off the river from Franklin, recorded in 1908 the greatest flood to ever hit the river. It measured forty-three feet and five inches. Old-timers remembered the flood of 1843 as the worst in history when it hit thirty-three feet. The Frisco railroad ran an excursion train from Paris to Arthur City for people to see the flood conditions. Hundreds made the trip. A new channel was cut west of Arthur City, going north several hundred yards and leaving a dry chasm in front of the place where Sam Fulton's trading house had stood and where his steamboats tied up to put off freight and load cotton that was headed downriver.[4]

Fulton operated a ferry across the Red River at Franklin. Evidently, the ferry was in use before the county was organized in 1840. His post at the ferry was established to trade with the Indians on the other side of the river.[5]

Boggy Creek Ferry

Morrison and Hamilton operated a ferry at the mouth of Boggy Creek (River) which was several miles upriver from Fulton's trading post. Before the Morrison and Hamilton ferry was in operation, two plantation owners, Isaac Williamson and Joshua Bowerman, operated a ferry, trading post, and distillery at the same location. When Bowerman died, among the claims against his estate was one which read:

> Due Robert Campbell for value received of him for services rendered up to date, eleven dollars 42 cents, which is to be paid in whiskey at $1 per gallon – 11½ gallons this April 20, 1844. Bowerman signed a note on May 12, 1844: "For value received I promise to pay to Sam. Houston or his order 40 gallons of whisky as soon as it is rectified." In November, 1843, Bowerman wrote this letter: "Henry Bingham, Esq., I am out of whisky and want you to oblige me with a couple of gallons. Either sell or lend it to me until we get started and then will replace it or pay you for it.

It seems apparent that whiskey was as good as gold and was traded, swapped, and bequeathed as something of value.[6]

Red River County

Red River County was settled starting in about 1814, when people began drifting into the rich river lands inhabited by the Caddo, Kickapoo, Shawnee, and Delaware Indians. James Burkham and Posey Benningfield were among the first and established the community of Burkham. In 1816 the settlement of Pecan Point was started by Claiborne Wright on the Red River. Jourdan J. Ward and his three sons settled nearby in the Riverview area. Jonesboro came into being in 1817 or 1818 and became the leading port for the area. James Clark moved to Henry Stout's land to start what grew into Clarksville. After Clark died in 1838, his wife married George Gordon.

The first school was a girls' boarding school in Clarksville, from the early 1830s to 1848, which was taught by Mrs. George Todd. A Presbyterian church was founded by Milton Estill at Shiloh in 1833.

In 1836 Red River County was created by the Republic of

Texas, and by 1847 all or parts of thirty-nine other counties were carved out of the original jurisdiction.[1]

In the late 1830s a few steamboats managed to circumnavigate the small logjams above Shreveport, and the little vessels made it to the landings to the northwest in Red River County. By the early 1840s, keelboat traffic out of the upper Red River began to come into Shreveport on a regular basis. Among the steamboats in the upper Red River trade on an intermittent basis were the *Cayuga, Swan, Yazoo, Frontier, Concord, Cotton Plant, Kate Ward, R. M. Jones, Frances Jones, W. W. Levy, Fanny Fern, Victoria, Hope, George, Vigo, LaFitte, Osceola, Ham Howell, Pioneer,* and the *Hempstead.* In November of 1843 the *Swan* arrived in Shreveport with nearly 500 bales of upper Red River cotton. Most of the steamboats that ran on the Red River were operated by Shreveport commission merchants. Two of these merchants were James H. Cane and Company and Lewis and Howell. Legend has it that Ben Milam ran a steamboat up the Red River in 1831. The next boat to work the Red was the little *Cayuga.* It was operating there when it was pulled out and sent to the Brazos to answer an offer made by upper Brazos merchants: 5,000 acres of land and $800 to the first steamboat to make it to Washington-on-the-Brazos.[2]

Pecan Point

Pecan Point Settlement was located at the mouth of Pecan Bayou where it entered the Red River in the northeast corner of present-day Red River County. Claiborne Wright is credited with being one of the first settlers in the area. He was born in North Carolina in 1784 and got a taste of steamboats when he took a voyage on the *New Orleans* in 1811 to engage in salt making in Illinois. During the winter of 1815–16, he built a keelboat, the *Pioneer,* that he used to take a party up the Red River. He reached Pecan Point in September of 1816 and found George and Alex Wetmore and William Mabbitt, Indian traders, and Walter Pool and Charles Burkham already there ahead of him. Wright probably settled in Pecan Point in 1818 and built a cabin; however, in 1819 he crossed the river and settled at Shawneetown in Arkansas. This area was referred to by Spaniards and early settlers as the Upper Red.[3]

Wright was the first to jot down notes about Pecan Point.

The next was Maj. S. H. Long, who headed an expedition of United States soldiers and naturalists. He visited Pecan Point in 1820 and observed that he considered Pecan Point to have been the most considerable village in the area. At that time he indicated that there were only a few rude houses in the community. In the summer of the same year the Rev. Jedidiah Morse came through and made these remarks:

> There is a settlement of twelve families, at Nanatscho, or Pecan Point; and one of twenty families at the mouth of the Kiamichi [Jonesboro]. At the lower settlement [Pecan Point] there are five, and at the upper settlement, three, traders, who in consequence of their contiguity to the fine hunting ground have taken the Indian trade of that country [southern Oklahoma] from Natchitoches.

Pecan Point could properly be classed as a river landing, rather than a port, since there is no record of warehouses, docks, or the like. Jonesboro was probably the port city for a wide area of Texas and later Oklahoma.[4]

Jonesboro

Jonesboro is accorded the distinction of being one of the first entry points for Anglo settlers into Texas – even before Stephen F. Austin started his colony on the Brazos River. From the beginning, in 1817 or 1818, settlers crossed over into Texas at Jonesboro in growing numbers. Sam Houston is said to have used the trail in 1832. A monument commemorating this event was erected in Clarksville by the state in 1936. Davy Crockett passed through the city in 1835. John Neely Bryan, who built a cabin at the forks of the Trinity (the beginning of Dallas), passed through the community. Ben Milam, one of the leaders in the first battle of the Alamo, stayed the night at James Clark's tavern and inn. An important early road ran from Jonesboro to Nacogdoches, and it was over this road that most people traveled into East Texas.[5]

Even as Jonesboro prospered as a river port, a group of people from Jonesboro and the area moved to the edge of the prairie and began building a new settlement just above the Delaware Indian Settlement. Isaac Smathers, with the help of James Clark, built the first log house in what eventually became Clarksville in the summer of 1834.[6]

Evidently, Jonesboro attracted some of the travelers to stay and become citizens. When Col. Juan Almonte toured Texas gathering statistical information for Santa Anna, he noted that a primary school existed in Jonesboro and that the town and surrounding area had a population of 2,350. This was probably overstated, as were most of his figures, but at least they showed that a growing number of people were settling in the area. District Judge E. W. Bowers, Red River historian, believed that the town of Jonesboro had a population of "several hundred people."[7] A community church building was erected in 1824 (which might have been the school) and any visiting preacher was welcome to use it. Benjamin Clark, father of the founder of Clarksville, frequently preached in the building.[8]

In 1836 John Hart organized a company of riflemen for service in the Texas Revolution, but by the time they arrived on the scene the Battle of San Jacinto had been won. Hart operated a store in Jonesboro, starting in 1832. Jonesboro was the county seat of Miller County, Arkansas, which at one time was on both sides of the Red River, but in about 1836 it ceased to be an Arkansas county seat. Arkansas did not give up its claim to the south side of the Red River, and this led to a dispute between the secretary of state of Texas and the United States. At least Jonesboro could lay claim to being the only county seat of a foreign country. In 1837 Jonesboro and Clarksville were incorporated by the Congress of Texas.[9]

Henry M. Jones (sometimes called William), a hunter who had visited in the area in 1815, moved to the area and shortly thereafter the community was known as Jonesboro. Mr. Jones apparently came to the settlement to establish a ferry. He left after several years. At the time he arrived, other settlers included Adam Lawrence, Caleb Greenwood, William Hensley, William Cooper, and John Ragsdale. Lawrence and Hensley located there as early as 1815.

Jonesboro became known as the head of the navigation of the Red River. As a result, cotton and other products were brought in by wagons to be shipped out to Shreveport and New Orleans. Quite a few merchants, or trading companies, opened businesses in the new port, including George W. Wright, and James F. Johnston, Thad W. Riker and Company, Williamson and Bowerman, and William M. Harrison. The new

COTTON would be brought to the river port of Jonesboro and stored, waiting for the spring rains which would bring the level of the Red River up to a point that small steamers could get around the raft and get in to pick up the cotton. If boats could not get through, the cotton would be sent overland to Jefferson for shipment.

city grew into an important river port with a number of steamboats calling, and thus many people came into Texas through Jonesboro.[10]

Jonesboro enjoyed a brief surge of commercial growth. With a number of brokers and merchants in place, the word spread. Farmers began to bring their cotton and other products in for shipment from the wharves of the Jonesboro merchants. Steamboats were regular callers at the port. Almonte in his 1834 report said that 1,000 bales of cotton were produced in the area that year.[11]

One of the largest businesses in Jonesboro was the trading firm of Williamson and Bowerman, operated by Isaac C. Williamson and Joshua Bowerman. In addition to their store they also owned a steamboat that made regular runs to New Orleans. Another large concern was D. Campbell and Company, owned by David Campbell and James Hogan. This company was in financial trouble in 1839 and was being liquidated by their agent, J. C. Woodall. The declining state of business in Jonesboro can be seen by the debt proceedings brought against these two firms. The New York firm of Clute and Mead brought suit against Williamson and Bowerman in the amount of $802.32. Judgment was rendered by Judge John M. Hansford in favor of Clute and Mead. In the case of D. Campbell and Company, suit was brought before Wm. Mays, justice of the peace in Jonesboro. The case was finally settled on appeal by Judge Hansford, who ruled in favor of the wholesaler, Peter B. Johnson. When another Jonesboro merchant, William Slingland, died in 1838, a number of claims were filed against his estate. Dr. George Bason was appointed administrator of the estate, and the sale of personal property was held on Saturday, October 6, 1838.[12]

A number of people settled in Jonesboro due to the fact that the U.S. Army removed all squatters from the lands in what is now Oklahoma, starting in 1819. This was done in order to move the Choctaws from Mississippi. In all there were about 5,000 white settlers in this area. It can readily be seen that with all of these people on the move, the ferry at Jonesboro was a busy place.[13]

Jonesboro's brief glory as a port city and trading center was abruptly ended in 1843, when a big flood hit the Red River. When the floodwaters finally receded, the damage was overwhelming at the old port. Most of the port-side businesses had been either washed away or damaged heavily by the flood. But the worst thing was that the main channel of the river moved almost a mile north, leaving the old port site high and dry. To compound matters, Clarksville had obtained the county seat, and people were moving there in large numbers. Another blow was the fact that so many competing steamboats began to push farther and farther up the river. There was no incentive to rebuild, and in a short time all that was left of the once bustling city were a couple of large sycamore stumps which steamboaters had used to snub their boats to the shore.[14]

All physical evidence of Jonesboro has completely disappeared; only a historical marker commemorating the site is there now.

James Clark, the founder of Clarksville, moved to Jonesboro to supply food and other supplies to the Choctaws and Chickasaws. While living in Jonesboro, he and his wife, the former Isabella Hadden Hopkins Hanks, entertained Sam Houston in their home for several days. Mrs. Clark always said that General Houston and his men were very well behaved and were gentlemen. In 1835 Clark and his family moved to the skirt of timber that is now the heart and center of the city of Clarksville.[15]

Rowland

Rowland was a small landing about fifteen miles downriver from Jonesboro. It evidently was used to ship cotton from the area to the south and west. Clarksville also used this landing to receive the bulk of their supplies.[16]

Pat Clark, grandson of the founder of Clarksville, remembered steamboats coming to the landing during periods of high water to pick up cotton from the prairie around Clarksville for delivery in New Orleans. In ascending the boats would bring sugar, molasses, and farm supplies in general. The steamers also took passengers, and on one occasion a newlywed couple, Buck Morrison and Belle Gordon, took the boat to New Orleans on their honeymoon.

There were two stores at Rowland, one owned by Rowland Bryarly, town founder, and the other by John Monkhouse, Sr., who had arrived many years earlier from London, England. Bryarly and Company continued to do a large business, wholesale and retail, until as late as 1874. In that year a heavy overflow of the river resulted in a change of the channel, and the boat landing and wharf were washed out and cut off from the town. Capt. Joe L. Bryarly, who was in charge of the family holdings at that time, built a new town, Mound City, a short distance from the old town. Much of the lumber from the old town was used in the new one. The account books of the store are still in the family. Mound City had a brief life. In August of 1876 the first train on the Texas and Pacific Railroad ran through Clarksville, virtually ending river traffic on the hazardous upper Red River.[17]

Bryarly and Company had perhaps one of the largest stores in northeastern Texas from 1850 to 1859. There a person could buy anything, including a slave. The store did a big business with Indians, buying deer skins, snake root and pink root, and selling them whiskey and groceries. Capt. Joe Bryarly, descendant of the founder, named his last steamboat the *Bonnie Bell* after his daughter, Mrs. Bonnie Harvey.

R. T. Bryarly had come from Virginia (about 1840) as a bachelor to claim his land grant and start a store. In addition to the store he established a ferry over the Red River that stayed in the family into the early 1930s. During the life of the ferry, it was necessary to move the physical location of the ferry dock due to the changing course of the river. At one time the river changed its course to the extent that 350 acres of the Bryarly Texas land ended up in Oklahoma. The family continued paying taxes in Texas on the property until it was sold. During his course of business he became interested in finding a market for snake root, a plant that grew wild and had healing powers. Family legends tell that Bryarly gathered up a supply of the snake root and headed for New York to try to find a market for the product. He died while on the trip, and the project died with him. He was buried in his native Virginia.[18]

Mrs. Mary Kate Hale, a granddaughter of R. T. Bryarly, of Clarksville, has several old steamboat bills of lading. One that was made out to the R. T. Bryarly Company calls for the shipment of two bales of cotton aboard the steamboat *Texas* to New Orleans, consigned to Rodgers Norwood and Company. The bill is dated May 12, 1860. Freight on the two bales was listed at $12 per bale, plus "charges" of $3.38. A shipment of merchandise consigned to R. Davis, Rowland, was shipped on the schooner *John H. Bell* on July 12, 1848. This list of goods included: 2 boxes tobacco, 10 barrels whiskey, 12 bags coffee, 7 bales ---, 1 cask powder, 1 keg salt, 1 box ---, 1 keg ---, 1 keg nails, 1 box mdse., 2 bales tobacco, 5 bags salt.[19]

A post office was registered in Bryarly, Texas, in 1892.[20]

The Bryarly Spanish land grant stayed in the family until recent years, when it was all sold to the Chapman Ranch.[21]

In a diary kept by E. W. Bowers, several entries pertained to the port of Rowland:

> April 15, 1873: I hauled 8 bales of cotton to Rowland to be shipped. Weighed 3,902 pounds in all.
>
> April 16, 1873: The cotton started to New Orleans, 8 bales in all.

> August 14, 1873: The cotton I sent to New Orleans brought $422.10 greenback. It paid only $382.86 specie at one ten. [This was during the Panic of 1873, when United States greenback sold at a discount.][22]
>
> This 7th day of February (1874) I sent ten bales of cotton to Mound City to be shipped (I went). This ten bales of cotton weighed 5,250 pounds in all.
>
> April, 17th, 1876 on Tuesday. Cloudy hauled my groceries from Mound City. Cost $173.29. [This was the last mention of Mound City, which coincides with the arrival of the railroad in Clarksville.][23]

The port of Rowland and John Monkhouse made the news in 1844. It seems that M. W. Davis, who was in the mercantile business in Red River County, ordered a bill of goods to be shipped from New Orleans to him at the port of Rowland. Instead of delivering the goods as directed, Capt. Joseph Claiborne of the *John H. Bills* decided the river was too low and left the merchandise at Fulton, Arkansas. When the goods were finally reshipped to Rowland to the warehouse of John Monkhouse, who was also the customs agent for the Republic of Texas, Davis was displeased and brought suit for damages for loss of profits, among other reasons. Since Monkhouse refused to deliver the goods until the freight was paid, Davis asked the court to place the goods in his possession by order of the court. The court agreed, and the sheriff seized nine barrels of whiskey, thirteen sacks of coffee, and six barrels of sugar and turned them over to Davis. Davis lost interest in the case once he had the goods, without paying any freight, and Monkhouse also lost interest. Case closed.[24]

Rowland T. Bryarly had battled the Red River for many years, but it finally got him. The diary of E. W. Bowers tells the story: "Rowland T. Bryarly got drowned on Thursday, April 28th, 1881 and was found on Friday, April, 29th. and was put on the train on the 30th. to be carried to Virginia."[25]

The rapid settlement of the Red River Valley was attributed in no small part to the availability of river transportation to move in settlers and supplies as well as take cotton and other products to market in New Orleans. The decline of the Red River ports can be attributed directly to two factors: first, the coming of railroads, and second, the popularity of Jefferson as a growing port that offered more than the smaller Red River ports.[26]

Wright's Landing

Wright's Landing was founded by Travis Wright, son of Claiborne Wright, who had come up the Red in a keelboat to Pecan Point and lived there the rest of his life. Travis made his financial success by trading goods in New Orleans. He operated a store in Jonesboro, where he traded for hides, furs, beeswax, and other products. When the season was right, he would load his keelboat and float downriver to New Orleans, where he would swap for merchandise to be sold in his store at Jonesboro. Each trip would take several months – but time was not essential.

Later he purchased land opposite where the Kiamichi River entered the Red from Oklahoma. At that site he located his home and a trading post, which became known as Wright's Landing. This landing was on a great bend in the Red River in the northwestern corner of Red River County. His landing was regarded in 1840 as the head of navigation until some steamboat captain pushed still farther up the river. Pine Hills or Bluffs was about twenty-five miles upriver from Wright's Landing and in Lamar County.

Wright operated a store at Wright's Landing in partnership with Ashbrook. He and some Indians also operated a ferry.

Keelboats were the workhorses of this part of the river. The keelboat was essentially a flatboat with a rounded bow and stern and a board in the center to keep it from turning over like a flatboat. Since it had no power, it was floated down the river by the current. On the return voyage the keelboat men tried to keep close to the banks, where the current was not strong, and they were able to use poles to move their boats back upstream. On occasion they had to attach lines to trees ahead and ease the boat forward by a windlass or warping.

Keelboats could make it through the Red River raft better than steamboats most of the time. There was a passage through the raft known as Willow Chute, and when it became blocked Captain Wright found a route through Red and Black bayous and lakes to Shreveport. Rivermen were not apt to share a secret like this with competitors. Capt. Jim Gamble was said to have made a practice of cutting heavy timber to fall across the river to harass his competitors. Other keelboaters during this period were Harrison Brummett, Capt. Dick Finn, and Abram Block.

Once steamboats were running regular on the river, Wright retired his boats but kept one that he could put back into the water on short notice if low water stopped the steamers. In October of 1842 the Clarksville *Northern Standard* estimated that more than 2,000 bales of cotton had gone down the river. In May of 1846 the *Harvey* arrived at Wright's Landing to take on a load of cotton. In May of 1848 the *Fulton* and *Shaw* were loaded at Wright's Landing when they were caught by falling water and had to take some cotton off. By late May the water was rising, and the *Duck River, Monterey, Shaw,* and *Texian* arrived to take on cotton. Two of the boats had full loads, and after discharging they went on upriver to Fulton's Landing (now Arthur City in Lamar County) for cotton. The river was falling by early June, and all four boats departed with their cotton.

In 1851 steamers were still running. Travis G. Wright & Co. advertised that the steamer *Texas* was due to arrive with a full load of merchandise that would be sold at low prices.

In May of 1854 the Clarksville *Northern Standard* reported that the river rose ten feet the previous Monday after a heavy rain. The steamers *Wm. Young, R. M. Jones,* and the *Runaway* had used the rise to head downstream. In March of 1856 the paper listed the *Fannie Fern, Hope,* and *Runaway* as having called, with the *Runaway* bringing much needed paper. The editor observed: "We have more at Jefferson, but it is impossible to haul it over the roads at this time."

In 1857 Travis and George Wright had an excellent wheat crop. They engaged the *Swamp Fox,* the largest boat to navigate up the river, to come to Wright's Landing and pick up their crop. Captain Kimball headed the boat up Black Bayou until it reached a place that was six feet too narrow for the ship to pass. The problem was solved by removing four trees, and the *Swamp Fox* continued up the channel. Kimball got the wheat and cotton loaded and made a successful return to Shreveport with 790 bales of cotton and 100 bags of wheat before running into trouble. The *Swamp Fox* went down with the full load.

In 1849 the little *Mustang* from the Trinity and Brazos was sold to four Paris men, Ulysses Mathiessen, Cyrus Holman, Hopkins Davidson, and Martin. The little ship worked the area until 1861.[27]

Fort Towson

Fort Towson was at the mouth of the Kiamichi River on the north side of the Red River and almost directly across the river from Wright's Landing. Fort Towson was established in 1824 and had a direct link to Fort Smith, Arkansas. This terminal of the National Road was once well furnished with facilities for both land and water transportation. The trail from Arkansas to Fort Towson evidently was used by many settlers headed for the new communities in Red River County.[28]

Doaksville

A large civilian settlement that grew up adjacent to Fort Towson was called Doaksville. Some historians credit Gen. Zachary Taylor with founding the fort. Robert M. Jones, a Choctaw, arrived on the scene in about 1836 and opened a trading post with goods that he had brought from New Orleans. He traded with the Indians for hides, furs, snake root and pink root, and other produce. By 1860, when the Civil War was approaching, he was considered a wealthy man, with 500 slaves and several steamboats on the Red River. He also owned several plantations along the river from Aransas to Lake West in present Bryan County, in Oklahoma. His home, "Rose Hill," was considered one of the finest in the Oklahoma Territory. A man by the name of J. R. Berthelat operated a large store in Doaksville.[29]

Dayton's Landing

Lewis B. Dayton settled on the Red River in about 1832 at a point across the river from Fort Towson and about five miles upriver west from Jonesboro. He built a store and warehouse, and after Texas independence he became a customs collector for the Republic while continuing to run his store. Just as business was beginning to grow, in 1838 a fire completely destroyed his store. He did not rebuild.

Evidently, Dayton had accounts unsettled, as well as land with unsettled boundaries. On June 25, 1838, justice of the peace for Beat No. 5, Red River County, Dayton, and Robert Ragsdale were in court to settle a dispute over the boundary between their land. A jury trial was held, with six men serving as jurors: John Robbins, William Becknell, Sherrod Rowlin, Joseph Reed, John Spain, and Robert Maxwell. Each man had his set of witnesses. The jury returned a verdict, but apparently Dayton did not agree, as he appealed it to district court. Judge John M. Hansford heard the case on October 1, 1840, with a jury. The foreman brought in a verdict affirming that of the justice court.

On March 12, 1840, Dayton charged that Daniel Bell broke into his home and stole merchandise valued at $235, including a barrel of whiskey valued at $100. It was noted that he placed a high value on the thirty-one gallons of whiskey, since it was considered a necessity on the Red River to use in case of malaria.

The case was settled by agreement of all parties.

Dayton disappeared sometime after May 1, 1841, as did his port.[30]

New Berlin

New Berlin was located near the county line between Bowie and Red River counties on the Red River.

Mrs. Gaffney's Landing

Mrs. Gaffney's Landing seems to have been located a few miles above New Berlin. It was a port of call for a number of steamboats picking up cotton from plantations in the area. In May of 1859 Capt. James M. Broadwell, captain of the *Lafitte,* pulled into the landing and took on 500 bales of cotton. Before he got them all loaded, the river dropped to a point that he was fearful that his loaded ship could not make it downstream. He banked his fires and waited for the next freshet.

On May 10 a rise started coming down the river, and the captain started getting up a head of steam to make the dash down the river. Just about the time he was ready to cast off, a Red River County deputy sheriff served him with a writ of attachment filed by John Pasley of New Orleans to fulfill a debt of $1,400. The captain scrambled and finally managed to raise $500. The sheriff told him to cast off; however, by that time the water level was falling again. He got under way but got stuck at the mouth of Black Bayou, damaging his cargo and wrecking his boat. More than likely, Pasley never got his $1,400 and Captain Broadwell lost his ship. The life of a riverboat captain is glorified in song and story, but it appears that they had more than their share of trouble meeting their expenses.[31]

Buried Treasure — Whiskey!

Do you like pirate gold stories? How about buried 100 proof whiskey aged over 138 years? Well, there may still be some good whiskey buried in the wreck of the *Jim Turner,* a river steamer that went down in 1854 somewhere in the vicinity of Albion's Ferry. There were 200 casks, or 40,000 fifths, on board.

Gold stories, or 100-proof stories, have a way of surfacing when someone stumbles on the old story, or, in the case of the *Jim Turner,* when the river makes a change in its course and uncovers part of the wreckage. Such was the case in 1957, when fisherman Benny Badgett tied his trot line to a timber sticking out of the Red River and discovered that he was standing on the decks of an old riverboat about 120 feet long and 30 feet wide. As the legend goes, more than 200 casks of good China whiskey are still locked in its watery grave.

It seems that Badgett uncovered more than he had bargained for when Mrs. Merle Ferguson of Clarksville showed up and claimed that she owned the rights of salvage on the *Jim Turner.* She had a bill of sale written on the stationery of the Fannin County Bank to G. D. Hoffman, dated December 28, 1889, to back up her claim. Hoffman had secured permission to raise the ship but was unsuccessful. The bill of sale was signed by S. B. Allen, who was the captain of the *Jim Turner.* Mrs. Ferguson was G. D. Hoffman's heir. Allen quit the river after the sinking and went to work for the Fannin County Bank, later becoming its president.

Old Man River probably ended the dispute in the late 1850s, when the river changed its course and the wreck site ended up on the Oklahoma side of the river, completely covered by river sand again.

Metal detectors can find buried treasure and trained dogs can locate marijuana. But what would one use to detect 200 casks of China whiskey?

There have been no more sightings of the phantom liquor

boat. Imagine the Feds showing up and applying 1993 revenue stamps on the old casks as they came out of the sand! Supposedly, a true story sequel developed in 1911, when a crew of workmen managed to scrape away fifteen feet of earth and then pumped out enough water to bring up one cask. Before the salvage party got sober, the excavation caved in and the crew retired.

An ad in an early newspaper tells about the *Jim Turner:* "Ho! For the Red River. The new, splendid, light Steamer *Jim Turner,* Allen, master, will commence as regular packet, from New Orleans to all points on river above the Raft, on or above the 1st of June next and continue throughout the Season . . ." (December 24, 1852).[32]

Bowie County

Bowie County was named for James Bowie and was formed in 1840 out of Red River County, with Boston as the county seat. At one time Miller County, Arkansas, claimed land in what is now Texas. In 1819 Ben Milam established a store on the Red River at Long Prairie, and when he discovered he was in Arkansas he moved into Texas. Milam had settled on the Red River in a deal with Arthur G. Wavell to help him settle and

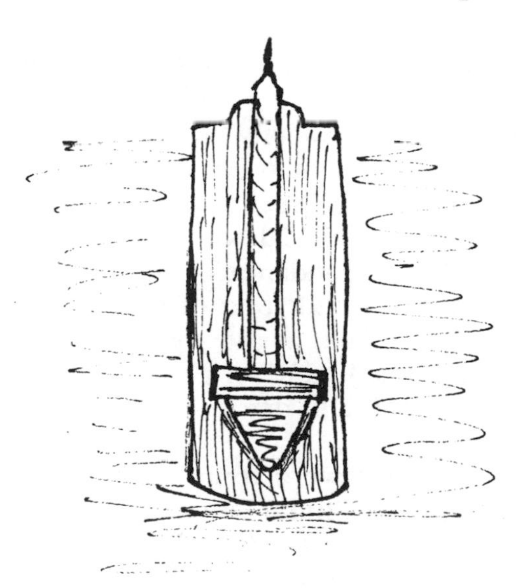

develop an empresario grant he had received in 1826. The project failed when the United States claimed that the land lay east of the Mexican border line in the United States.

While on the Red River, Milam became interested in steamboats on the Upper Red River. He managed to get a small steamboat past the raft in 1831. In 1835 he made a trip to Mexico to ask the land commissioner to give title to settlers in the Red River area. On his return he was captured by men under Martín Perfecto de Cos. He managed to escape and joined Texian forces at Goliad that were planning an attack to retake San Antonio. Milam was killed in the successful attack.[1]

Actually, Miller County, Arkansas, extended into what is now Texas and Oklahoma. In two separate treaties with Indians and the United States, Arkansas gave up their claims to land north of the Red River. Difficulties in the disputed territory of Miller County and Texas (Red River County) finally led the Arkansas legislature to abolish Miller County and pull out of the area. Another Miller County was established in 1874 with its present boundaries.

Families dispossessed in the Oklahoma Territory, which was turned over to the Indians, as well as families in Arkansas wanting to have a Texas address, moved into Bowie County. They joined a group of adventurers and explorers who had been living in the area since about 1800. The first town created was started where the South Fork of Mill Creek empties into the Red River, which is about ten miles north of present-day DeKalb. Some of the first families to settle were the Burkhams, Cutrights, and Spurlocks. Shortly afterwards, Nathaniel Hickman settled in what is known as Hickman's Prairie.

The settlement at Mill Creek grew, and a surveyor by the name of F. Seidikum officially laid out the townsite of Berlin on the Red River. With an abundance of lumber on hand, several enterprising carpenters built one of the first steamboats in Texas on ways at Berlin.[2] Just as the town was getting started in 1844, the unpredictable Red River changed its course and left the town of Berlin high and dry two miles from the river. It withered and died.[3]

Two other landings were founded upriver from Berlin: Long Prairie and Spanish Bluff. Plantations along the Red River and also on the Sulphur River all had their own landings. No records of them have been uncovered.

Fulton, Arkansas, was one of the most important ports north of Shreveport, and a lot of business that moved into Texas was routed through Fulton. Twelve steamboats regularly moved between Shreveport and Fulton, and when water conditions were right all of these boats continued on up the Red River. Boats included were the *Texarkana, Flavilla, Morgan, Texas, La Belle, Selma, George, Lightest, Era, Rudolph,* and *Gladiola.* Capt. Matthew Moss and his brother, William, owned the steamboat *Hempstead* based out of Fulton. Once Captain William took the boat up the river alone, and on his return trip a big overflow caught up with his boat. The whole country was covered with water, and when the captain came to a bend in the river he decided to just cut across and save time. The water looked deep, but halfway across the cornfield he went aground. Records tell the story: "... boat lost on Lost Prairie." Fulton remained a steamboat oasis even after the railroads took most of the river traffic. The steamer *Waukesha,* owned by W. H. McWhorter of Fulton, continued hauling cotton out of the upper Red River as late as 1894. Two other ships, the *Ellen* and the *Kingfisher,* both owned by Dan Harkness, operated on the Red even after the *Waukesha.*[4]

A letter published in the *Dallas News* in 1893 from T. J. Crooks, of Denison, explains how he came to Texas, crossing the Red River near the mouth of Mill Creek in 1843. It tells the story about the old landing of Berlin and about the building of the first steamboat there. Parts of the letter were taken out of district court records of Red River County.

> My personal advent into Texas was when I crossed the Red River at the mouth of Mill Creek in December, 1843, and there and then saw the first evidences of civilization in Texas. It was a real steamboat in course of construction already launched and almost completed. It was no doubt the first and last real live steamboat ever built on Red River above the Raft. It was being constructed under the auspices of a man by the name of Dyer. That Spring, 1844, occurred the biggest overflow ever known in Red River. The whole upper Red River Valley was inundated except a few artificial hills thrown up by the "Moundbuilders," a pre-historic race. On one of these mounds near the mouth of Kiamitia rested the dwelling of Capt. Travis Wright, another was the Pecan Point farm residence. The evidences of this flood were visible on

the second bottom by drift and sand marks in and on trees fifteen to twenty feet from the ground for many years after. It came so suddenly and not being anticipated, that the settlers were unprepared for it. There was great loss of stock and some (human) lives. Whole families took refuge in trees, where they remained for days before rescued.

In this catastrophe the Dyer steamboat did valiant service in rescuing the unfortunate inhabitants, and about all the good it ever did do, for its first attempted trip down the river it sank somewhere in the neighborhood of the Raft. But it was a North Texas enterprise. Every stick of lumber in it was cut from Texas forests, and not exceeding five miles from where the boat was constructed was any of the lumber cut. The lumber for the steamer was all sawed by hand "whipshaw" fashion. A trestle was built up a number of feet from the ground on which the saw log was rolled. Then one man took his position on top of the log and another on the ground while each pulled at the respective ends of the straight up and down saw and thus the lumber was made.[5]

When Dyer died, his estate was taken over by John Dyer, not to the satisfaction of brother Robert, who filed actions in district court. The suit probably caused the story of the first steamboat on the Red River to be preserved.

Further court action shows that the engine that was placed in the first steamboat had cost $800. The boat went down on its first voyage near the raft, and the engine was sold to James Latimer and Dixon Dyer. The paper trail ends with another suit seeking to recover the engine or $1,000. Steamboat stories that end up in court have a way of ending without revealing how they turn out. It is not known how the case of the missing engine was resolved. Probably if it was as tough as most of the old steamboat engines, it was put into another boat and served until its new owner also struck a snag.

Jefferson: An Impossible Dream

Tourists by the thousands come to Jefferson and listen with rapt attention as historians, guides, and coffee shop operators tell of great riverboats that tied up at wharves at one time to disgorge manufactured goods and load cotton, hides, beeswax, and other products produced by farmers and ranchers of northeastern Texas.

Visitors look at their maps, shake their heads, and try to figure out if someone is trying to pass an old legend off on them as the gospel truth. But then, truth is stranger than fiction. And so is the tale of Jefferson, Texas, which at one time was running Galveston a close second as the busiest port in Texas.

Jefferson's brief glory was made possible by a quirk of nature that defied the law of gravity and caused water to run upstream. This paradox was made possible because of the Great Red River Raft. Actually, it wasn't a raft at all but a gigantic logjam that was anything but a raft. It was a solid mass with logs stacked in all directions and held together with dirt, trash, moss, weeds, and vines. Stretching for a distance of up to twenty-five to thirty or more miles, in as many as two different locations, the raft was an ever-growing, yet crumbling mass of uprooted trees, brush, debris, and rotting animal carcasses. In some areas the raft had been in place long enough that the tangled mass was filled with soil, and grass and trees grew in the raft. Men and animals could easily cross on this solid bridge. The raft started about twenty-five miles north of Natchitoches. The ultimate top was perhaps as much as a hundred miles upstream.

When the first white men entered the Red River Valley, the Indians told them that the raft had been there many years. So, actually no one knows just when it really got its start. On the raft's lower end it was constantly coming unraveled, but at the same time new debris would be added to the upper end. During times of extremely heavy rains, the raft would be shaken and broken but always seemed to mend itself.

Even when the raft was at its greatest lengths, some riverboats always managed to find a way to bypass it and make their way up or down the river. The lower part of the Red River Valley was laced with bayous, creeks, and rivers that fed the giant river. As the water backed up into the bayous, the adventuresome riverboat captains would manage to find water links to squeeze around the big raft and make it into the upper Red, where the rafts did not exist.[1]

It was this backing up of water that made a deepwater river port out of Jefferson of Marion County. The water backed up 12 Mile Bayou, through Soda Lake, into Caddo Lake, and finally into Big Cypress Bayou, which flowed past the ferry established by Allen Urquhart sometime in 1841. The earlier date of establishing the ferry in 1836 is not supported by historical research.[2]

Before the steamboats ventured into the Big Cypress Bayou, they had been running into Soda and Caddo lakes for several years. Henry M. Shreve, captain of the *Velocipede,* explored and opened the Sabine River up to steamboat trade. He is also credited with making the trial runs on 12 Mile Bayou that proved that the system was navigable. He sailed the *Archimedes* into Caddo Lake in 1834. Shortly thereafter, Ben V. Crooks, master of the *Rover,* started making regular runs into Caddo Lake. During the 1830s, more and more steamboats began to service the landings in Caddo Lake. As early as 1834 the steamboat *Indian* explored Big Cypress Bayou, but probably did not go as high as where Allen Urquhart eventually established his ferry.[3] In January of 1845 the State of Texas established the Soda Lake Customs District. The collection of taxes at Port Caddo was somewhat of a failure, and collection efforts virtually ceased with the murder of a customs officer.[4]

Some historians confused Jefferson of Jefferson County with Jefferson of Marion County, thus giving a date of 1836 for the founding of Jefferson of Marion County. Actually, it appears that a group of would-be settlers of Smithland, on the north bank of Big Cypress, became disgruntled because they could not get clear title to land in the area and jumped at Allen Urquhart's offer of a place to settle legally. An interview with a grandson of Allen Urquhart, published in the Jefferson *Jimplecute* in 1937, tells of the events leading up to the laying out of the townsite. After Urquhart's offer to sell part of his land to the Smithland settlers, a meeting was called with Urquhart at his ferry.

Evidently, Urquhart had experience in selling land, as he had a barrel of whiskey under a brush arbor with enough tin cups to go around. It goes without saying that everyone enjoyed the party, with a cup of whiskey going for ten cents. Probably all of the land being offered for sale was spoken for long before the barrel ran dry.[5]

The ferry owned by Urquhart was operated by Berry Durham, who also purchased sixty acres of land with an agreement to operate the ferry for five years. This agreement was altered in 1843, when Durham took Tinsly Weaver into the operation. Urquhart, Durham, and Weaver each apparently received one-third of the proceeds of ferry operations. By 1845 trouble between Urquhart and Durham developed, according to documents filed requiring a strict accounting from Durham on lot sales. A plan of the townsite was drawn by Hugh Hensey on January 5, 1846, and was laid out with provisions for commercial lots on the water front. The commercial streets were laid out parallel to Big Cypress, giving plenty of space for warehouse districts and wharves. Even though Urquhart is considered the founder of Jefferson, he never lived in the city, maintaining his residence in Daingerfield. He died in 1866 and is buried in Daingerfield.[6]

In addition to the town plat laid out by Urquhart, a subdivision known as the Alley Addition was created by Daniel N. Alley. In contrast to Urquhart's subdivision, which envisioned the commercial potential of Big Cypress Bayou, Alley had dreams of stately homes filling his subdivision. Perhaps there was a need for both types. Jefferson became a shipping giant, and at the same time the affluent plantation owners created the ante-bellum setting for the finer things, with the wealth generated by the plantation system. Fine homes were built in Jefferson and on the plantations in the area. In 1860 the population of Marion County was thought to be 3,977, including 2,017 slaves. Plantations as large as 23,000 acres were the rule.[7,8]

After the steamboat *Indian* made an exploratory trip part of the way up Big Cypress Bayou in 1834, there seems to be no further record of boats venturing up the bayou, probably because there was no reason to probe past known landings. The steamboat *Llama,* W. W. Withenbury captain, made it all the way to Jefferson in 1843 or 1844. William Perry was responsible for the voyage, either under contract or through some other arrangement. Tradition tells that his wife, Sardinia, gave birth to the first child born in Jefferson.[9]

The *Jimplecute* carried a good description of those early steamboat days:

> Capt. Withenbury's *Llama* picked up 154 bales of Texas cotton at Smithland on March 23, 1845 destined for New Orleans. The shipper was Todd and Brander and the charge was $1.37 per bale.
>
> Many steamers and boats of all descriptions treaded Jefferson waters. The *Bloomer* was a small 79-ton packet which steamed through these waters frequently. The *Daily Picayune,* dated Feb. 17, 1858, carried the following news concerning the *Bloomer's* cargo which had arrived in New Orleans from Jefferson. "It carried 610 bales of cotton, 300 sacks of cotton seed, 600 hides and five barrels of beef." [The *Bloomer* almost sank in November of 1858 when it struck a snag a short distance below Jefferson. The boat leaked so rapidly that there was one foot of water in the hold before the problem was discovered. The *Bloomer* was kept afloat until it reached Jefferson, where the damage was repaired. The cargo was but slightly injured. (*Marshall News Messenger,* November, 1857)]
>
> The *Daily Jimplecute,* dated March 29, 1875, carried an advertisement by the Independent People's Line, which stated that the splendid new and fast passenger packet, *Col. A. P. Kouns,* mastered by Mart H. Kouns, and E. F. Gillen, clerk, would leave on Saturday, April 3. On the same date an article was carried to the effect that this same boat would make special round trips to Shreveport for the sum of $4.00.

> Another boat, which was listed as a passenger packet, *Lotus No. 8*, was shown as a regular Jefferson and New Orleans packet. The master was D. D. Dannals, and the clerk was H. C. Heatt. The agent at Jefferson was W. B. Chew.
>
> Other boats of 1874 were the *Magnet* and the steamer *O. H. Durfee*. Many, many others steamed into Jefferson waters, bringing immigrants, household furnishings, and other necessities of life. These craft were very important in carrying passengers on the great rivers. A passenger traveling to central Georgia, via steamboat from Jefferson to James' Landing on the Mississippi and to Memphis, Tennessee, where train could be taken, would be en route for two weeks.

The Clarksville *Northern Standard* reported in April of 1844 that Jefferson was the head of navigation.[10] Several times before the coming of the railroad to North and East Texas, the *Northern Standard* reported a shortage of newsprint due to the inability of steamers to get up the Red River in dry weather. In each instance the editor wryly noted that he had newsprint in warehouses in Jefferson, but due to travel conditions had not been able to get the paper to Clarksville.[11]

As soon as the first riverboat made it to Jefferson, the backers of the town organized to clear the overhanging obstructions from Big Cypress Bayou and began to make plans to develop Jefferson into an inland river port. One point that made Jefferson a good natural river port was the fact that it was located where two branches of Big Cypress Bayou came together again after the stream had divided to flow on either side of Saint Catherine's Island. This afforded a wide area in the bayou and an excellent place to turn steamboats around. Around this natural harbor a concentration of warehouses and wharves were built up during the next fifteen years.[12]

The first passenger steamboat arrived in Jefferson during 1854, with 130 passengers. The boat was evidently headed someplace else and went to Jefferson to discharge some cargo.[13] It was obvious that during these early days the people in Jefferson were not ready to accommodate steamboat passengers. Buck Barry, a Texas Ranger who wrote of his experiences, had this to say about Jefferson in 1845: "There were several houses under construction but there was only one finished. It was a log cabin built without a nail in it. It was covered with split boards and they were weighted down and held in place by small logs on top of them. It had a puncheon floor and a stick and mud chimney."[14]

By 1859 Jefferson was on a Maj. William Bradfield daily stage route that ran between Shreveport, Marshall, and Jefferson. The trip was made in one day, using four horses and post coaches.[15] In 1866 Bradfield established a daily line of hacks running from Marshall to Jefferson in the morning and returning in the evening. He called it "The People's Line." A post office was granted for Jefferson in 1846.[16]

Capt. Sid Smith, of the steamboat *Afton Jr.,* announced in 1857 that he would run his freight and passenger packet regularly between Jefferson and New Orleans, touching at all intermediate landings. "No pains will be spared to protect the interest of the shippers and to insure the comfort of passengers." (Advertisement in the *Marshall News Messenger,* September 19, 1857.)

It did not take long for Jefferson to move to the forefront as a shipping center. Wharves were built along the bayou for a mile, and great brick warehouses were erected – but not overnight. Businessmen began to open retail and wholesale houses for hardware, clothing, groceries, and furniture. The years before the Civil War were ones of steady growth. Marion County was formed in 1860, and shortly thereafter Jefferson was named as the county seat.[17] The town was undergoing a building boom, and the Texas legislature appropriated $304,000 for Texas waterways, with Jefferson slated to get $21,298 for an improved turning basin. Unfortunately, this project was not completed before the Civil War stopped thoughts of construction.[18]

Growth in Jefferson was fast, and by 1848 the people decided that it was time to incorporate their city. S. H. Ellis was elected the first mayor and was succeeded by J. W. Brickell the following year. The city charter provided fines for indecent conduct, abusive language, and drunkenness. A touch of puritanism was inserted with a provision that only druggists and physicians could operate on Sunday. Taxes included a toll on bridges, ferries, and steamboats, plus a poll tax of every white male over twenty.[19]

One interesting aspect of steamboat shipping throughout Texas was the use of symbols rather than names to identify recipients of merchandise and towns. For instance, Marshall was known as "King of Diamonds." Merchandise headed for Marshall would have a "King of Diamonds" inscribed on the package, together with the brand or initials of the person for whom the shipment was consigned. Longview was known as the "Ace of Hearts," and Jefferson as the "King of Spades." This was done since a great many workers and slaves, who could not read, worked as deck hands. They could readily identify symbols and in this manner load and discharge freight at the various ports. Many ranchers used their own cattle brand as their mark.[20]

With the opening of navigation on Caddo Lake in the early 1830s, plantations in the area began to grow and prosper. Just as soon as transportation became available on Big Cypress Creek, more large plantations were put into cultivation. When the Civil War started in 1860, a substantial number of regal homes had been built in Jefferson and the immediate area. The lifestyles of the plantation owners and their ladies closely paralleled those on the Brazos River. Fortunately, a number of these homes built before 1860 have been preserved in Jefferson. The plantation owners used slave labor, reflected in the hand-hewn timbers found in some of the stately homes.[21]

Before the Civil War, thousands upon thousands of immigrants came through Jefferson simply because this was the deepest penetration into North Texas for mass transportation on the rivers. Families could board a river steamer in the heart-

RIVER BRANDS – To assist rivermen who could not read, the destination of all merchandise shipped on steamboats was indicated by pictures that anyone could understand.

land of the eastern United States, and by riding down any river leading to the Mississippi they would soon be in New Orleans. There boats would take them up the Red River to the mouth of 12 Mile Bayou, where they began the last leg of their trip to Jefferson. The city of Jefferson had become a center of hotels and boardinghouses of all types. Westward-bound immigrants could purchase a wagon and team and all of the necessary supplies to tide them over until they could set up their own homes.[22]

As the Civil War loomed near, a number of men enlisted in a Marshall Company headed by Walter P. Lane. Two additional companies were organized in Jefferson in 1862. Col. W. B. Ochiltree formed a company consisting of ninety-eight volunteers that became John K. Cocke's Company D of the Eighteenth Texas Infantry Regiment. W. P. Saufley organized the "Marion Rifles," consisting of 107 mounted men, that formed Company A of the First Texas Cavalry Regiment, John B. Hood's Brigade. By the end of 1862, more than 500 men from Marion County were serving in the Confederate Army.[23]

The pinch of the war was not felt immediately in Jefferson. In fact, in some ways business remained steady. Cotton was still brought in from the surrounding area for shipment to New Orleans in the early part of the war. The Confederates established a slaughterhouse and packing plant in Jefferson, and during the period of its operation thousands of head of cattle and sheep were processed in the plant. The meat products were shipped down the river to New Orleans, where they were reshipped to Confederate forces throughout the South. Despite all of the efforts of the Union forces to cut off the meat supply, the plant continued operation until the end of the war. As a by-product, a tannery was set up and boots and shoes were manufactured during this period. Candles and soap were made from the surplus tallow by the firm of Nusabaum and Lindsay. While the meat-packing plant operated until the end of the war, it drew criticism from the very beginning due to lack of sufficient cattle, no system of inspection, and undesirable products. The same was true with the candle and soap plant that was unable to secure enough old wood to burn for making alkali. Green wood was not a satisfactory substitute for old wood.[24]

Kellyville, Texas: While not a part of the city of Jefferson, the products of the Kelly Plow Company were shipped out of Jefferson in large quantities. Originally called Four-Mile-Branch because it was four miles west of Jefferson, the business was started by Zachariah Lockett and John A. Stewart in 1843, when they began to make plows and operate a general repair shop. In 1852 George Addison Kelly joined the group, and when he became part owner the townsite was called Kellyville. The firm's name was changed to Kelly and Stewart in 1858. Kelly became full owner in 1860 and brought out the Blue Kelly Plow that was accepted universally because of its simple and effective design. A community with a population estimated from several hundred to 1,000 grew up centered around the plow factory. Two churches and a school were built, and in 1883 a post office was established. During the Civil War, the Kelly Plow Company turned out cast-iron cannon balls by the thousands, as well as civilian utensils and plows. Other than a small part of their products that were consumed locally, all of the output of the Kelly Plow Company was shipped out of Jefferson. The plant burned in 1880 and in 1882 was moved to Longview.[25]

At the end of the Civil War, life did not return to normal immediately. Since Jefferson was a prosperous community and a growing seaport, carpetbaggers were soon a force to be reckoned with as they took over governmental affairs. Capt. William Perry was killed in the street in front of the J. R. Cornelius home on January 2, 1869. His death triggered the murder of a carpetbagger named George Smith, which brought a contingent of Federal troops into the city. A stockade called "Sand Town" was built on a hill just outside of town, and the troops were quartered there. Also, Jefferson County citizens were imprisoned at the stockade and suffered through cruel treatment that took quite a few lives. Colonel Loughery, publisher of the Jefferson *Daily Times* of 1869, was instrumental in ending the tyranny of the military tribunal by exposing their deeds in his paper. He sent copies of his newspaper to members of Congress and leading newspapers throughout the country. The Yankees finally left and the carpetbaggers were voted out of office as quickly as citizenship was restored to Confederate soldiers. Reconstruction days in Jefferson have long been remembered. During that time, a military appointee, A. G. Malloy, held the office of mayor by order of General Reynolds and sustained it by armed soldiers. He and his city council of union sympathizers ran up a debt that exceeded $250,000. This deficit remained on the books for ninety-two years, with the last payment made in 1962.[26]

It took a few years for productivity to return to Jefferson and the surrounding area, but by 1867–68 the steamboats were again running on regular schedules and cotton was once again being brought in for shipment. By 1870 the town reached a population in excess of 10,000. It was during this time that Jefferson was said to be second only to Galveston in tonnage handled by the ports.[27]

The heart of Jefferson's commercial district, including the huge warehouses and main business houses, were on Dallas, Polk, Austin, and Walnut streets. Fires gutted this area several times, but most of the businesses were rebuilt. The city had numerous wagon yards on the outskirts of town, and on Walnut Street there were accommodations for travelers who carried their own bedrolls. Dallas Street was the center of town during the 1870s. The Haywood House, built by Gen. H. P. Marby in 1865, was a four-story brick building that covered almost an entire block.

Another brick building on Dallas housed a bar and dancehall downstairs, and a meeting room upstairs was used by the Masons, Elks, Woodmen of the World, Knights of Pythias, and Odd Fellows. There was also a cotton mill on Dallas that made denim cloth. The Excelsior Hotel, still going strong in 1993, was noted as being one of the leading hotels in Texas. It was furnished largely with original rosewood, mahogany, and cherry wood furniture. In the lobby today are old registers bearing such historic signatures as Rutherford B. Hayes, Ulysses S. Grant, Jacob Astor, W. H. Vanderbilt, Jay Gould, Oscar Wilde, and Mrs. Lyndon Johnson, to mention a few. On display across the street from the Excelsior Hotel is the Gould family private railroad car. Its lavish furnishings reflect Gould's lifestyle.

Jefferson's business district had something for everyone. In all there were about a hundred businesses, eighteen commission markets, twelve wholesale grocery houses, seven drug stores, five banks, four wholesale dry goods houses, four dealers in hides, four wagon yards, three hardware stores, three livery stables, and several machine shops. The big commission houses/merchants included Graham & Taylor; Goyne, Harper & Murphy; A. Gilham; Middlebrooks & Hall; and A. C. Allen.[28]

A report issued by the Army Chief of Engineers in 1873 for the year 1871 gives an insight into the amount of merchandise shipped out during one of the Golden Years:

Shipped:		
Cotton (Sept. 1, 1870 to Sept. 1, 1871)	76,328	bales
Dry hides	84,762	
Green hides	18,471	
Peltries	84,623	
Bois d'arc seed	9,721	bushels
Cattle	5,381	head
Lumber	121,000	board feet
Pig Iron	Amt. not ascertained	
Received:		
General supplies	67,822	tons[29]

It is interesting to note the large shipment of bois d'arc seed. When planted in a row, these trees made an almost impenetrable fence. The seeds were in great demand in the North and Northeast. When barbed wire was invented, the gathering of bois d'arc seed stopped abruptly.

During this period Jefferson installed a system to manufacture artificial gas by burning pine knots at an intense heat. A few of the old gas retorts are still around, with one being at the corner of the Excelsior House.[30]

In 1874 Jefferson boasted one of the first artificial ice plants in Texas. The plant was operated by Boyle and Scott. B.J. Benefield delivered the ice in a wagon for ten cents per pound. Tradition says that Boyle left Jefferson to go north to raise money to develop his idea; however, J. E. Hasty says that he raised the money before he went north. Anyway, Boyle never returned, and Scott claimed bankruptcy. Probably Mr. Hasty lost his job delivering ice. In about the same year, U. B. Uden manufactured the first commercial beer in Texas. Mr. Uden probably was seeking a "long cool one."[31]

Another first was accomplished in Jefferson in 1883. Despite the fact that steamboat days were gone, Capt. Ben

Bonham built and successfully launched the *Alpha.* The *Alpha* was regularly inspected by William Applegate, local inspector of boilers, and by Capt. W.E. Riddle, inspector of hulls, of Shreveport, and both pronounced the steamer "O.K. in every particular." The *Alpha* had a capacity of 450 bales of cotton and was assigned to work the coastal trade.[32]

The years from about 1867–68 through 1873 have been described as the "Golden Years" in Jefferson. Of course, the years before the Civil War were also full of growth, bustle, and entertainment. During this period the Jefferson Opera House came into being and flourished.

Practically all frontier towns, especially those that boomed, were notorious for murders. Jefferson was no exception. Murder Alley, a short off-shoot from Line Street, ran down to the river. It earned its name because for a time a body, or even two, could be found there every morning.[33] And, of course, there was the famous "Diamond Bessie," who met her death in Jefferson on Sunday, January 21, 1878. Annie Stone, daughter of a New York businessman, was seduced at age fifteen and afterwards became a high-class prostitute. She became famous for her beauty and for the diamonds that she collected from her many admirers. She met Abe Rothschild about fifteen months before she traveled with him to Jefferson, registering in the Old Capitol Hotel. On Sunday, January 21, Abe and Annie went on a picnic in the woods across Big Cypress Bayou. Rothschild left Jefferson alone, telling folks that Annie had already left. Her body was found two weeks later. Rothschild's three successive trials attracted national press. He was finally acquitted despite an impressive array of prosecuting attorneys. Annie still "lives" in Jefferson. The trial of Abe Rothschild is reenacted each year at Pilgrimage time, with the stage production sponsored by the Jessie Allen Wise Garden Club. Many have looked but none have reported finding the fabulous diamonds that Bessie was wearing the last time she was seen.[34]

Through the years Washington legislators heard from two different camps concerning the removal of the rafts from the Red River. Interests on the Red River wanted the obstructions removed in order for steamboats to be able to travel to the upper reaches of the river, mainly in the counties of Bowie, Red River, Lamar, Fannin, and Grayson. Small riverboats had been detouring the raft for years, but larger boats could not get through. The interests in Jefferson, Marshall, and in the area surrounding Caddo Lake believed status quo was their best bet. Eventually, the pressure for the removal of the raft reached a point that Congress took action.

The first attempt to remove the raft was made under the direction of Major Shreve, who battered his way through the mass with a snagboat; however, within a short time the raft was building anew. In 1852 efforts were made to build canals around the raft, but this was halted as unsatisfactory. It was 1872 before Congress finally appropriated $150,000 to remove the raft. Previously, most efforts to remove the obstruction had been with conventional means and snagboats. This time Capt. C. W. Howell, engineer in charge of the project, used cans containing ten to twenty pounds of nitroglycerin, which were sunk as near the bottom as possible and then exploded. The plan worked and gradually the raft diminished, until on Thanksgiving Day of 1873 the last portion of the raft was blasted loose and the water and steamboats returned to the main channel.[35]

Life went on in Jefferson after the raft, but at a different tempo. Small steamers still picked times when the water was high and called at Jefferson. In March of 1877 it was reported that the Red River was falling to sixteen feet and two inches above the lowest water of the season. The steamers *Col. A. P. Kouns* and *R. W. Dugan* were in Jefferson. It was reported: "The *Kouns* carried off one thousand bales of cotton at twenty-five cents a bale. The two boats ran heavy against each other. The *Dugan* offered to take cotton at fifty cents. Such prices are simply ruinous."[36] It appears that boats were choosing their times to run to Jefferson during high water and cutting prices trying to keep business.

While merchandise was still flowing on the river, it was at a diminished rate. Merchandise in tons for the years 1877 through 1910 were compiled under the direction of the 63rd U.S. Congress, 1st session, as follows: 1877, 7,650 tons; 1878, 16,000; 1883, 5,000; 1885, 3,550; 1886, 3,050; 1888, 1,900; 1897, 578; 1903, 4,550; 1904, 1,849; 1905, 5,897; 1907, 1,703; 1910, 2,111.[37]

An insight into the effort that Jefferson interests made to

keep traffic flowing to Jefferson was carried in the *Marshall News Messenger* of 1877:

> Mr. Wm. Perry, informs the public through the *Jefferson Herald,* that he has been engaged with twenty hands in cleaning out the Lake, and that the work on the banks from Jefferson to Smithland is finished. He is now ready to commence work on the body of the stream [Big Cypress Bayou], but the water is too high both above and below Smithland. He says: "We have a dam in progress above the bridge at Jefferson, which will be finished next week, the object of which is to throw all the running water out through a slough or chain of lakes on the Harrison side, which will convey the water some six miles below Jefferson, and will, doubtless make all the shallow places dry, if the lower lake comes down to near low water mark."

From the time that the first steamboat entered Jefferson in the winter of 1844–45 to the day that the last boat blasted a fond farewell in 1903, many boats visited the Queen City on the Bayou. A partial list includes *John Strader,* 1853; *Steamer Echo,* 1853; *Pister Miller,* 1853; *Steamer Caddo,* 1853; *National,* 1860; *Fleta,* 1875; *Col. A.P. Kouns,* 1875; *R.W. Dugan,* 1877; *Bell Gates,* 1858; *Caddo Bell,* 1857; *Music,* 1856; *White Cliffs,* 1857; *Starlight,* 1858; *Mollie Fellows,* 1866; *Edinburg,* 1875; *Seminole,* 1875; *Lessie B.,* 1875; *John G. Sentell,* 1875; *Dixie,* 1875; *Lizzie Hopkins,* 1868; *C.H. Durfee,* 1875; *R.T. Bryarly,* 1875; *Belle Rowland,* 1875; *Katie P. Kouns,* 1875; *Lotus No. 3,* 1875; *Texas,* 1872; *Edinburg,* 1871; *New Era,* 1868; *J.M. Murphy,* 1869; *Red Cloud,* 1875; *Mittie Stevens,* 1875; *John T. Moore,* 1875; *Llama,* 1844; *Pioneer,* 1865; *Fanny Gilbert,* 1866; *T.D. Hine,* 1867; *Carrie,* 1868; *Era No. 10,* 1869; *Alpha,* 1880; *Duck River,* 1847; *Maid of Osage,* 1849; *Sylph,* 1849; *G.W. Sentell,* 1889; *Lillie M. Barron,* 1900; *Vesta,* 1846; *Danube; Bessie Warren; Iron Cities; Hempstead.*[38] From other sources: *New Era 9 & 10, Silver City, Ashland, Port Caddo No. 2, Osceola, Cleopa, Lotus No. 8, Magnet, Telegraph.*

A lot of river ports died a graceful death, drying up and fading away into history book pages, but not Jefferson. They struggled to keep their lifeline open by dredging, clearing obstacles, straightening channels, and diverting water. Federal appropriations, starting in 1873, reflect this effort: 1872,

$10,000; 1873, $50,000; 1876, $13,000; 1878, $15,000; 1879, $6,000; 1886, $18,000; 1890, $10,000; 1892, $2,000; 1894, $10,000; 1896, $5,000; 1907, $10,000; 1909, $6,000; 1910, $5,000; 1910, $100,000; 1911, $2,500; 1912, $5,000; for a total of $266,500.[39]

After the raft was removed from the Red River, people began to drift away from Jefferson to find employment. Merchants closed and sought other towns. But the hard core of people stayed on, and the county seat remained firmly fixed in Jefferson. Back in the "Golden Days" an annual Queen Mab celebration was staged to rival New Orleans' celebration. This featured a parade more than a mile in length. But in modern times, a group of historians and civic workers began a campaign that has brought Jefferson to front and center in the world of tourism. The Pilgrimage is a yearly celebration that has grown until now it offers something for everyone. The Jefferson Historical Parade draws interest from a wide area. A part of the celebration features historical window displays in the downtown area. For those who really want to relive the days of the steamboaters, float trips down Big Cypress Bayou to Caddo Lake are offered throughout the year.

The Diamond Bessie Murder Trial is now a yearly event staged by locals and based on the old court records. Key roles have been passed down in families. To back up all of the celebrations, a large number of restored homes are opened during festive days for tours. Jefferson boasts having more homes, sites, and structures bearing Texas State Historical Survey Medallions than any town in Texas. Tour buses can be seen on Jefferson's streets almost any day.

Jefferson's past is remembered in the Oakwood Cemetery. Many of the steamboat captains are buried in Jefferson, as well as other figures such as Diamond Bessie. At least one marker is unique. Two graves are bound together by a chain anchored to two iron posts. The men buried in these graves fell in love with the same woman and settled the matter on Polk Street with a shootout. Both were killed. Graves of veterans from all wars, and of many who died during the infamous carpetbagger days, are scattered throughout the old cemetery.

Countless newspapers and regional magazines have paid recognition to Jefferson's comeback. The city is proud of its ghosts, and has them all dressed up and ready to perform.[40]

Caddo Lake

Caddo Lake, one of the largest natural lakes in Texas, has been all things to mankind since its mystic beginning.

Caddo Indians loved to tell the legend about how the lake was formed. Old chiefs would get a mysterious, far-away look in their eyes as they looked back into the past when the Caddo Nation covered East Texas with their lodges. One night a great Caddo chief had a vision as he sat beside the still waters of the lake. The moonlight, filtered through the sheltering cypress trees, cast a mystic light on the peaceful scene. His vision was of an impending disaster unless he moved his people to high ground. His people listened to the warning and abandoned their village in the valley. Soon the earth trembled, the ground sank, and a flood filled the space they had inhabited. The Indians were thankful for the new and beautiful lake, and they rebuilt their lodges along its shores.[1]

Another Indian legend tells of how a great Caddo chief displeased the Great Spirit, who sent an earthquake to form the lake and swallow the chief.[2]

Scientists do not like legends. They like to be able to apply their scientific rules to everything – even Caddo Lake. They theorize that in 1811 there was an upheaval along the New

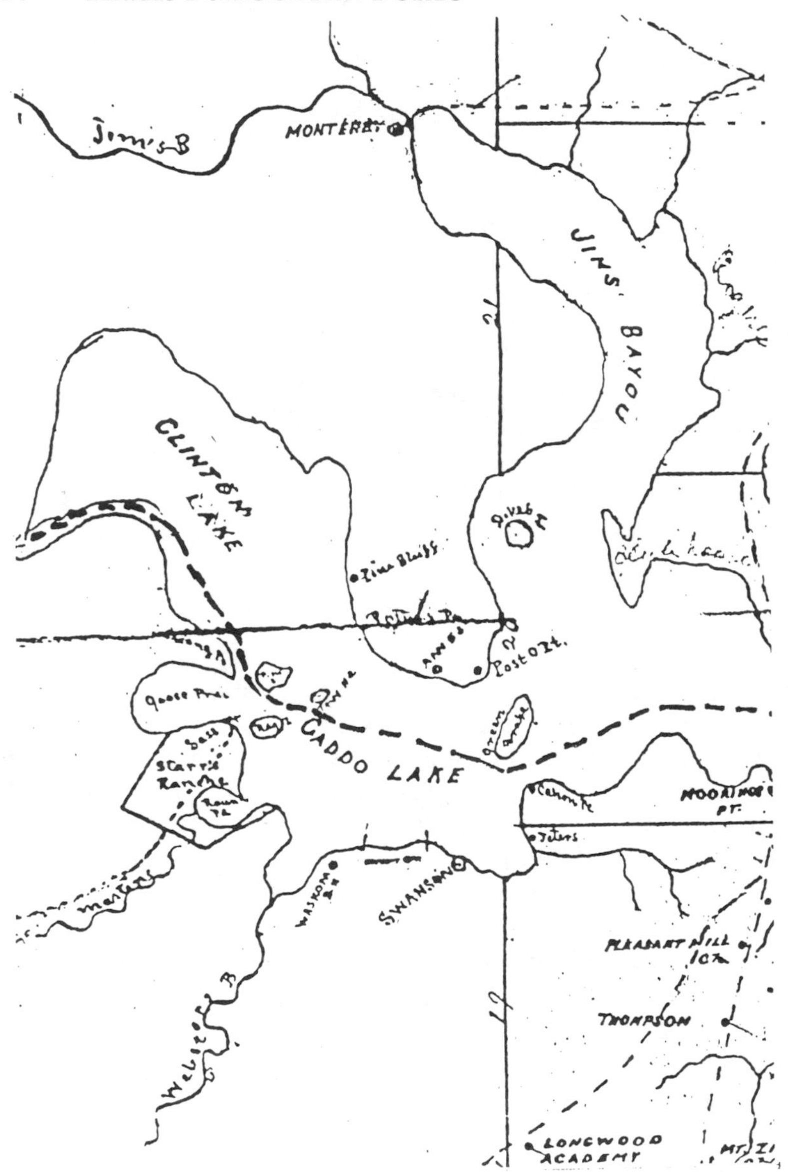

BACKWATER caused by the Great Raft that blocked the Red River for scores of years led to the waterway into Jefferson being "discovered" by steamboat captains in the early 1830s. On the right-hand page it will be noted that 12 Mile Bayou leads off the Red River. Follow the line of dots to the top of the right-hand page through Soda Lake and then shift to the left-hand page through

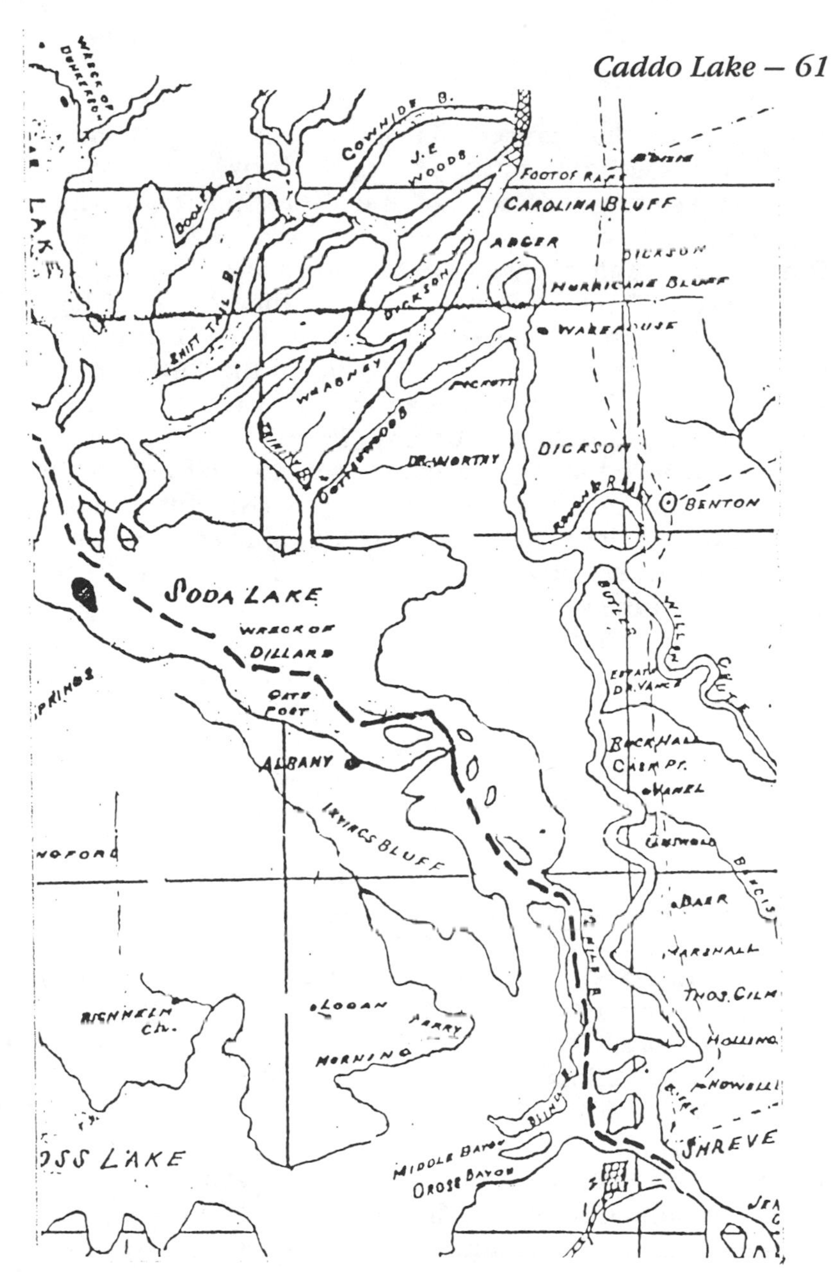

Caddo Lake into Clinton Lake. Off Clinton Lake the Big Cypress Bayou led to Jefferson. As long as the raft was in place, enough water backed up through this system of waterways to give safe passage to steamboats. Jim's Bayou leads off Caddo Lake with Monterey at the top of the Bayou. (Original map from files of Marion County Historical Society)

Madrid Fault that caused many unusual things to happen across the southern states. The earth broke open and gave forth with sulfurous fumes, and the Mississippi River ran backwards for a few minutes. Reelfoot Lake in Tennessee was formed as a result. So, why not Caddo Lake?[3]

There is the school that contends that the great log raft which formed in the Red River sometime in the late 1700s was the culprit. The water just backed up in the low places, and liked it so much that when the raft was removed the lakes remained behind as a souvenir. People of this school of thought believe that a great conspiracy existed in Shreveport to destroy the raft, thus destroying Jefferson and sending all the business to Shreveport. Capt. Henry Shreve, the army engineer who successfully blew up the raft in 1873, was supposedly a part of the scheme.[4]

Then there are the practical folks who blame the Regulators and Moderators. Their logic holds that the Regulators were miffed when Robert Potter switched sides, and so they flushed him out of his house so that he could be bushwacked. Times were a bit out of kilter for this story to be credible, but a storyteller has to have a few years of latitude.

Regardless of the scenario one chooses, Caddo Lake, along with its surrounding bayous, lagoons, sloughs, and inlets that seem to disappear into the walls of moss-draped cypress trees, has an air of intrigue and mystery that few lakes can match.

The Caddos, made up of the Kadohadacho proper, Masoni, Upper Natchitoches, Nanatsoho, and the outlying Cahinnio tribes, were discovered by the Spanish in 1541 by the Moscoso Expedition (Luis de Moscoso de Alvarado took over after DeSoto died). LaSalle is thought to have passed through the area trying to find the Mississippi in 1687. A Frenchman, Henri Joutel, recorded a number of Indian tribes. Spanish missionaries came in 1690 but had trouble making a permanent settlement until much later. French missionaries, working out of Fort Natchitoches starting in 1714, made contact with the Indians—much to the displeasure of Spanish authorities and to the detriment of the Caddos.[5]

One thing that bothers scientists is the fact that archaeologists are constantly finding evidence of ancient Caddo villages on what was the bed of the old lake.

Evidently, the Caddos liked the land and Caddo Lake. Sam Houston is quoted as having said that he traveled from the Red River to Nacogdoches without losing sight of an Indian village.[6] Artifacts dating back 20,000 years to the late Pleistocene man have been found in Caddo country. The removal of the Caddos from East Texas is not an event that Texans can view with pride. But to the frontiersman, the Indian was in the way and had to be removed.[7]

Red River County at one time took in thirty-nine northeastern Texas counties. Bowie County was separated from Red River County in 1840. When Cass County was created in 1846, the land around Jefferson was included. After Jefferson grew into a city, Marion County was created from Cass and Harrison counties in 1860 and Jefferson was the county seat. Harrison County, to the south, was created in 1839 from Selby County. Harrison and Marion share the present-day Caddo Lake.[8]

Anglo settlers evidently started coming across the Red River and down into present Harrison, Marion, and Cass counties as early as 1819, when the Adams-Onis Treaty was signed by the United States and Spain. This attempted to fix the western boundary between the United States and Spain as the Sabine River up to 32nd parallel and then straight north until it hit the Red River, then following the river. That was fine until Mexico won her independence from Spain in 1821 and refused to recognize the border. This state of confusion can be seen on early maps that will show Port Caddo sometimes in the United States and sometimes in Texas.[9]

This did not keep Mexico from issuing land titles, and in 1835 the land commissioner of the Nacogdoches district issued twenty-two land patents to Anglo-Americans in the vicinity of Caddo Lake. They went to Hiram Blossom, Wm. Chas. Brookfield, John Chisum, John M. Dow, Patrick Dougherty, Wilson E. Ewing, E. M. Fuller, Franklin Fuller, Clery Guillet, Hudson H. Hall, Henry Harper, James Harris, Wm. McIlwain, Samuel Monday, Samuel Murphy, Joseph Nations, John Patterson, Wm. Paton, Aaron Poe, Bethany Rogers, William Smith, and Elihu D. Spain.[10] During the days when steamboat traffic was at its height on Caddo Lake, strangers were sometimes treated to an unusual sight. Amory Starr, a Caddo plantation owner who had a flare for history and the flamboyant, had built an ancient galley ship that he would staff with a crew of black oarsmen. Starr liked to direct his stately ship while standing in the prow. The plantation owner had cut a passageway near Pine Island that led to his dock. For many years old-timers could still identify this passageway.[11]

Port Caddo

In this period the name of Port Caddo creeps into the records, and in 1845 the Soda Lake District was organized with Port Caddo as the headquarters.[12] In action taken by Santa Anna in 1833, Harrison County was separated from the Nacogdoches and put in a new district called Tenehaw. In 1836 the Tenehaw district became Shelby, making Port Caddo a part of Shelby County. Old boat records show that the steamboat *Indian* had entered Big Cypress Bayou and that the *Nicholas Biddle* identified Port Caddo on their manifest.[13] Port Caddo was located on the south bank of the Big Cypress Bayou near Caddo Lake State Park.[14]

During the 1830s it appears that boat traffic out of Caddo Lake to Shreveport was steady. The steamboat *Charleston* seems to have been the first steamboat to come up the river to Shreveport. It made news because it brought the first two white women to travel as passengers to Shreveport.

Henry M. Shreve, captain of the *Velocipede,* explored 12 Mile Bayou, probably in preparation of making a run into Caddo Lake. He also used the *Archimedes* along 12 Mile Bayou in 1834.

Ben V. Crooks, master of the steamboat *Rover,* seems to have been the first to begin regular runs into the Caddo Lake system. Since Monterey was an established port at this time, he probably called there as well as at Port Caddo on his first trip in 1835.

In 1836 Capt. Ben V. Crooks made a run in the steamboat *Nicholas Biddle* and identified the following ports: Swanson's Landing, Chamards Landing, Port Caddo, Hawks Ferry Landing, and Schenks Ferry Landing.

After making the rounds of the Caddo Lake landings in 1834, the steamboat *Indian* also explored on the Cypress Bayou. Evidently it did not go as far as Allen Urquhart's ferry at

PORT CADDO was a growing port on Caddo Lake that was first visited by paddlewheelers in the early 1830s. It grew rapidly into quite a thriving trading post where Indians and Anglo settlers sold their hides and produce and purchased supplies brought in by the steamboats. As with many other ports of this type, the steamboats could tie up to a wharf that was part of the store, or they could nose into main street and unload directly into waiting wagons. (Drawing by M. B. Cole, used by permission of Harrison County Historical Museum)

soon-to-be-established Jefferson. Other steamboats and their captains who worked this Caddo Lake trade included *Texas*, Capt. Ivy Young, 1837; *Yazoo*, Capt. Ivy Young, 1837–42; *Maid of Kentucky*, Capt. Ruth Edwards; *Little Yazoo*, drew only eleven inches of water empty, Capt. W. W. Wethersbury, 1840; *Robert T. Lytes*, Capt. Lodwick, 1840; *Vista*, 1840, drew only twelve inches water empty; *Washington*, Capt. Ruth Edwards, 1840–41 on regular run from Shreveport to ports on Cypress Bayou; *Water Witch*, Capt. Dan Smoker, 1840–41; and *Swan*, Capt. Rhodes, 1840–45.[15]

In 1837 the Republic of Texas established a customshouse at Port Caddo in an attempt to collect duty on the large volume of freight that was entering the Caddo Lake area. Records show collection of taxes was poor. All ships bound for ports past Port Caddo were registered and customs levied. Farm tools and

COLLECTING TAXES was a dangerous job in Harrison County. The Republic of Texas established a customshouse in Port Caddo in an attempt to collect taxes on merchandise coming into Texas. It was an unpopular tax and so incensed the residents of Port Caddo that on January 23, 1841, a mob shot the sheriff, Dr. John B. Campbell, and burned his tax records. (Drawing by M. B. Cole, used by permission of Harrison County Historical Museum)

implements (when individually owned), clothing, and Bibles were exempt.[16]

On January 29, 1845, Congress decided that taxes must be collected in the Red River and Soda Lake districts and thereby established the collector district of Soda Lake, with L. H Mabitt as collector stationed in Port Caddo. The belligerent attitude of merchants and residents alike in Port Caddo had reached a point that Judge Ochiltree wrote to President Anson Jones that "every peaceful means had been explored to collect the taxes but without success." He asked that fifty men be sent to force collections. No action was taken, probably due to the approaching annexation of Texas to the United States and because the elimination of the hated taxes was near. In fact, the number of people protesting taxes reached the point that Dr. John B. Campbell, coroner and acting sheriff, was assassinated on the main street of Port Caddo in 1840 and robbed of his official papers, including his tax book, which they burned.[17]

Henderson Yoakum, a leading historian in early Texas, once described the East Texas Badlands as "one section of Texas where law was only a passive onlooker."[18]

WITH THE SHERIFF out of the way, a mob tore down the customshouse office and ran one of the deputies out of town. (Drawing by M. B. Cole, used by permission of Harrison County Historical Museum)

Undoubtedly, mail was being brought in on the steamboats plying the waters of Caddo Lake; however, no records have been found. In 1843 as many as three to four steamboats were on the river and lake daily. In January of 1839 a weekly route was established from San Augustine to Port Caddo, via Shelbyville and Shelton's Store, with post offices at Shelton's Store, Bristow's Ferry, at Thomas Timmon's, and Port Caddo. This route was extended from Port Caddo to Coffee's Station in Fannin County on the Red River.[19] The first postmaster was John H. Walker. The office was discontinued in 1866.[20]

Port Caddo continued to prosper after annexation, chiefly because of a system of plantations in the area that were feeding a steady stream of cotton to the port for shipment. But it also developed into a trading center as Caddos brought in their furs to trade for supplies. Gamblers and saloons were commonplace. Port Caddo was known as a boisterous frontier town, and with the murder of a sheriff and the near lynching of a customs officer, the town's reputation stood it in good stead to compete with Monterey as the city devoted to having a good time.[21]

A large warehouse, general mercantile stores, and saloons were clustered at the port. Merchants included John B. Webster, John F. Womack, John F. Williams, Ed Rowe, – Orville, Col. Rene Fritzpatrick, J. D. K. Andrews, Dr. Baldwin, Capt. Josiah Perry, Dr. Howard Perry, Leorin and Joshua Perry, and Judge Geo. B. Adkins, the first chief justice of Harrison County. There was usually at least one commission representative in Port Caddo. J. D. Todd and Co. operated in 1849; W. H. Cobbs in May of 1852; W. B. Perry, 1852; and W. H. Farley, who advertised in the *Texas Republic* in 1855–56: "Dry goods, groceries and receiving and forwarding merchant."[22]

A hotel and tavern on a hill overlooked Port Caddo and several cotton warehouses. The road was heavily traveled in the fall, with ox wagons carrying cotton to be shipped north via Port Caddo. The Port Caddo Road was known in earlier days as Stagecoach Road, and coaches came in over the road blowing a horn for the stop at the Old Stagecoach House on what is now Highway 59.[23]

During the Civil War, Port Caddo experienced a brief flurry of activity, especially with the shipment of gunpowder from the Marshall Powder Mill. The cotton that was on the piers and in warehouses was confiscated by Union troops. Cotton seed destined for the coming crop was also seized by the government.[24]

Travel along the Stagecoach Road junctioned with the Caddo Lake–Cypress Bayou waterway route at Port Caddo, the first important shipping point established on the lake and near the plantations of Walter T. Scott. Scott developed five plantations in northern Harrison County and no doubt was a big shipper out of Port Caddo. Monterey, on Jim's Bayou, was on the overland route of entry into Texas, the Coushatta Trail. That trail was connected to Port Caddo. The commissioners court in Harrison County also ordered a road opened from Marshall to Port Caddo. The ferry at Port Caddo kept this north-south traffic flowing, connecting Port Caddo with Trammel's Trace, the Shreveport road, the road to Marshall, and the route to Nacogdoches. It also linked Port Caddo westward along the Comanche Trail.[25]

SCHENK'S FERRY – This ferry crossed Big Cypress Bayou to connect Port Caddo with Trammel's Trace as well as the Shreveport road and Marshall road. This type of ferry was hooked to a cable and pulled across by a rope tied to the far shore. (Printed in *Port Caddo – A Vanished Village* and reproduced with permission of Harrison County Historical Museum. Artist, M. B. Cole.)

Dr. William Baldwin and his son practiced medicine in and around Port Caddo for a number of years. In the late 1840s Dr. Seaborn J. Arnett moved into the Benton area and began a practice which took him on the riverboats from Port Caddo to Jefferson. Port Caddo was without any church for many years, but ministers of several faiths began holding camp meetings in the area. There was a Baptist church at Leigh, a few miles north, that later moved to Port Caddo.[26]

Port Caddo's star set as Jefferson's started to shine brightly. The first steamboat made it into Jefferson in 1844, and after that the old port faded away into the sunset. Port Caddo's business declined steadily; however, some traffic did not desert until the raft was removed from the Red River in 1873. It had been a flourishing pioneer village and an important shipping point for cotton and other commodities for more than twenty years. It is estimated that the population of Port Caddo may have reached 500 at its peak.[27]

Swanson's Landing

Swanson's Landing was on the south bank of Caddo Lake, as was Port Caddo. Peter Swanson, a slaveowner who operated a plantation in the area, settled on the lake sometime in the early 1830s and was on the list of stops for steamboats that started plying the waters of the lake. Swanson built a log cabin on his land and worked as a surveyor and civil engineer. He died in 1849 (date on tombstone) and his two sons, Dr. W. C. Swanson and Thomas F. Swanson, operated the landing. Buried in the old family cemetery are Swanson's wife, Amelia, and some children, along with several slaves. The cemetery is near Leigh on FM 1999.[28]

The landing was a port of entry for inland Texas points. Swanson's granddaughter, Henrietta, once boarded a river packet at Swanson's Landing and went to St. Paul, Minnesota, without going ashore.

Swanson's Landing was the starting point for one of Texas' first railroads. It extended from the landing to Jonesville and later to Marshall, twenty-three miles distant. When the little line was finally finished, a big celebration was planned for February 1, 1858. Southern Pacific Railroad Company, the owner, was to send a locomotive by steamboat to pull the first train to

Marshall. Crowds lined the route, and some families gathered several days before and camped to witness the smoke-belching locomotive.

The locomotive failed to arrive. But not to be outdone by the lack of a locomotive, someone came up with the idea: four yoke of oxen! The oxen had to do some hard pulling on upgrades, but downhill it was a cinch. Soon Southern Pacific replaced the oxen with real locomotives that earned names and reputations of their own. One was called the *Bull of the Woods* because it had a habit of leaving the rails and crashing through the trees. Another was named the *Ben Johnson* in honor of the banker who evidently put up some money.

Abandoned during the Civil War, the train was taken over by Charlie Hynson, who used mules to pull the cars. After the mules pulled the cars to the top of a grade he would unhitch the mules, load them on the flatcar, and let them ride downhill. A man will do anything to keep workers happy![29]

Swanson's Landing is remembered for the tragic burning of the *Mittie Stephens.* On February 11, 1869, the palatial packet was on her maiden run out of New Orleans, by way of Shreveport, headed for Jefferson. The ship left the dock in Shreveport at 4:00 P.M. and headed down the 12 Mile Bayou that led to Caddo Lake. The luxury ship offered everything to its guests, including fine cuisine from a complement of chefs. Chamber maids, servants, a barber, and a barkeeper were also members of the crew to insure that the guests had an enjoyable trip.

Capt. H. Kellog had been warned that it was unsafe to travel in the waters of Caddo Lake at night, due to many snags, but gaiety was in the air as guests enjoyed the primitive moonlit bayous from their haven of luxury. Perhaps the captain was in a hurry, as he had a $100,000 payroll on board destined for Federal troops. He also may have been nervous about a shipment of gunpowder in the ship's hold, especially since he had a number of bales of hay stacked on the bow.

Darkness caused the captain to light the fire baskets and the torches at the ship's bow so that he could see how to guide his ship through the waters with a full head of steam. The fire baskets were metal cages filled with rich pine knots that gave off a glowing red light when burning bright.

THE MITTIE STEPHENS *caught fire near Swanson's Landing on Caddo Lake the night of February 11, 1869, on its maiden voyage out of Shreveport, Louisiana. At least sixty people either drowned or were burned to death in one of the greatest steamboat tragedies of all times.* (Drawing by M. B. Cole, used by permission of Harrison County Historical Museum)

A grinding shudder went through the speeding ship about midnight. She had struck a snag. The shock apparently caused a fire box to spew red hot coals onto the bales of hay, and within minutes the prow of the ship was a mass of fire. An alarm sounded, and the captain quickly decided to jam his ship into the mud bank so that passengers could get ashore. In a few minutes the ship shuddered again as she ran aground close to Swanson's Landing. The captain kept the stern wheel churning under full steam to hold it to the shore.

It was a tragic scene of confusion. Since the bow of the ship was on fire, the passengers rushed to the stern to jump overboard in order to get ashore. A number were sucked into the whirling blades of the stern wheel. A lone horseman passing nearby saw the accident and rode into the waters again and again to help people ashore. Captain Thornton, skipper of the

Dixie, saw the fire and rushed to the scene, managing to take some of the passengers onto his ship.

The charred remains of the once regal ship was all that was left the next morning. More than sixty of the passengers either drowned or were burned to death in one of the worst steamboat accidents in the Caddo.[30]

Other Landings

Success is sure to be duplicated. The same holds for ports. Every plantation owner wanted his own landing to have the prestige of steamboats stopping at his place to pick up *his* cotton. Every promoter felt that he could surely make a million dollars by promoting a successful port. Many tried; few were successful.

Taylor's Bluff: Obediah Hendricks' new town got off to a running start when it was incorporated and more than 1,000 lots were surveyed and staked out. Richard Hooper and John S. Ford were the surveyors. The description of the property indicated that his 660 acres were in Shelby County, south of Ferry Lake. Almost 100 shares of stock and lots were sold. Each share allowed the owner five lots that he could either retain or sell. The price of the lots ranged from $25 to $200, depending on the location of the lot. Homes and other buildings were started on the townsite almost immediately. Evidently, the investors either tired of their investment or moved to greener fields. There is no record of the community lasting. Hendricks was a native of San Augustine.[31]

Ray's Bluff: This community was surveyed by Richard Hooper and John S. Ford. It was located just a short distance from Port Caddo. Later this landing was known as Benton or Haggerty's Bluff. S. M. Haggerty was one of the people who purchased land in Taylor's Bluff. There is no evidence that this landing was successful.

Rock Landing: Located on Cypress Bayou.

Wyatt's Camp: Located on southern tip of Caddo Lake.

Potter's Point: On the north side of Caddo Lake at the mouth of Jim's Bayou. Robert Potter received the land as his headright due him as head of a family. In October of 1836 Potter and his hired hand, Hezekiah, built a permanent home at Potter's Point. Potter served as senator from the district while living at Potter's Point. Potter was shot in the water off Potter's Point by Dr. Rose. It is doubtful that Potter ever had an opportunity to develop the landing he planned, since the times were troubled and his affairs were in a complex state of unrest.[32]

Wray's Bluff: Located on south side of the lake across from Potter's Point.

Pine Bluff: Located on north bank of Clinton Lake across from mouth of Big Cypress Creek.

Baldwin
Clinton
Smithland: (See Jefferson segment.)
Bonham Landing
Stacy Landing
Uncertain[33]
Chamards Landing
Schenks Ferry Landing
Hawks Ferry Landing

Caddo Lake Stories

Stories out of Caddo Lake derive from the very core of people who have lived in the region for many years. Wyatt Moore was one of these "characters" – a modern link to the early beginnings of settlements in the area, a bridge to the past. He was born in 1901 and grew up listening to tales about the "old times" until they were a part of his thinking. He missed the steamboat age but savored all the pursuits of rivermen who lived deep in the woods. At different times he farmed, hunted, timbered, manufactured moonshine, and was a commercial fisherman. He described himself as a "lake rat." The people who lived in the depths of the Caddo Lake region knew the paths, the winding bayous and perilous swamps. Those who did not understand how to survive in this environment – such as game wardens and revenuers – were at a disadvantage.

Franklin Jones, Sr., Marshall attorney, became a friend of Wyatt Moore and through the years recorded hours upon hours of his life experiences. (Jones furnished the author a complete set of these tapes, from which the following incidents were preserved.)

In 1931 the Texas side of Caddo Lake had a closed season on white perch during March and April. Moore was "hungry," and if he remembered the season rule, he pushed it to the back of his mind as he set out on Friday, March 13, to catch fish. Just how he caught the fish didn't much bother him either, but when he brought his load of forty-seven nice fish up from the landing to his house in a wheelbarrow, he found two game wardens waiting for him.

Perhaps fisherman Moore had a plan in mind as he visited with the game wardens, who were planning to take him into town to file charges. "Could I milk my old cow and shave before meeting you in town?" the fisherman asked in a dejected manner. Probably knowing that they had the goods on Moore, and wanting to try to nab some other fishermen, they agreed to the slight delay as they packed up the evidence and left Moore's place.

Moore lit out for Shreveport in his Model-A Ford and arrived there just as the sheriff's office opened. Being a visiting type, Moore soon had struck up a friendship with the clerk, a Mr. Pitchford. They had mutual friends. Moore made his pitch: "Me and my wife is down here from Texas visiting friends in Shreveport and they want to go fishing . . . . I understand you can get a week's license." As Mr. Pitchford agreed and got down his book, Moore played his other card. "What is today?" he asked.

Pitchford chuckled as he told the fisherman that it was Friday the thirteenth.

"I don't want to be superstitious, but it's early this morning," said Moore. "Couldn't you date them yesterday? I've had some things happen to me on Friday the thirteenth."

Finally, after Moore said that he wanted a license for his wife also, the clerk laughed and wrote him out two Louisiana licenses at $1.50 each.

Moore took the licenses and took off to Marshall, stopping in Waskom just long enough to get a shave. He arrived at the courthouse in time to meet the county attorney and did a bit of visiting with him. The game wardens arrived and told the story about catching Moore with forty-seven fish. About that time the county attorney brought out the license Moore had given him. The game warden was mad: "Why didn't you show me those licenses before?" Moore's slow reply: "You didn't ask me."

The case beat around in court for almost two months

before it went before a jury. The prosecutor insisted that the lake was too rough for fishing on March 12. The defense made points when he told the jury that a lake rat like Wyatt Moore could go out on the lake whenever he pleased. The jury agreed with Moore.

Years later, the county attorney, who had moved to Longview, went to fish on Caddo Lake and met Moore at his fishing camp.

"Wyatt, don't I recall having the pleasure of prosecuting you once?" he asked.

"Well, yeah," Wyatt conceded. "I guess so, if you want to call it a pleasure. But if you recall a little closer, you might remember having the displeasure of losing the case, too!"[34]

Monterey

"What was your name before you came to Texas?"

A way to start a conversation? Perhaps. But if you lived in Monterey, Texas, in the olden days, it was a good way to end up dead.

Monterey was located in East Texas, Cass County, just a few miles from the Louisiana line. This was the No-Man's-Land of Texas, between the French in Louisiana and the Spanish in Mexico, between the Republic of Texas and the United States. For several hazy years this No-Man's-Land was a haven for fugitives from the law from Texas, from the United States, or from anywhere. Usually the fugitives didn't use their own names, and native fugitives knew this and asked no questions. If someone did happen to ask "What was your name before you came to Texas?" then it was obvious he was a newcomer, or a damn fool.[1]

It is possible that Monterey, Texas, was founded by the Spanish as far back as 1776. In 1787 the two northern provinces of Mexico were formed into two divisions, namely, Eastern and Western. Texas was in the Eastern province. In 1810 Father Miguel Hidalgo was waging a war to gain independence for Mexico from Spain. In 1812 a session of Eastern Prov-

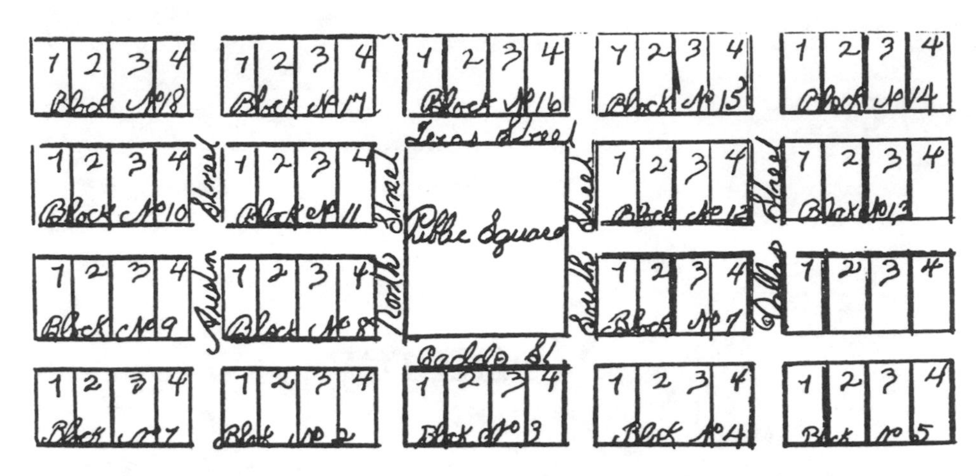

THE ORIGINAL plat of the city of Monterey on Jim's Bayou has been long lost, if it ever existed, but some historian years ago put together this map that shows the public square and principal streets. Steamboats called regularly at the old port in the 1830s and 1840s.

inces was held in Monterey. Since the old Spanish records definitely record the Monterey with one "r" (as opposed to two, used in the Spanish spelling of Monterrey, Mexico), it is possible that this 1812 meeting was held in Monterey, Texas.[2]

Historian Boon suggests that few records, such as census records, of Monterey exist for the simple reason that most of the people did not want to be counted. And, more than likely, the census takers knew why they did not want to be counted. But the existence of a town cannot be completely hidden. Postal records and deed records tell the story about the old town. A post office was established in 1847, and in 1851 N. Gupton was the postmaster. This office was discontinued in 1867. An office was reestablished in old Monterey on August 1, 1878, with S. B. Williams as postmaster, followed by Robert H. Harrell, who served from March 23, 1880, until the office was discontinued.[3]

Probably the best description of Monterey came from "Uncle Ned" Rambo, who was eighty years old when he was asked to reminisce about Monterey:

> I was born in Monterey on February 5, 1856. My father was Gayel Rambo and my mother was Lydia, from Lions

County, Alabama. They lived at Monterey, a little rough town on the line of Texas and Louisiana. I had three brothers, no sisters. Monterey had whiskey houses, a Mason house (Masonic Lodge building) and some stores. Judge Gupton who used to live up there at Linden run one of the stores, Jim Noel run a store, Charles Hotchkin (or something like that) run one and Billie Browning run one. Mr. Browning had a big warehouse and stored cotton during the war.

Captain Clim Marshall had a company of men that he would drill at Monterey every Saturday, for the war.

They had plenty whiskey, plenty of fights, they had no laws, no church, no school, just a rough town.[4]

The following letter, written some years ago to R. T. Douglas in Gilliam, Louisiana, and now in the vertical files of the Jefferson County Historical Society, sheds a few more rays of light on Monterey. (Part of the letter is lost.)

. . . . as to Monterey. I may be able to help you find it. About 20 years ago my husband and I went to find it. We drove from Jefferson, Tex., on the road to Vivian, La., and after a good many false leads, and some misunderstood true directions, we found it on Jean's Bayou. A man by name Tom Williams had a fishing camp there. He took us down the steep bank and we saw the remains of old brick work through which huge trees were growing. This crumbling brick work was presumed to be the foundations of old warehouses and landings. Up the bank the ground was level and open and I believe had been used at other times as a cotton field. Tom Williams showed us the location (supposedly) of the old blacksmith shop and the race track and told us of many curios and relics found thereabouts – silver spoons, bits, spurs and other metal things made by a blacksmith. I have a photostat of an 1871 map of Marion Co. upon which my grandfather had located Monterey. He placed it in Texas almost on the Tex.-La. line and in the J. E. Miller Survey.

During the time that Norphlet Gupton was postmaster, he also ran a saloon in a two-story building near the boat landing. He later moved to Linden and served as county judge of Cass County. Browning operated a store, sawmill, grist mill, cotton gin, and a large cotton warehouse between 1870 and 1876. He had a connection with a firm in New Orleans believed to be

Henderson Terry & Co. John Lester ran a blacksmith shop.[5] S. L. Williams operated a business from 1877 to 1879. In some old records Monterey is referred to as Williams Bluff, Cass County.[6]

Sam Williams, son of S. L. Williams, visited Monterey in 1878 and left a record of what he had seen: "Besides the S. L. Williams store, there were 6 or 7 vacant houses which showed very plainly there had been a village in more recent years." Williams came by the steamer *Hornet,* skippered by George A. Turner.

Williams continued his observations: "R. H. (Bob) Harrell operated the only store in Monterey in 1849. Mr. Harrell moved from Monterey to his farm some one and one-half miles north of town, and built a house where his daughter, Mrs. Fanny Carver, lived." Mrs. Carver said: "My father moved here and ran the Monterey post office back there in that little room (she pointed to a room in the corner of the house). It was in that room and in the post office that my father taught me to read."[7]

All accounts of Monterey left the impression that the town was in the disputed land, or No-Man's-Land, with absolutely no law and order. Entertainment was the name of the game, with plenty of drinking, gambling, horse racing, cock fighting, and fist fights. The fights live on in legend.

Things were done in a big way in Monterey. Take, for instance, a triple murder. Mr. Collins, an overseer for Rube Harrison, and John Lester had been involved in a little clean fun – cock fighting, which was popular in Monterey. An argument ensued, and Lester shot and killed Collins. That afternoon (July 7, 1847) Lester met Harrison, who was returning to town on the afternoon steamboat from a business trip to Benton, Alabama, and told him of killing his overseer. Harrison replied: "Yes, you killed my overseer and I am going to kill you." The argument continued as they walked toward Lester's Blacksmith Shop. When they got into the shop, the argument grew heated. Lester picked up a pair of blacksmith tongs and Harrison picked up a sledgehammer. They faced off and swung at the same time. The well-placed blows were fatal. Three murders in twenty-four hours may have been a record in Monterey.

Bob Hunt ran a saloon in town. A man by the name of Mabern came in and continued downing whiskey until he was intoxicated to the point that he was a nuisance. Hunt and his clerk, Dan McCann, threw Mabern out of the saloon. Mabern waited outside until McCann and Hunt came out, then attacked McCann, cutting him with his pocketknife. Hunt pulled his gun, and in the ensuing brawl he shot and killed Mabern. As was the custom in those days, Hunt left Texas and went to Arkansas, which was only a few miles away. Years rolled by and Hunt returned to Monterey, only to be arrested by Deputy Sheriff Will Rand. Hunt's remark: "I've been expecting this for twenty-five years." To which the deputy replied: "That's right. I've heard all my life that I was born the day that Hunt killed Mabern, and I'm twenty-five today!"

The Rambo family had a unique background. Col. Gayel Rambo, a white man from Lyons County, Alabama, settled in Monterey. One of his slaves was the mother of his children, Ben, Alonzo, Rowe, and Na Dan. When the colonel got old he was afraid that the mother of his children might be used as a slave, should he die. He therefore took her to Ohio and kept her there six months so that she would be free under the Dred Scott Decision. He brought her back to Monterey as a free woman. One of the children, Uncle Ned, is the storyteller in earlier accounts about life in Monterey.

Monterey, like many of the early Texas towns, had a strong Masonic Lodge. The Clinton, or Van Zant, Lodge No. 42, A.F.&A.M., was organized in 1848. Signers of the original petition for the lodge were John H. Cole, Amasa White, David Lee, R. R. Harrison, W. W. Head, J. W. Green, John M. McReynolds, Robert Lowe, J. C. Rhett, S. F. Newby, J. R. R. Harrison, John W. Scott, W. H. Moore, James E. Harrell, N. Gupton, and John Freeman.

Members were Chas. Ames, J. L. Y. Blackburne, J. H. Cole, W. H. Crow, G. W. Fortune, Jos. W. Green, McNary Harris, B. F. Hill, A. P. Jones, John A. Lester, W. Meredith, J. M. McReynolds, Sam Perkins, G. J. Pyland, Thos. Ritchie, John W. Scott, E. P. Smith, Amasa White, W. F. Arrington, R. H. Browning, B. F. Cooke, R. V. B. Eddins, B. Foster, N. Gupton, J. R. K. Harrison, J. R. Hill, John T. Ketchings, Jas. C. Love, W. H. Moore, S. F. Newby, S. G. Peters, A. T. Rhea, W. H. Robinson, B. F. Smoot, C. J. Willard, John Barlow, W. D. Browning, Wiley Coor, Jesse Fitzgerald, R. C. Graham, Jas. E. Harrell, Wm. W. Head, R. E.

Hines, David Lee, Robert Lowe, M. S. Mullins, J. L. Nuget, David Pinkerton, J. C. Rhea, J. H. Rodgers, Jas. Rodgers, and John Viermand.[8]

The membership seems to show that Monterey drew its support from a rather wide area. There is no lodge No. 42 in existence in Texas today.

Rooster fighting was viewed in Monterey as entertainment, a hobby, and a business. Large crowds would gather from all over the area for the cock fights that were held regularly. The betting often led to more serious trouble. Witness, for instance, the triple murder.

Horse racing was the *big* entertainment, with numerous races held at the town racetrack. Pari-mutuel betting hadn't been invented, but gambling was on a large scale, with stakes running high enough that a man could lose everything on a single race. The Monterey Race Track was in the shape of a circle with a lookout tower in the center. Individuals who had horses running were allowed to climb into this tower, where they had a better view of the race. The extent of the gambling is evident in a story about Bill Rieves, a gambler, drunkard, and owner of a prize race horse. Before the race he told his black jockey that the race *must* be won since he had wagered everything that he owned, including his home, on the race. If he won, he told his jockey, he would have plenty of money for life. If he lost, it meant that he would have nothing. He also told his jockey if the race was lost he was going to kill him. By the time the race got under way, all of the men in the tower were drunk and were leaning out, screaming at the top of their voices for their horses. Rieves' horse finished one-half his length ahead, but as it crossed the finish line the horse staggered against one of the posts of the tower, thereby shaking it, and the owner of the horse fell out and broke his neck.[9]

Probably the murder that best typified the utter disregard for law in this No-Man's-Land was the murder of Col. Robert Potter just a few miles from Monterey. The story is told best by Charles Dickens, who visited America in 1842, the year that Jefferson, Texas, started. Dickens was impressed by the murder and told the story in one of his books:

> From the *Caddo-Gazette* of the 12th inst. (March 12, 1842) we learn of the frightful death of Col. Potter . . . . he was

beset in his house by an enemy named Rose. He sprang from his couch, seized his gun, and in his night clothes, rushed from the house. For about two hundred yards his speed seemed to defy his pursuers; but, getting entangled in a thicket, he was captured. Rose told him that he intended to act a generous part, and give him a chance for his life. He told Potter he might run, and should not be interrupted till he reached a certain distance. Potter started at the word of command and before a gun was fired he had reached the lake. His first impulse was to jump in the water and dive for it, which he did. Rose was close behind him and formed his men on the bank ready to shoot him as he rose. In a few seconds he came to the top to breathe; and scarce had his head reached the surface of the water when it was completely riddled with the shot of their guns, and he sank to rise no more.

Potter was buried on a high bluff near his home at Potter's Point, only a few hundred feet from where he was shot and killed. In 1929 his remains were moved, by an act of the state legislature, to the State Cemetery at Austin.

Perhaps it should be noted that Potter was not the saint that Dickens might have painted. He was a highly regarded attorney, with a promising political career just starting in North Carolina, when he castrated ("potterized") two men he suspected as being his wife's lovers. After serving a prison term, he joined the list of people who had "Gone to Texas" to escape their pasts. In Texas he was a signer of the Declaration of Independence, the first secretary of the Texas Navy, and a senator in the Texas Congress. However, men like Sam Houston said: "Robert's infamy is wider than the world and deeper than perdition."

Potter was caught up in the Regulator and Moderator war that wracked Texas during this period.[10]

Monterey's zenith probably was reached when steamboats were able to penetrate Lake Caddo and Jim's Bayou. After the raft was removed from the Red River, and steamboats stopped running into these regions, Monterey and other interior landings died on the vine as the promoters and residents moved on to greener fields.

Brazos River

Great rivers produce great legends.

The Brazos River – perhaps the greatest of all Texas rivers – has inspired countless legends about its past. All seem to reflect its mystic abundance where man not only had great respect for the might of the river but knew that it offered an abundant life.

The river was called Los Brazos de Dios by the Spaniards, who learned respect and awe for the river from the Indians. Translated, the name means "the Arms of God." Several legends speak to the origin.

One legend ties in with the Legend of the Lost San Saba or Lost Bowie Mine. A rancher befriended an old Mexican who was ill. After the man recovered he offered to tell his new friend about the mine's location. The rancher didn't find the mine. Coronado and his men were found by Indians wandering on the Staked Plains in the west, about to perish from thirst. The Indians guided them to a small stream then named Brazos de Dios. Other Indian legends give the river the name Tokonohono, which is mentioned in the expedition led by Rene Robert Cavelier, Sieur de la Salle. LaSalle may have called the river by the name of Maligne.

Other stories tell of men adrift in small boats in the Gulf

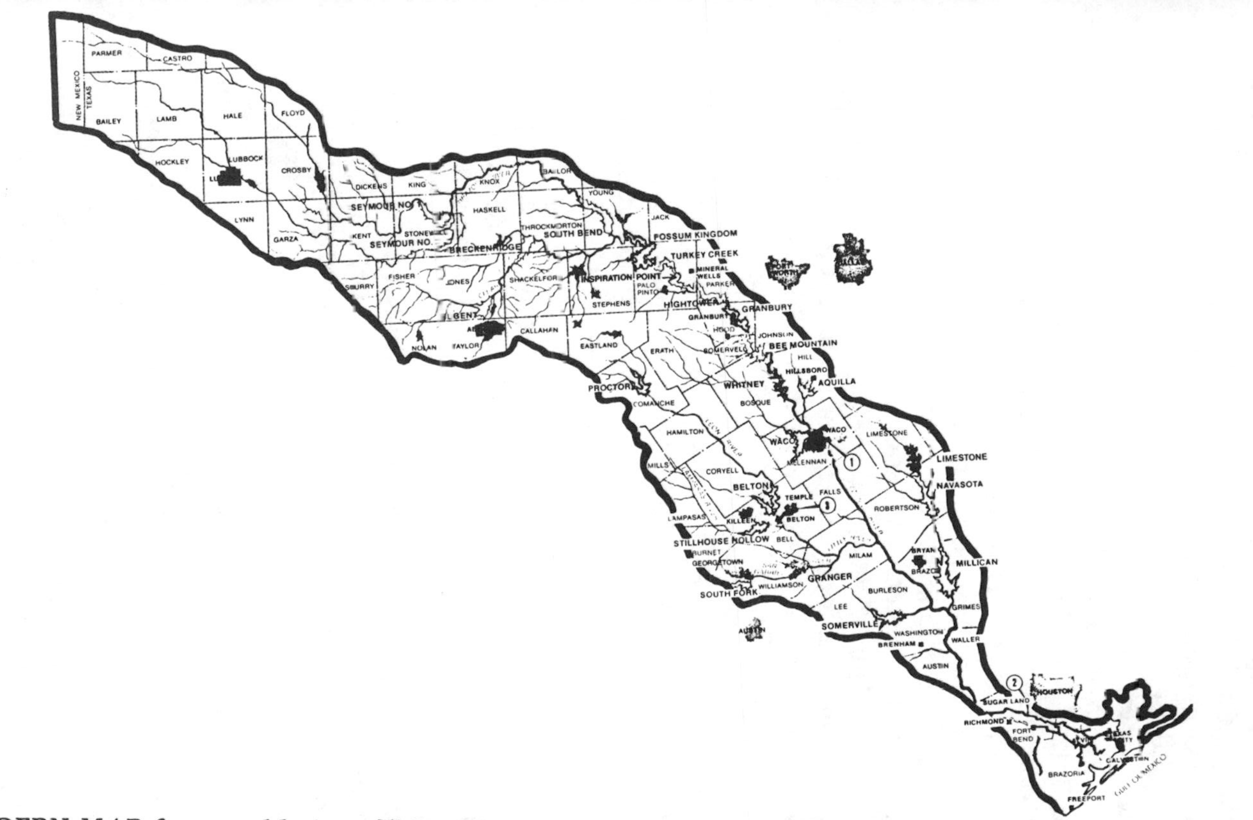

A MODERN MAP for an old river. This map was prepared by the Brazos River Authority to show their existing and proposed projects. The old riverboats had a hard time making it all the way up the river to Port Sullivan, but today it would be much harder. (Map taken from *Waller County History*)

who discovered the river by following a muddy streak in the water and finding, by the current, the mouth of a wide river. There is also evidence that the Colorado and Brazos were misidentified by several early explorers. All of the stories depict the waters of the great river as life-saving. What better name than the Arms of God?[1]

The Brazos River lays claim to being Texas' longest river and also one with the greatest discharge of water into the Gulf of Mexico. It has three branches that furnish it life: the Double Mountain Fork, the Clear Fork, and the Salt Fork. The Double Mountain Fork is the longest. It rises in New Mexico and enters Texas in the northwestern corner of Bailey County and flows through Bailey, Lamb, Hale, Lubbock, Crosby, Garza, Kent, Fisher, and Stonewall counties. In Stonewall it is joined by the Salt Creek Fork and now becomes the Brazos River, flowing into Knox, Baylor, Throckmorton, and Young counties. In Young it is joined by the Clear Fork. From this last junction the river gains volume as it drains Palo Pinto, Parker, Hood, and Somervell counties. It then flows between Bosque and Johnson and Bosque and Hill counties, cuts through McLennan and Falls counties, and then forms the boundaries between Milam and Robertson, Burleson and Robertson, Burleson and Brazos, Brazos and Washington, Washington and Grimes, Washington and Waller, Austin and Waller, and Austin and Fort Bend counties. It loops through Fort Bend and cuts across the middle of Brazoria before it empties into the Gulf.

The river is approximately 840 miles in length and drains an estimated 41,700 square miles with all except 600 square miles in Texas. The larger rivers that join the Mighty Brazos include the Navasota, Yegua, Paluxy, Little Brazos, Little, and Bosque.

Early Spanish explorers found many Indian tribes that lived on the banks of the Brazos River. The first Anglo settlement was made by Stephen F. Austin's Colony at San Felipe at a point where the Atascosito Road crossed the Brazos.[2]

The Brazos River has been described as moody, vicious, unpredictable, and a muddy giant. The first settlers immediately began using the river for transportation. Some of Austin's first colonists built boats to make their way upstream to found the community that grew into Richmond in the great bend of the river that gave Fort Bend County its name. Velasco and Quintana, at the mouth of the river, were the forerunners in using the river, but they found that the river could be a curse as well as a provider. In dry years the water level dropped so low that snags could rip the bottom out of boats in a few seconds. During its flood stages, the river swept everything to the sea and left behind destruction and stagnant pools of water. Sailing vessels crossed the bar early and probed the lower portion of the river. The powerful paddlewheelers could buck the swift flow of water, but they were no match for the falls and shoals that lay across the river like protecting giants in the upper reaches. Despite all of the river's efforts, the tough rivermen always found ways to push the head of navigation farther and farther upstream. They were finally stymied by a falls above Port Sullivan that they were never able to breast—even when the river was at flood stage.

River captains were a tenacious breed of men. Where a challenge seemed impossible, they sought to conquer it with a back-door approach. The people in Waco had always looked with longing eyes at the Brazos, hoping someday to be able to have boats serve their city. In 1875 the *Katie Ross* was built in Waco. For a short time it made trips upstream and brought freight down the river to Waco. But that wasn't enough—the *Katie*'s master wanted to take the boat down the river. One day, when the river was in flood stage, the captain headed the ship's bow south. By the time the vessel reached the falls, the river was falling. The *Katie Ross* got stuck for good after a valiant effort to ram her way through the rocks. The falling water left her high and dry, and the ship was eventually broken up for salvage. A few months later, the *Lizzie Fisher,* a much smaller sternwheeler, was built in Waco and made a few trips upstream. But one night, when the river was at flood stage, the ship disappeared from its moorings. It is thought that the skipper left in the dead of night to keep his creditors from stopping his dash for the coast. Despite rumors of disaster, it is believed that the *Lizzie Fisher* ended up in New Orleans. These are the only two vessels known to have attempted the downriver trip.[3]

Lists of landings and ports on the Brazos River have been compiled by historians, starting with D. E. E. Braman in 1857. Some made lasting ports, others served as loading places for a

LOADED for the trip down the river. Some old riverboats could load as many as 1,200 bales by stacking the bales all the way over the top decks. (Photo courtesy of Institute of Texan Cultures)

short time, and others were just a gleam in the eyes of some promoter. Starting at the Gulf: Velasco, Quintana, Brazoria, East Columbia, West Columbia, Marion, Bell's Landing (last four same), Bolivar, Orozimbo, Richmond, Gaston's Landing, San Felipe de Austin, Groce's Landing, Ralston, Newport, Lancaster (last three ferries), Warren (landing for Chappel Hill area), Rock Island, Washington-on-the-Brazos, Hidalgo's, Cole's, Munson's, Moseley's, Port Sullivan, and Nashville. Some listed by Braman (the author does not know their approximate location) include Calvers', Cashe's, Crosby's, Payne, Sayre's, Tinsley's, Hill's, Towne's, Menard, Lobdell's, Manadue's, Big Creek, Waters', Crumb's, Caney, Peebles', and Cole's (port for Independence).[4]

Some historians put the head of navigation in the Brazos River at The Falls, located near the present town of Marlin, Falls County. An early town called Buckshot was located at The Falls.[5]

Shippers, boat operators, and plantation owners worked constantly to get meaningful work done toward clearing the Brazos of snags, shoals, falls, and sandbars. For the most part, none of their plans were completely successful. In 1857 the Texas legislature passed a bill offering matching money to private firms to clear the river. Of this amount, $50,000 was earmarked for the Brazos. It is thought that twelve miles of the river below Richmond can be credited to this project. In 1874 Congress appropriated funds for a study of the Brazos by the Army Engineers. Lt. R. B. Talfor built several small boats and started down the river from Waco on the project. His report indicated that shallow-draft navigation was feasible as far north as Washington. The report was largely ignored. In 1891 the Corps of Engineers concluded that the Brazos could be made safe for navigation, but only at tremendous cost. Another report, issued in 1895, summarized that a system of locks and dams was the only solution. R. L. Henry, congressman from Waco, managed to get funds for a lock-and-dam system approved. Eight locks and dams were envisioned, and work was started before World War I stopped all work. It was never renewed.[6]

One of the first counties on the Brazos that sought protection from the disastrous floods was Burleson County. In 1908 an Improvement District was organized and, after fighting off legal challenges, a levee for the protection of the rich valley farms from inundations and overflows was started along the Brazos opposite Bryan. This was one of the first of many flood-control measures taken to keep the river in confines.[7]

The Brazos River Authority was created by the Texas legislature in 1929 with responsibility for the entire Brazos River Basin. The original plan, conceived in 1930, called for thirteen major dams on the Brazos and its tributaries. This has been expanded to include twenty-three reservoirs. The first project completed was the Possum Kingdom Reservoir in 1941. In 1967 the authority expanded its scope with two canals in the Gulf Coast that provide water directly to water users through a system of canals from the Brazos River. Currently, the authority is concerning itself with water quality.[8]

Surfside Beach

Actually, the history of Surfside is the history of Velasco and old Velasco. From the earliest days of Stephen F. Austin's Colony, settlers have made their homes in the area. The old port of Velasco, together with Fort Velasco, were important places in the 1830s–40s.

Hurricanes have always been a nightmare for the residents on Gulf Islands, and Velasco and Surfside were no exception. The community that existed in the area was completely washed from the face of the earth by the Hurricane of 1875. Yet, despite everything that Mother Nature has thrown at the island, the love of the beach is stronger. People keep returning to rebuild their homes and enjoy the Gulf breeze.

The 1993 population listed for Surfside Beach in the *Texas Almanac* was 605. A new bridge connecting the island with the mainland has brought more beach lovers to the area to make their homes in the past several decades. As long as real estate promoters can match a spit of sand with a dream, Surfside Beach will continue to exist.

The inland waters have as much appeal today as they had back in the early 1800s. It is doubtful that Jean Lafitte's men took part in sunbathing and pleasure boating, but once the plantations were established up and down the Brazos the favorite pastime of the gentlemen and their ladies was a day at the beach.[1]

A fire department helps keep modern Surfside free from the fires that helped to destroy a lot of old Surfside. The Surfside Hotel, a famed recreation spot for tourists at the turn of the century, withstood hurricanes but was completely destroyed by fire.

While modern Surfside follows the paths of the twentieth century, its citizens also spend a lot of time looking back. Efforts to restore the old Fort of Velasco have been under way since the early 1970s and will probably continue for many years to come. Secrets of the past are sure to be uncovered from the site, as well as other historic sites in the area.[2]

The local chapter of the Texas Society of Professional Engineers has established that the original Velasco was situated on approximately the same site as the location of old Fort Velasco. A project to restore the old fort began in 1969. The engineers

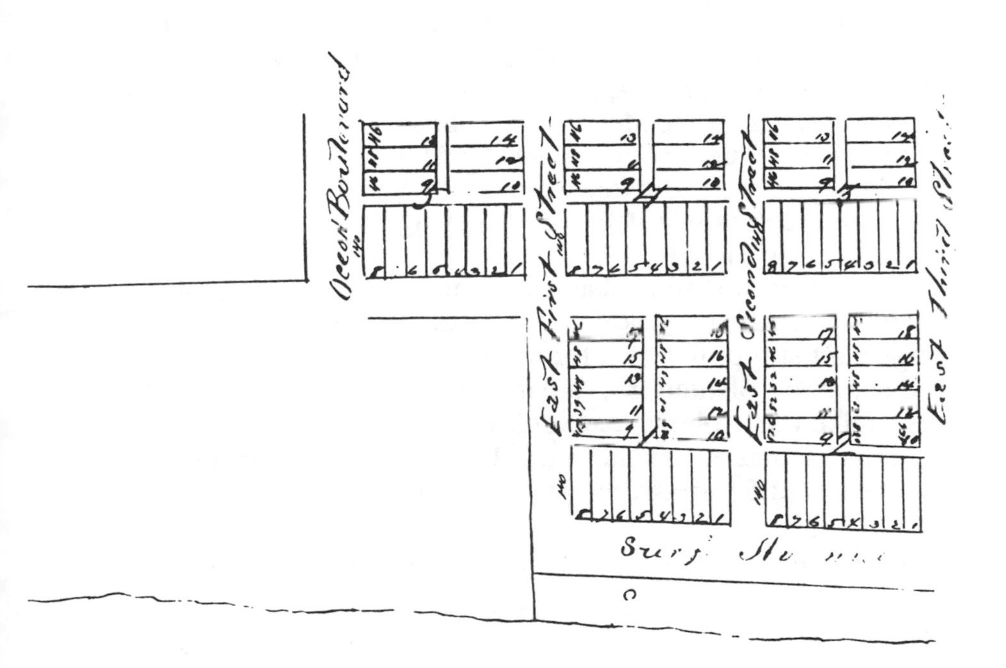

SURFSIDE was a promoter's dream, and while it prospered for a short time, its big day was not to come until modern times. (From files of Brazoria County Historical Museum)

placed the location of the fort in a block of Surfside Beach bordered by Ave. C, 14th Street, and 13th Street. This area had been known as Old Monument Square. After several changes, an organization called the Gulf Coast Parks and Historical Restoration Association is in charge of the project.[3]

Quintana

Quintana! Romance, adventure, intrigue — it is all buried in Quintana's past, folded into the pages of time that reach back more than 360 years.

Cabeza de Vaca and his companions were perishing from thirst when their hand-crafted horsehide boats drifted ashore at the mouth of a great river, where the explorers were able to "take fresh water from the sea." At the spot where this 1528 Spanish explorer fell down on his knees to give thanks for their deliverance from the sea, the unique city of Quintana came to life in 1821 when the Mexicans established forts at the mouth of the Brazos. The fort on the west side of the river was named for Gen. Andreas Quintana, a Mexican official who was sympathetic to Stephen F. Austin and his struggle to found a colony on the Brazos River.[1]

Quintana was started as a trading post, and along with its twin-city on the east side of the river, Velasco, it became an important shipping point for cotton and other products from the adjoining plantations. What made it truly unique was the resort-like atmosphere that took over the new city. Scores of wealthy plantation owners built homes overlooking the Gulf, and a way of life fitting their station permeated the community.

In 1838 Mary Holley, Stephen F. Austin's cousin who traveled and wrote about early Texas, had this to say about Quintana:

> We passed a day or two with Mrs. McKinney at Quintana — Mr. Toby was there from N. Orleans — & Mr. Williams, just from the States. It is very pleasant there, was delightful riding on the beach — where 5 miles of our road lay. Mrs. Perry has given me 2 town lots there — They live remarkably well there — having everything they want from N. Orleans.[2]

The business section of Quintana was built on the Brazos River, in order to accommodate the river steamers, and fronted

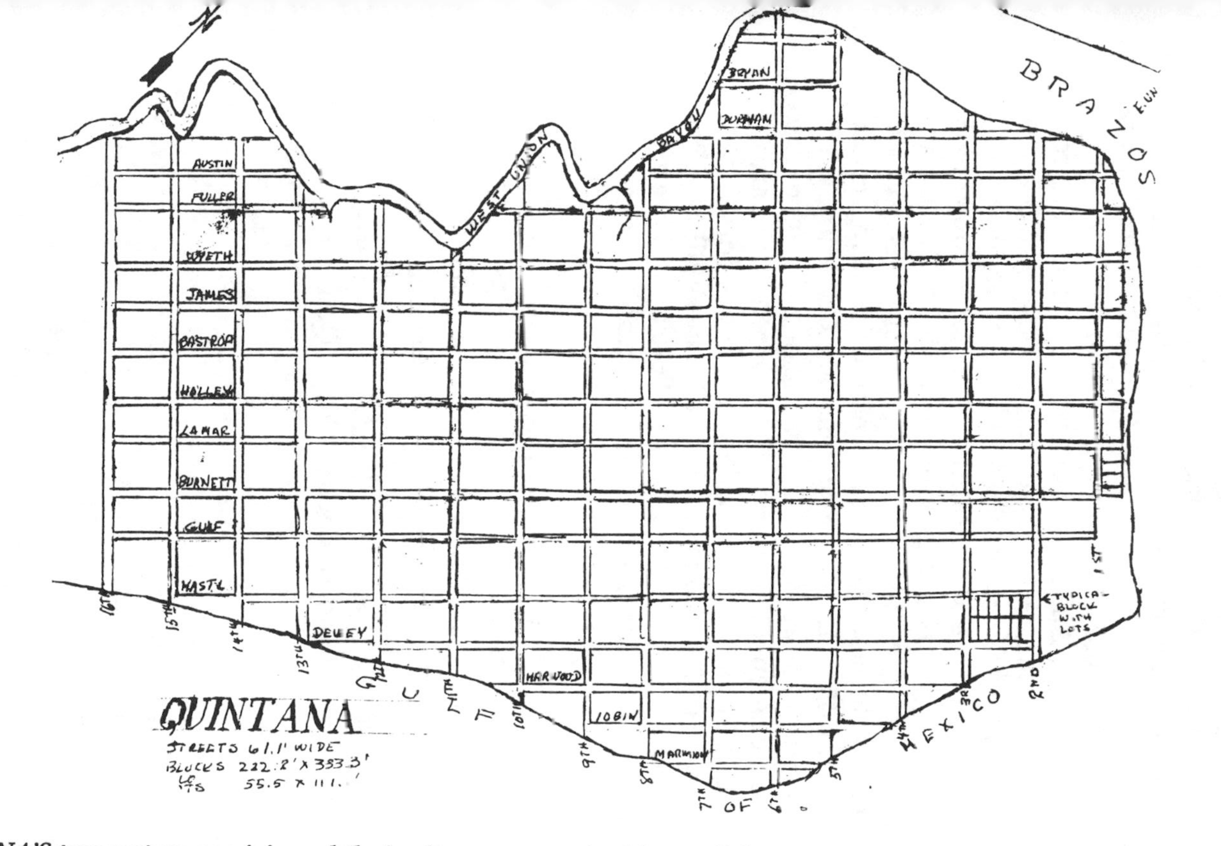

QUINTANA'S promoters envisioned their city as a resort with a solid commercial base, and for a while their dreams came true. Most of the big plantation owners had summer homes at Quintana, while basic industries like shipbuilding gave the city an industrial base.

the Gulf to give the city a magnificent view. Actually, the town was laid out between the Gulf and West Union Bayou.[3] The Intracoastal Canal now has its junction with the Brazos at the original mouth of West Union Bayou. Most of the streets running parallel to the Gulf were named after leading figures of the day: Bryan, Durman, Austin, Fuller, Wyeth, James, Bastrop, Holley, Lamar, Burnet, Gulf, Washington, Dewey, Harwood, Tobin, and Marmon. The vertical streets ran numerically.

In 1836 Quintana was established. The town contained a two-story proprietor's house, belonging to Mr. McKinney, and a large warehouse. The Hill House was built for travelers, and a pavilion, pool halls, and dance halls were opened for amusement.[4] The firm of McKinney, Williams and Company, established in Quintana before the town was laid out, was formed to handle the large amount of cotton that was grown in the area. It is believed that in 1834 as many as 5,000 bales of cotton were grown by Brazos plantations. The McKinney-Williams firm established houses, or at least offices, in Velasco and Brazoria, and did business there until 1838, when its main offices moved to Galveston. There it became the forerunner of the Moody interests.[5]

McKinney was known as a man who would find a way to accomplish what he had set out to do. Once he found himself some distance up the Brazos River from his Quintana headquarters and with no means of transportation. He found a pig trough that had been hollowed out of a log and turned it into a canoe and paddled it down the river.[6] Thomas Dwyer, from Tipperary County, Ireland, opened a store in Quintana in 1845, to be followed by stores in Brazoria and Columbia. In 1858 he moved to Brenham.[7]

Like many other coastal cities, Quintana had at least one packery that slaughtered cattle for hides, tallow, and bones. The meat was taken out to sea to dump. Evidently, there were some smaller slaughterers who had no concern for whose cattle they killed. After all, the tallow looked the same when it was in barrels on the way to New Orleans. At least one firm made an effort to pickle part of the meat that was being dumped; however, it failed after a short run. People were not apt to buy pickled beef when fresh was cheap.

Quintana also had one unique business: a coal elevator.

Since many ships that called at the old port were coal burners, an enterprising businessman built an elevator, three or four stories high, near the waterfront so that ships could replenish their supply of fuel. The failed real estate promotion at Velasco by the Boston Syndicate brought a beneficial side effect to Quintana. They drilled a deep well in the area and got an artesian well, which was still flowing as late as the 1960s.[8]

Legends tell of a cork tree plantation near Quintana with a business on the waterfront to ship the bark of the tree to foreign ports.[9]

Several business houses were shown on a map made from memory by C. Ohlhausen in 1965. They included Syndicate Office, Cheap John's Store, Shannon's Store, Bar Pilot office, City Docks, Bowers Store, Runyon Store, Dry Dock, Rail Ways, Wittlers Store, Geiseke Store, Hedcalf Saloon, Bynums Boarding House, Old Bunk House. Homes shown: Gus Stevens, Fred Johnson, Church, E. Seaburn, Will Seaburn, Digger's, James, Jarvis, Milligans, School, Seaburn, Foster, Lewis, Locke, Pizzara, Wilson. A hospital was thought to have existed in the 1880s, when the Chicago Land Company was promoting the port. It consisted of a long frame building described simply as "a barrack." The hospital was destroyed in the Hurricane of 1900.[10]

Every coastal city had problems with the weather. Quintana was no exception. Storms remembered by old-timers include the terrible storm that struck the Texas coast in 1875. It dealt a severe blow to many coastal towns, including Quintana. One group of people took refuge in the schooner *Verbena,* which was built by the Seaburn Shipyards and was tied up in a sheltered spot behind a clump of salt cedars. The ship was loaded with baled hides that were soaked. The refugees dumped the stinking hides and took shelter in the boat, but the remaining stench, plus the roll of the boat, made people deathly seasick. Nearby residents, thinking that Quintana had been obliterated by the storm, made a batch of coffins and arrived to help bury the dead. Finding out that those arriving had a load of coffins and not food, one spirited lady lashed out at the would-be gravediggers: "Dead, my foot! We're hungry."[11]

Floods in 1899 almost washed the old city into the sea, and to make matters worse a storm struck in 1900 to send families scurrying to find shelter. Mrs. John S. Caldwell remembers her family moving four times during the night to seek standing shelter. One ship with people aboard washed ashore at Quintana. After this double whammy, a part of the shrinking populace left Quintana for good.[12]

In 1835, when recruits for the Texas Army were flooding in from the United States, one group landed at Quintana, where they remained for something over two weeks. John C. Duval, who was to become well known in Texas as a survivor of the slaughter of Fannin's men at Goliad, later wrote about the Quintana visit: "We landed upon the Quintana side [Brazos River] and pitched our camp upon the beach, adjoining the camps of several other companies which had arrived a few days previously. Here we remained two weeks or more, and as we were liberally supplied with rations by the patriotic firm of McKinney & Williams, and game and fish were to be had in abundance, we fared sumptuously every day."[13]

Along the ridge of the beach the plantation owners built their summer homes. Some were cottages, but most were mansions befitting the financial stature of the planter. The life carried on by this "plantation set" was apart from frontier life; in fact, it was closer to the feudal life of the Old World. Most of the homes had ice cellars. Ice was brought in from the north on packets and was packed into the cellars with sawdust to keep until the summer months, when it was brought out to cool drinks. Slaves were on hand to do all the work, leaving the women free to preside at social affairs and the young men to amuse themselves with their hunting dogs and to attend the horse races.[14] During the Texas Revolution, Quintana was in the thick of the fighting, with the Battle of Velasco waged just across the river. A number of men from Quintana took part in the war. After San Jacinto, President David G. Burnet and his cabinet set up shop for a brief time at Quintana, giving the old city the right to claim that it served at one time as the capital of the Republic. When the *Invincible* took Santa Anna away from Galveston, he was kept in Quintana for a short time before being removed to Velasco.[15]

When votes were taken to select the new capital of Texas, Quintana received three votes on the first ballot but none on the second, third, and final ballots. Houston won with twenty-one over Washington-on-the Brazos, with fourteen.[16]

The men from Quintana had gone to war, but once the war was over things soon returned to normal on the plantations that gave life to Quintana. It was during this period of lavish plantation life that summer homes were built by a great number of plantation owners. Families would go to the beach to live for the entire summer, while owners returned to the plantation on occasion to see that the work was being carried out. The young ladies did their swimming and sunbathing in discreet attire. Slaves were in constant attendance.

Hospitality reached new highs during this period, with relatives from the States visiting for months at a time. Balls and other social gatherings were held frequently. Mary Holley, who was visiting Emily Perry (S. F. Austin's sister), wrote of San Jacinto Day festivities on April 21, 1838, celebrating the victory two years earlier. She remarked that "festivals are everywhere" in honor of the occasion.[17] Hospitality also had its humorous side. A small, wiry Irishman, who worked as a carpenter, would on occasion tire of his work and go to the

EARLY SETTLERS along the coast at Surfside, San Luis, Quintana, and Velasco were drawn to the pristine beaches backed by sea oats and presided over by sea gulls that kept the beach patrolled.

nearest saloon to buy a full keg of whiskey. He would put it in a wheelbarrow and proceed to wander all over town, stopping anyone he met to give them a drink of his whiskey. When he ran out of friends, or whiskey, he would return to work, probably to save up enough for another turn of the hospitality wheelbarrow.[18]

Probably one of the biggest assets to Quintana's business community was the shipbuilding business carried on by Henry Seaburn and his sons. It is believed that the shipbuilder, who had been a cabinetmaker in Germany, arrived at Quintana as early as 1837. Some historians say that he settled first in San Luis but left there because he had been "washed out" several times. He built eight sailing vessels capable of river and Gulf commerce. It is not known how many steamboats that he built, but probably as many as three or four.[19] The ways for his shipyard were said to have stood high in the air and were known as the Crab House. In order to haul ships out of the water to be repaired, or to launch new ones, he had a winch that was hooked up to a windlass powered by a horse, which was rigged up to walk in circles – a one-horse-power rig. According to a hand-drawn map made by C. Ohlhausen and in possession of the Brazoria County Historical Museum, it appears that several docks and "rail ways" were located near the entrance of West Union Bayou into the Brazos River. This would probably have been a good place for a shipyard because other old papers seem to indicate that other businesses were located on the lower end of the bayou.[20]

Since the Seaburns worked on ships from all over the world, and were paid with foreign coins, they probably had quite a collection of foreign money that not everyone could convert into American money. Once when they made a deal to purchase a large tract of land for a certain amount, it took a couple of days to agree on the value of the many foreign coins offered in payment.

Any time there is gold, there are gold stories. One story tells of gold kept in a hollow fence post. When high tides flooded the area, the post was washed away. Another tale tells about the gold being stored in a trunk, but the same storm destroyed the house and the trunk was never found.[21]

In addition to the Seaburn Shipyard, a man by the name of Bradbury Follett also had a shipbuilding business.

The McKinney and Williams firm expanded their business in 1841 and contracted with John Bradbury Follett to build the *Lafitte* for them. The sidewheeler was 138 tons burden and about 120 feet in length and drew three feet of water unloaded and five when loaded to capacity (with 300 bales of cotton). The *Lafitte* was used in the Brazos River trade but probably never went above Columbia.[22] The lumber schooner *Quintana,* thought to have been built in Quintana, went down at Pass Cavallo in 1887, a complete loss. She was loaded with 28,000 feet of lumber and 50,000 shingles.[23]

Not all shipping on the Brazos came to a halt once the railroads arrived. Capt. Henry Locke and his brother, William, operated sailing ships on the river for many years, making regular trips up and down the river picking up such things as watermelons, cabbage, potatoes, sugar cane, and molasses from the various plantations and farm landings. William's wife was Lilly Webber, a native of Quintana. The Locke brothers operated several boats, the first being the *Susie,* followed by the *Golden Arrow* and then the *Laurel.*[24]

Quintana's first school probably opened in 1866 and was held in a building close to the river. The school was closed after a boat with children from the other side of the river sank within sight of the teacher, Miss Nina Sweeney, and several were drowned. Free schooling was offered in the one-room log building for three months, and then those who wanted additional teaching were required to pay tuition of $3.00 per month. A fireplace in one end of the cabin afforded heat, and the window that overlooked the harbor scene provided something for the students to kindle their daydreams. The building was destroyed by the Hurricane of 1875.[25]

Quintana had a high school in the mid-1800s that was attended by Stephen Perry. He also worked in the Quintana post office after school and in the summers.

During the 1890s, the Presbyterians built a church on Burnet Street in Quintana.[26]

Quintana, platted in 1835, grew and prospered as a trading port and summer resort until about 1854, when a canal was built connecting the Brazos River at a point above its mouth with waterways leading to the port of Galveston. This routed ships through the new canal and not up the river and past Quintana and Velasco.[27]

During the Civil War, forts, made out of liveoak wood surrounded with earthenworks, were built at Quintana and Velasco. These guns were instrumental in preventing the Federal forces from ever attempting to enter the Brazos River, and as a result quite a number of ships made it out of Quintana and Velasco, running the blockade. The Quintana fort was about one and a half to two miles from the mouth of the river on the west bank. General Bates was in command of the Brazos forts. During the four years that the forts were in operation, scouts would ride out on the beach every day with spyglasses to keep a check on the Federal warships. If a ship looked as if it was coming toward shore, shots would be fired to let the Yankees know that the Rebs were on alert. On occasion the Yankees would bombard the coast. One day they started shelling Quintana, and women and children were scurrying for cover. A group gathered on the porch of the Seaburn home just about the time that a shell hit the porch, taking about half of it away, as well as one foot of a Confederate officer who was on leave visiting the Seaburns.[28]

Quintana residents were accustomed to being hit hard by rising water and hurricanes, but they were not prepared for the storm which covered the entire area with twenty inches of snow on February 14, 1895. When the weather warmed up and the snow melted, the prairies were covered with dead cattle. It was years before the livestock industry recovered.[29]

The *Texas Almanac* still lists Quintana, with a population of thirty. When the great industrial wave hit the Gulf Coast, the towns and communities of Lake Barbara, Richwood, Freeport, Lake Jackson, Clute, Gulf Park, Jones Creek, Surfside, Quintana, and Oyster Creek decided to form one large, 214-square-mile geographical division all represented by a single chamber of commerce and named Brazosport. Roughly it is the same territory covered by the Brazosport Independent School District today. Velasco was absorbed by Freeport in 1957.[30]

Quintana will probably live on forever. There is romance and adventure to be found on the seacoast even today. And, who knows, you just might find some of the gold coins lost by boatbuilder Seaburn.

Velasco

Being first seemed to appeal to the pioneers who called Velasco home.

The *Lively,* a small sailing vessel hired by Stephen F. Austin in 1821 to deliver colonists to their new homes in Texas, eased its nose into the sandy shore at the mouth of the Brazos. There was no chamber of commerce representative to herald their arrival and congratulate them for being the first to land at the port of Velasco.

During the next fourteen years, probably as many as 25,000 settlers passed through the port, or up the Brazos, on their way to their new homes. If the river was low, which happened most of the time, early boats did not attempt to cross the bar, which usually did not have over two feet of water. The larger boats would unload at Velasco, with the colonists going the rest of the way by wagon or transferring to small boats to continue up the river. The spring freshets allowed larger boats to make it over the bar and proceed up the river. Small sailing vessels, like the *Lively,* could get across the bar. A sailing ship

WEALTHY PLANTATION families gathered each summer on the Gulf beaches, unspoiled by anything except driftwood and sea shells.

had a hard time tacking back and forth to get up or down the river if the wind happened to be in the wrong direction.[1]

On January 8, 1836, a Lone Star flag was raised over the American Hotel at Velasco. The flag, made by Miss Joanna Elizabeth Troutman of Knoxville, Georgia, came to Texas with a Georgia Battalion dedicated to helping Texas gain her independence. The flag was made from one of Miss Troutman's white silk skirts with a blue, five-pointed star stitched on each side. She gave it to the Georgia Battalion that reached Velasco in December of 1835 and was soon placed under the command of Col. J. W. Fannin. After reaching Goliad, the Lone Star flag was hoisted over LaBahia Fort. In the process of lowering the flag in a high wind, it was torn to shreds. These shreds were left on the pole to witness the later massacre. There were other similar flags, but Velasco and Brazoria County claim kin to the Lone Star flag made by Miss Troutman. After her death, Miss

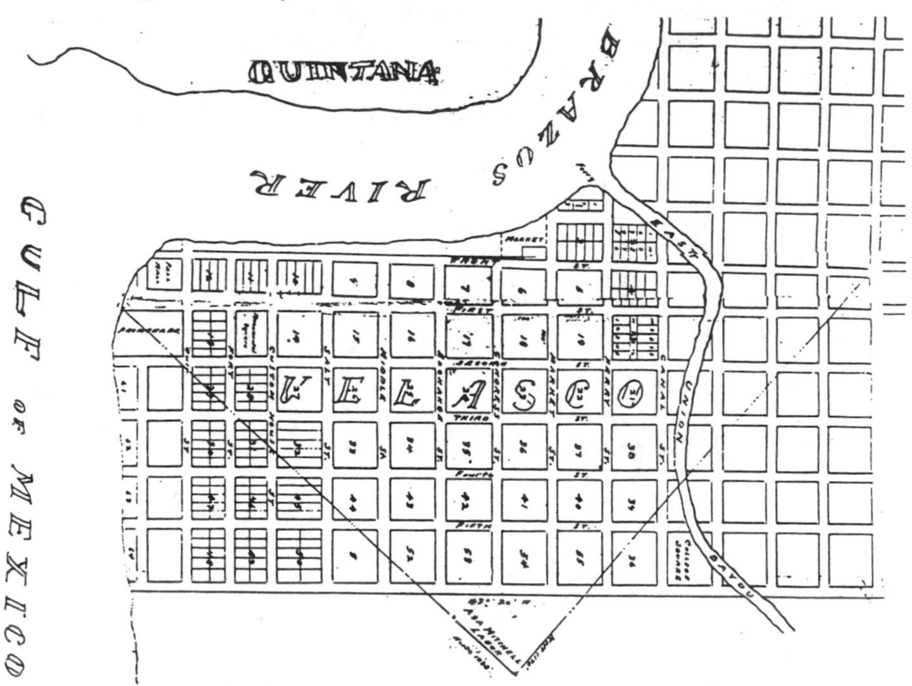

VELASCO was laid out on the east side of the Brazos River facing the Gulf of Mexico. It had a varied life but at its peak was known as the horse racing headquarters of Texas, as planters brought their horses here to race.

Troutman's remains were brought to Texas and reinterred in the State Cemetery in Austin. The inscription reads: "The tattered shreds of that flag silently witnessed the murder of Fannin and his men at Goliad, Sunday, March 27, 1836 . . ."[2]

Mary Austin Holley, Stephen F. Austin's cousin, wrote extensively about Texas in the early 1830s. Her writings may have given early colonists the wrong idea about the Brazos River. In her book she glowed about the Brazos:

> Never, was a river better calculated than the Brazos, whether we consider its depth, its placid current, or unobstructed channel, for the perfect operation of the steam engine. At present, they say, there is not enough of business to defray the expense of a steamboat. The experiment has been made. But the tide of population is setting so strongly and trade increasing so rapidly, that this objection, must of course, be speedily removed.[3]

When the *Lively* landed at Velasco in 1821, it was by accident. Actually, the colonists were supposed to have been landed at the mouth of the Colorado River destined for the city of Matagorda. There is a possibility that the skipper knew about the old Spanish landing at Velasco and brought his ship there on purpose. Legends tell that the old port was named for a prominent Mexican general, and it is thought that a Spanish village may have existed at the site once. A Mexican fort was built a short distance from the village, and in the early 1830s this fort was armed and improved in an effort by the Mexican government to exert control over the trade entering and leaving the Brazos River.[4]

There were business houses, nice homes, a hotel, boardinghouses, wharves, and a Mexican customshouse at the old port by the mid-1830s. In a number of instances, larger ships, like the *Columbia,* would come in from New Orleans with supplies for Austin's Colony and land at Velasco. There the supplies would be put onto small coastal schooners that were of shallow draft and able to get across the bar at the mouth of the Brazos. It is believed that the firm owned by Samuel M. Williams and Thomas F. McKinney established a trading post in Velasco at an early date, possibly in the early 1830s. Asa Mitchell operated a tannery and salt works at Velasco. By the late 1830s, Velasco was a community with a population approaching 1,000.[5]

Without a doubt the early settlers were so busy setting up new homes, clearing land, and surviving that they did not pay too much attention to their Mexican landlords. All of this changed on April 6, 1830, when the Mexican government issued a decree directing the construction of forts at Velasco and Anahuac. Fort Velasco was built about 150 yards from the Gulf of Mexico and overlooking the Brazos River. Two concentric circles were formed by sinking rows of posts in the ground six feet apart and extending about ten feet in the air. After sand was packed into the space between the posts, a formidable wall was in place. A customshouse office, housing for 120 soldiers (lean-tos or tents), and a large cistern for water were built inside on the river side of the fort. In the middle a large mound of dirt was placed and topped with a nine-pounder cannon. The cannon was mounted on a circular track surrounded by a

AIR CONDITIONED – This drawing of the Goodcheer Hotel, the first hotel in Velasco, gives an idea of what life was like in frontier river towns. (Photo courtesy of Institute of Texan Cultures)

wooden parapet. When the colonists saw this cannon frowning down on them each time they passed in front of the fort, it gave them an uneasy feeling. Every time a duty was collected, or a boat was stopped to inquire of its cargo and destination, this uneasy feeling gave over to wrath.[6]

First, there was trouble at Anahuac, and then the soldiers at Fort Velasco attempted to stop Capt. Jerry (Jeremiah) Brown as he brought the *Sabine* up the river. He sailed past, ignoring the command to stop, despite shots being fired at his vessel. There were no casualties or damage to the ship. This was the fuse that ignited the men in the area. The invitation went out: "There's going to be a fight, and everybody's invited."[7]

More than a hundred men gathered at Brazoria, where John Austin had called a meeting for June 20, 1832. An air of uncertainty prevailed in the community but it did not stop their preparations for a battle. John G. Rowland, master of the *Brazoria,* was instructed to have his ship ready to sail by June 22. Thomas Westall, G. B. McKinstry, Reese, and Caldwell led a group to the Brazoria customshouse, presided over by Mr. Dulcor, to seize all of his arms and ammunitions in exchange for a note from Austin expressing his regret. The *Brazoria* was put in charge of Capt. William J. Russell. The two cannons, one a brass nine-pounder mounted on a carriage, and the other a four-pounder mounted on a swivel, were put aboard and about thirty men were also consigned to the ship. The rest of the troops, numbering slightly beyond a hundred, were divided into two groups and put in charge of John Austin and Henry S. Brown. In addition to Austin and Brown, other commanders were Henry Smith, A. C. Buckner, Thomas B. Bell, John W. Cloud, W. H. Wharton, and Thomas Westall's rear guard. The women of the community busied themselves molding bullets and making patches used in loading muzzle-loaders.[8]

Settlers were alarmed due to rumors that the troops at Velasco were trying to incite slaves to revolt. The story is told about a black man known as Big Jim who ran away and consorted with the Mexican soldiers, agreeing to return and incite the slaves to rebellion. He returned the day before the battle and began to lay his seeds of insurrection. Turned in by loyal slaves, Big Jim was captured. The next day Jim's wife managed to cut him free, and he jumped out of the window and took to his heels. Pleasant D. McNeel called to him to halt, but Big Jim, more than a hundred yards away, turned and defiantly screamed: "Shoot, God damn you." Shoot he did, and Big Jim's brief career as an insurrectionist was over.[9]

The *Brazoria* reached the fort at Velasco, and when stopped and asked what their cargo was, they replied: "Cannon headed for Anahuac!" Col. Domingo de Ugartechea, commander of the fort, ordered them to return to Brazoria. They turned around and went back up the river to confer with the men on foot led by Austin and Brown. A battle plan was drawn that called for the foot soldiers to arrive at the fort at about midnight and build breastworks before morning. They had evidently made portable barricades out of heavy lumber to be used in the battle. The plan was compromised when one of the soldiers tripped on a root and fell, and his gun discharged. A keelboat is also mentioned as being used to bring troops to the battle scene. The men moved in close to the fort and were clear of the Mexican cannon fire since the gun could not depress enough to bear on the Texans' positions.

When morning arrived, Texan sharp-shooters picked off every Mexican sent to man their cannon. Any head that poked over the embankments was a good target. Meanwhile, the two cannons on the *Brazoria* inflicted enough damage and casualties that when Austin demanded that the fort surrender, a white flag was run up. Seven Texans were killed and the Mexican forces suffered at least forty-two dead. The Mexican forces were allowed to surrender, and arrangements were made for them to be transported by ship back to Mexico, at their own expense of $600. Officers were allowed to keep their side arms. The number of men taking part in the battle, as well as those in command, is a bit confusing due to the many accounts written by men who saw the engagement from a different spot.[10]

The Battle of Velasco was a battle that both the Texans and Mexicans did not want to happen. As a result, both sides embraced General Santa Anna's Plan of Vera Cruz, which declared that the Texans at Velasco acted in support of his cause. It was a ploy, but one that the Texans embraced. When Col. Jose Antonio Mexia arrived in Texas to investigate the battle, he was invited to a grand ball given in Brazoria on July

22, 1832. The dinner party turned into an occasion of patriotic rejoicing. Each side drew back to make plans. The Texans had accomplished one of their main goals, that being to get the Mexican army out of Texas. Now the War Dogs, mainly the men who had led the Velasco and Anahuac battles, set to work by political means to gain separation from Coahuila, and eventually, they wanted independence.[11]

As affairs with Mexico were put on hold, business at Velasco began to pick up – only to be squashed with the disastrous flooding of 1833, followed by a cholera epidemic that struck almost every family. The *Arkansas Gazette* of September 10, 1833, reported that Velasco was a "depopulated community." When Col. Juan Almonte published his statistical survey of Texas in 1834, Velasco had a population of 100, probably still not recovered from the cholera epidemic. By August 20, 1835, conditions in Velasco must have improved a great deal, since an important committee to consider the calling of a consultation was chaired by Branch T. Archer of Velasco and Brazoria. Henry Smith and John A. Wharton were members. Further recognition came in October of 1835, when a mail route was formed to run from San Felipe to Velasco. I. C. Hoskins was the postmaster in Velasco. The First Congress of the Republic of Texas considered Velasco as a permanent capital, but in the vote no one cast a ballot for the coastal city. However, for a brief time immediately after the Battle of San Jacinto, Velasco was the seat of government of President David Burnet. It was in Velasco that two treaties, one public and the other secret, were signed – thus ending the Texas Revolution and recognizing Texas as an independent nation. It was probably these events, and the fact that so many immigrants came through Velasco, that gave the city its name: "The Plymouth Rock of Texas." Santa Anna was held in Velasco until the summer of 1836, when he was sent to the United States.

Part of the New Orleans Grays landed in Velasco to assist in the fight against Mexico. Most of them perished either with James Grant at Agua Dulce, or with Col. James Fannin at Goliad. The Twin Sister cannons were also landed at Velasco and rushed to Gen. Sam Houston in time for the Battle of San Jacinto.

In 1838 Velasco had two schools offering boarding students everything from fancy needlework to French. Miss Elizabeth Warner, the teacher, announced that she would also accept boys under twelve. A Methodist church circuit rider came through Velasco in about 1838. Statistics compiled in 1840 showed that Brazoria had a population of 800 and that Velasco was the second city in the county.[12]

A new industry was growing up in the area: horse racing. It might appear to be out of place in the raw frontier, but it was in line with the lifestyle of the rich plantation class that was forming in the Brazos River Valley. The raising and racing of thoroughbred horses was becoming a way of life, with large purses being put down on many races. Traveler Mary Holley described the races held in Velasco:

> There will be a great Ball at Velasco tomorrow (January 22nd, 1838) night – being the period of the races. All the world, who can move, wind & Weather permitting, are to be there . . . . everything available for dresses in Texas has been brought up for the occasion . . . . the clothes being all brought from N York ready made & of the newest fashions. The steamboat plying constantly on the Brazos, will fetch and carry the people. They have only to ride to some convenient landing to embark.[13]

Mrs. Holley also dabbled in real estate and remarked that

> I will sell land at Velasco if I can to advantage . . . I am growing rich in Town Lots – all the town-makers, and they are not few, are ambitious to have me in their town and present me with a lot. Mr. Wharton has given me one in Velasco – Mr. Jones in Manhattan (mouth of Cannae) and Dr. Stone at Oregon and Galveston Bay . . . . Brother will have a sale of town lots in Bolivar 14th of April (for cash).[14]

A racetrack that had been in existence in Velasco since the early 1830s had evidently been upgraded and remodeled in 1838 enough to warrant publicity extending to New Orleans. The *Weekly Picayune* there reported: "The citizens of the neighborhood Republic pay considerable attention to the improvement of their blooded stock. Fine horses are raised and the sports of the turf are to be enjoyed in their full vigor." Branch T. Archer, who as president of the racing club invited a friend to attend the racing, said: "We shall have one week of racing and frolic in this town . . . . I will insure you a display of fashion and beauty." Another racing enthusiast added: "Many fine women and horses are in attendence all ready."

The purses for the races in Velasco seem to have been liberal. There were numerous $1,000 purse races, and one year a $10,000 purse was offered. Velasco seemed to have set the tone for the area in raising and racing fine horses. Early newspapers contained notices of races being held in Velasco, Columbia, and Brazoria in the lower Brazos Valley. In an ad in the *Columbia Telegraph and Register,* P. R. Splane offered to match one of his horses against all comers – horse, mare, or gelding – brought to his home, known as the Gin Place. The horse racing was also tied in part to the push to sell lots in the many towns that were being put on the market during this time. Gen. Thomas Jefferson Green, a soldier of fortune and one of the leaders of the Mier Expedition in 1842, was one of the movers to get the New Market Course established at Velasco. He owned a string of horses that he ran in Texas and the United States.

The racetrack being opened in 1838 in Velasco was known as the New Market Course. Officers, other than Mr. Archer, included Gen. Felix Huston, former commander-in-chief of the Texas Army; Gen. Thomas Jefferson Rusk, former secretary of war; and Edwin Waller, later to lay out the city of Austin and serve as its first mayor. The Archer House was the favorite hotel for the racing crowd in Velasco, while in Columbia the hotel owned by Jones and Robbins was used by the racing fans.[15]

The Texas Navy did not officially headquarter in Velasco, but a lot of their operations were out of the Gulfside port. In 1835 the Mexican sloop-of-war *Correro,* under the command of Capt. T. M. (Mexico) Thompson, attempted to stop the *San Felipe,* owned by McKinney and Williams and headed for Velasco. The ship finally eluded the *Correro* and made it into port. After unloading its cargo, the *San Felipe* crew rounded up an armed boarding party. With the *Laura* towing the sailer into battle, they captured the Mexican ship without firing a shot and brought the prize back into harbor.[16]

With the coming of the Civil War, the coastal defenses of Texas came to the forefront when the Federal fleet blockaded the coast. Velasco was one of the places picked to fortify. A fort made of oaken logs was constructed, surrounded by earthen breastworks. One twenty-four-pounder gun was assigned to the fort. In September of 1861 Joseph Bates was appointed head of the Fourth Texas Volunteer Regiment with headquarters at Velasco, which included two field batteries. The Federal forces raided a salt factory near Velasco, but on a whole the Brazos River remained free of restraint so that blockade running ships made it in and out on occasion. In fact, General Magruder was so confident that he issued the following proclamation:

> Whereas the port of Velasco on the Brazos River in Texas has ceased to be actually blockaded, by the forced withdrawal of the enemy, I hereby issue the following proclamation, inviting all friendly nations to resume intercourse with this port until a blockade has actually been re-established . . . .

Running the blockade became a way of life centered around the port of Velasco and Titlum-Tatlum, a small island near the entrance to the San Luis Pass, just a short distance from Velasco. One of the big blockade runners was Christy Delaney, who seemed to be able to get Brazos Valley cotton to Matamoros, Mexico, on a regular basis. It is evident that the guns mounted at Fort Velasco kept Federal ships from moving too close to the coast near the mouth of the Brazos.[17]

The completion of a canal from Galveston Bay to the Brazos River in 1856 started the decline of shipping out of Velasco. A killer hurricane hit the Texas coast in 1875, with the full brunt of the wind and waves being felt at Velasco. Practically the entire town was destroyed, even records of the old city government. Few people seemed interested in rebuilding the city on the Gulf.

Among the last boats to operate in the Brazos and out of Velasco was the *Eugene,* which took freight and passengers up the river as late as 1891. The 132-foot sternwheeler *L.Q.C. Lamar* operated out of Orange and then from Velasco and Galveston until 1893. By the late 1890s, Velasco had regained some of its popularity as a resort center. Capt. Travis Smith of the *Hiawatha* took a group of 500 campers from Velasco on a two-week ocean voyage. After this voyage the ship was taken to her home port of Columbia, where she was caught by a drop in the river and eventually turned on her side and sank after an oak stump stuck a hole in her bottom.[18]

However, a new real estate boom was in the making, and the people from old Velasco seemed to agree with the new town promoters. So, in 1888, the new town of Velasco was born about four miles up the river on the east side. The company was headed by William M. D. Lee, a businessman from Leavenworth, Kansas. His dream was to form a company for the purpose of constructing, owning, and operating a deepwater channel from the waters of the Gulf of Mexico to the mainland at the mouth of the Brazos River. What made this dream worth more than most was that it was backed by $1 million.

Deep water across the bar on the Brazos had been around as a dream since the days of Stephen F. Austin. In 1887 the U.S. Army Corps of Engineers had investigated the same possibility and labeled it as too costly and a doubtful job for the government. To back him up, Lee sought the counsel of E. L. Cothrell, engineer for developing the South Pass that opened the Mississippi to navigation.

Lee's master plan called for jetties, constructed of brush and rocks, to be built two miles into the Gulf. The flow of the river could thus be rerouted into a narrow channel in order to scour the ocean bed to a depth capable of handling oceangoing vessels. Once a deepwater channel across the bar was established, it would be no problem to dredge the riverbed upriver for four miles to Lee's new inland port, which would be connected by railroad to interior markets. Lee felt that he could tap inland exports that had been going to the Atlantic Coast, New Orleans, or Chicago. On March 20, 1888, Lee filed an application for a charter for the Brazos River Channel and Dock Company with the Texas secretary of state. He got an option of several hundred acres of land near the mouth of the river and 4,500 acres in the vicinity of the new port site. His thinking called for the Brazos River Channel and Dock Company to own a narrow, 300-foot strip on both sides of the river.

A Brazos bill was presented in the U.S. House of Representatives in May, and in August President Grover Cleveland allowed the bill to become law without his signature. Senator

Charles B. Farwell, part owner of the giant XIT North Texas ranch and a booster of the Velasco project, lobbied hard for the project. Rows of pilings soon appeared in the Gulf, outlining the coming jetties. Problems showed up at every turn, only to be met by Lee. By April 11, 1889, more than 10,000 cords of brush had been cut and placed on site for the jetties, as well as fifty carloads of rock parked on a spur near the Columbia depot. Even as the work on the jetties progressed, financial problems were ever present. Shortly, Lee and his partner, Congressman Abner Taylor, filed for receivership for their company.

Lee gradually worked out his problems, and construction work started on the syndicate's new office building in new Velasco. Over 650,000 feet of lumber was on the wharves and on site for the promised hotel.

A big breakthrough came on July 7, when the secretary of the treasury telegraphed the U.S. customs officer in Galveston that "in view of the fact that the water over the bar at your port is not sufficient depth for vessels of certain draught, such vessels, although foreign, may be allowed to go to Velasco." Large vessels followed immediately. A boom was building rapidly as the population of the new city approached 1,500. The 100-room Hotel Velasco opened on October 5.[19]

A railroad was finally built to connect with the International and Great Northern at Chenango Junction, near Anchor. Business at the port was booming, with over 175 vessels logged during 1891 bringing in assorted cargoes and taking 10,000 tons of outbound goods, mostly cotton and cotton seeds. During 1892, progress seemed apparent on all fronts. But trouble was on the horizon. The Financial Panic of 1893 hit, and money sources dried up like a mud pond in hot August weather. Velasco slowly began to die as removal of funds stopped all work, and the depressed financial condition of the nation cut land sales to zero.

In 1896 the Corps of Engineers recommended that the federal government take over the new ship channel, provided that the Brazos River Channel and Dock Company donate one mile of riverfront back to the public and turn over harbor improvements that cost $1,449,025 to the federal government.

What the Panic of 1893 did not ruin, the hurricanes of 1900 and 1907 put to rest. The dream of a new Velasco, along with the dreams of promoters such as Lee, were swallowed up by the shifting sands of the Brazos River.

But man and his dreams are hard to stop. By 1911 dredging was resumed, and water reached the depth of eighteen feet over the bar and up the river.

Man's dreams are somewhat akin to "breakers that build to a majestic height, crest and dissipate on the beach .... but another takes its place, and undaunted rises in height only to ...."[20]

Slave Ditch

The Slave Ditch was a glimmer in the eyes of early colonists, including Stephen F. Austin himself. The success of the Brazos River plantations probably had more to do with the idea than anything else. Crops planted in the rich Brazos bottomland produced excellent yields. It was imperative that an expeditious means of getting crops to market be found. The bar at the mouth of the Brazos River was the big stumbling block that stood in the way of getting products to Galveston – the number-one market during the early colonial period.

As early as 1839 a group of plantation owners got together to develop a plan. Leading members of this group included James F. Perry, owner of Perry Plantation, whose wife was Stephen F. Austin's sister; Abner Jackson, owner of a plantation on Oyster Creek four miles north of Eagle Island; Gen. James Hamilton, a plantation owner who went down on a ship off the Florida coast in 1857; and William G. Hill, owner of the Osceola Plantation.[1]

The route that this group of planters proposed was a canal between the Brazos River and Oyster Creek connecting Oyster Creek and Bastrop Bayou and down Bastrop Bayou to San Luis Bay, which connects with Galveston Bay. It was proposed to make the ditch twenty-four feet wide and at least three feet deep, with a slight slope on the banks. The first segment of the canal was dug in 1847, using slave labor, chiefly from the plantation owners who helped organize the project. The slaves used picks and shovels and fresnoes pulled by mules or oxen. It took two years to finish the first segment, at which time the promoters decided that it was costing them too much money.

The project, known to historians as "The Slave Ditch," dropped into oblivion.

In 1850 the idea was revived and a charter was granted by the state to the Brazos Navigation Company to build a canal from San Luis, or West Galveston Bay, to the waters of the Brazos River.[2]

It appears that the new venture was being financed by a group of plantation owners as well as cotton brokers in Galveston. According to the memoirs of Addie Hudgins Follett, granddaughter of J. L. Hudgins, work began in June of 1851 and was completed in 1854. Steam dredges were used to construct this ditch. At first there was just one dredge, but eventually another one started working on the Galveston end. Upon completion a toll collector's shack was installed, with John L. Hudgins as the collector of tolls.[3]

David Bradbury, contractor on the project, and James E. Haviland, a steamboat pilot who designed much of the machinery used in completing the canal, both deserve credit for the completion of the ditch to connect the Brazos with Galveston Bay.[4]

In the twentieth century some people will try anything in order to be the first to swim a river, climb a mountain, or ride a wild bull. It must have been the same in 1854. The dredge on the Galveston Bay side had been pulled out, but the dredge on the other end was plugging away to chew out the last yards of dirt. About this time Gen. Greenberry Harrison arrived at the mouth of the canal with his steamboat *Nick Hill.* He was hell-bent to be the first to enter the canal. Despite warnings, he headed his ship into the unfinished canal, and as he approached the spot where the dredge was working from the other end he grounded his boat to the point that he couldn't back out. He had to sit and wait until the lone dredge finally carved out the last chunk of dirt to complete the canal. The flow of water form the Brazos end was enough to float the *Nick Hill,* and he managed to make it to the Brazos. He was the *first* to use the shortcut.[5]

The canal was not a roaring success. They had trouble with the sides sloughing off and blocking traffic. Also, there was no channel across Galveston Bay and not all steamships wanted to risk feeling their way along this rather shallow bay. It was not until Travis L. Smith, under contract with the federal government, dug a channel across the bay that ships were able to use the shortcut effectively. The real benefit came after the Intracoastal Canal was opened early in the 1900s, making access to the Brazos River easy — but by that time there were few riverboats around to enjoy the scenery.[6]

Freeport's Diversion Channel

A bridge built on dry land!

A rare oddity?

It must have been, because it made Robert Ripley's famous "Believe It Or Not" syndicated column that ran in newspapers all over the United States.

Probably Brazoria County residents hadn't paid much attention to the new bridge being built near the Brazos River on State Highway 36 near Freeport because they were familiar with its history. But when Robert Ripley ran across the little news item he put Freeport on the map because *the bridge was being built on DRY land!*

But to have the same background that the citizens of Freeport had in 1925, it is necessary to know a bit about the century-old battle with the sandbar at the mouth of the Brazos River. Stephen F. Austin saw the need of removing the bar because of the many ships that were wrecked trying to cross its ever-changing channel. Eventually, the Slave Ditch was started in an attempt to bypass the mouth of the river. Later this ditch became a reality (see Slave Ditch in this volume). But as Freeport sought a solution to the establishment of a modern port on the Brazos and coast, some engineer came up with the brilliant idea of making a new river.

The Brazos River Harbor and Navigation District was organized in 1925 and shortly thereafter a federal grant was received "to dig a diversion channel to divert the muddy waters of the Brazos into the Gulf some distance from the mouth of the original river, in order to get rid of the sand and silt brought down the river by frequent rises."

The bonds were approved and the work started on the ditch. Again someone had a brilliant idea: "Why not build the bridge before the ditch was dug and save a lot of money?" The contract for the bridge was let on May 12, 1928, and it was completed in June of the following year at a cost of $220,000 for the 610-foot structure. The bridge features a 250-foot swing span between two fixed truss spans, each 183 feet in length. The river channel at this point is approximately 450 feet wide. With the approaches, the total length of the structure, from levee to levee, is 800 feet. The bridge's clearance was about twenty feet above mean low tide.

Original plans called for a lift bridge, but these were abandoned in favor of a swing bridge. The cost of the bridge was kept lower than a similar bridge over a river because the workmen drove to work in their cars, parked, and went to work. Materials were delivered to the site without bothering with the river. And, they didn't have to worry about a sudden rise in the river upsetting their work. Spectators wanting to see a bridge being built in the prairie drove out and parked to watch the job take shape.

The digging of the diversion channel started at Freeport at the sea end and worked back up the proposed route until it arrived at the bridge under which the diversion channel would run to link with the Brazos River. A big crowd was on hand to watch the dredge make its first cut and let some of the water of the Brazos into the ditch. After some widening of the channel, the spoilage and silt from the dredge was piped to the Brazos River and a dam was constructed, thus closing the old entrance and allowing the water to flow down the newly dug riverbed. Locals report that the nubbed-off end of the river turned into some of the best saltwater fishing on the Gulf of Mexico.

Freeport ended up with a thirty-two-foot deep, landlocked port bordering on the Gulf and capable of handling the largest of seagoing vessels.[1]

Old Brazoria

Old Brazoria was a town that storytellers love. It had everything.

The port of Brazoria played host to thousands of immigrants as they entered Texas seeking their fortune. It had a Mexican flavor, but a Texas twang. Heroine Jane Long played hostess to plain Joe and to renowned heroes, and she probably listened as "hotheads" planned for greater political freedom. Tides of war swept the town's streets. Great plantation squires

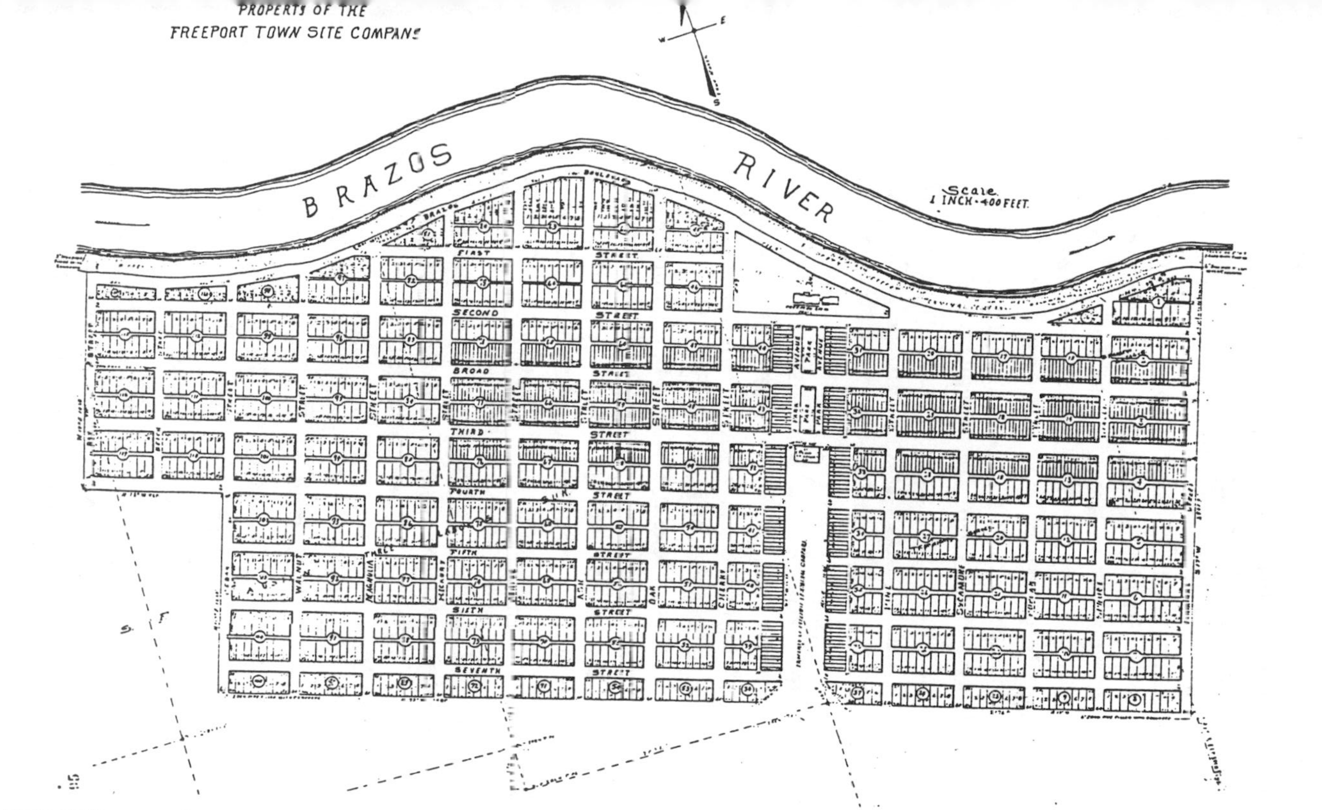

FREEPORT owes its very existence to a diversion of the Brazos River that was accomplished in "modern" times. Now oceangoing vessels call here to serve the vast petrochemical industry that has grown up in the Brazosport area.

and their satin-clad ladies rode their fancy carriages into town. Boom and bust, tides of hope and fear; horses, wagons, steamboats, iron horses all had their day. What greater place than old Brazoria to visualize the changing Texas?

Perhaps the area surrounding Brazoria, dotted with plantations, typified the period in Brazoria County that is known as the "Olden Golden Age," which really got under way in earnest after Texas was admitted to the Union in 1845. However, even before the Texas Revolution, plantations in the area were already producing large cotton crops and getting their sugar cane kettles on line to the extent that wealthy planters were the rule rather than the exception. The plundering of Gen. José de Urrea in 1836 set the planters back, but by 1838 the plantations were running smoothly and cotton was flowing down the Brazos River, out of Brazoria and plantation landings, at an increasing rate. Records of the Republic of Texas customs-house in 1838 showed that imports from Brazos County were second only to Galveston, with $380,639 recorded for the fifteen months ending September 30, 1838.[1] Mrs. Dilue Harris wrote that her father, Dr. Pleasant W. Rose, and other men who had cotton on the banks of the Brazos, built flatboats to ship their cotton to Brazoria. Other planters assembled cotton at William Little's plantation, where the steamboat *Yellow Stone* would pick it up.[2] The great plantations of the area were built with slave labor: The more slaves a plantation owner had, the more acres he could put into cotton and sugar cane. One slave could take care of five to six acres, so it took several hundred slaves to work and manage a large plantation. The plantation homes were usually large, two-story mansions built out of brick by slaves. Hospitality was the rule of the day, and entertaining was done on a regular basis. The young men followed the hounds or amused themselves with genteel sports such as horse racing. The ladies were properly gowned in silks and satins when they ventured forth to balls. These families reached a peak during this "Olden Golden Age." They were refined, cultured, and prosperous; however, they had great fortitude to survive the hardships of the frontier, live through a war and endure hurricanes of 1837 and 1854, as well as to survive the floods and disease of 1833 and 1854. They were very strong, but they lacked the work ethic to survive the Civil War

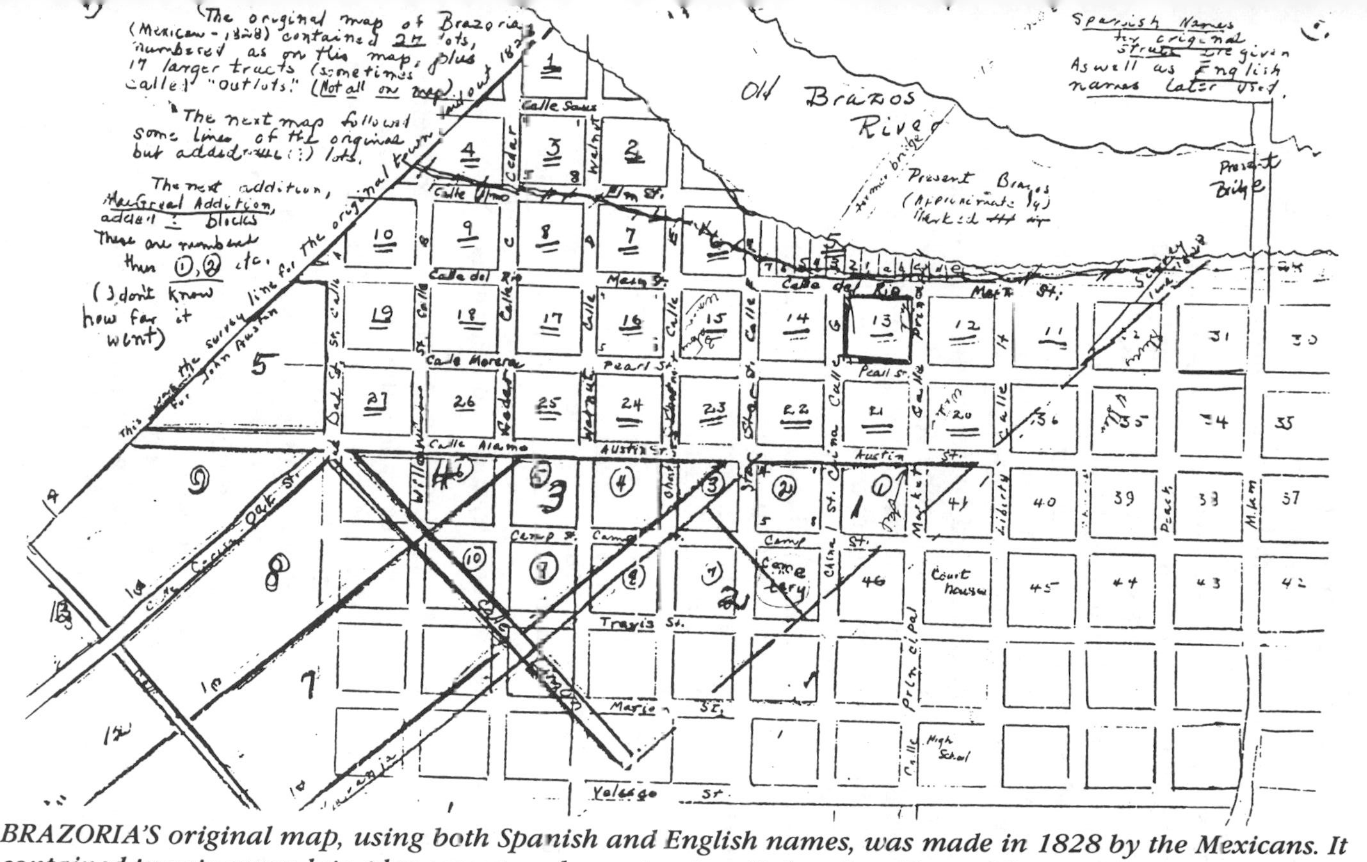

BRAZORIA'S original map, using both Spanish and English names, was made in 1828 by the Mexicans. It contained twenty-seven lots, plus seventeen larger tracts called outlots. Two additions followed as the need for more lots was felt. The commercial riverfront lots were numbered one through seven and "a" through "e."

and the destruction of the life that they had grown to believe was their right. Traditions and institutions, when divorced from wealth, perished, as did a great many of the plantation manors.[3]

Brazoria was conceived by Stephen F. Austin as the trading center for the Austin Colony. It was laid out by John Austin, a distant relative of Stephen F. Austin, in 1828. From the very beginning, it served as a funnel for people coming to Austin's Colony and as one of the first ports to receive and ship exports. A customshouse was established in 1831 at Brazosport on the Brazos River by the Mexicans, with John Austin in charge. In 1832, when Mexico decided to form the municipality of Brazos, Brazoria was named as the captial.[4]

Actually, the old town of Brazoria was laid off in two parts. John Austin laid out two streets that ran parallel to the Brazos River, with other streets intersecting them at right angles. Stephen F. Austin laid off another part of the town, adjoining and attached to the river section. The town grew rapidly. Mary Austin Holley, Stephen Austin's cousin, who kept a diary on her travels in Texas, noted in 1831 that

> Twenty excellent families have been added to Brazoria since I was there .... This spot was chosen as the most commanding and healthful, besides combining other advantages .... A stranger is more surprised to see brick stores and frame dwelling houses, than disposed to complain that he does not find more elegance and convenience.[5]

Lots in Brazoria sold for $20 to $120, according to their location. By 1831 a newspaper called the *Texas Republican* was in operation. During the next ten years, at least six newspapers were published for varying time periods. Merchants were opening shops at a regular pace. Robert and David G. Mills were planters, merchants, and bankers who got an early start in the city. Their store was noted for its very large stock of merchandise. In their banking business they advanced money to plantation owners to buy equipment and were proud of the fact that they never closed a man out because of debt. Their bank was on the corner of Market Street and River Road. Later the building was occupied by the People's Bank. The next bank, the First State Bank, was started in 1909 and continues to operate today in "new town" as Bank of Brazoria. They operated three plantations and their banking customers came from all over the county.[6] Thomas J. Pilgrim, who established the first school in Brazoria, joined Morgan L. Smith in opening stores in Bell's Landing and in Brazoria. Later Smith joined John Adriance to pioneer a method of shipping cotton called "floaters," which was unique on the Brazos:

> In Oct. 1842, experiments were made by the mercantile firm of Smith and Adriance in transporting cotton in gum-elastic floating bags, and so well pleased was the firm, that, until a steamer was put into trade, and even after, this method was used. These bags were made of stout linen sheeting folds, inbued with gum elastic. A bale of cotton was placed in the river with lower side enveloped in one of these wrappers and sunk 3/12 inches in water. A raft was formed in subdivisions of four to six bales. The bales of each subdivision were separately lashed together before the hole was formed into a platform and fastened with poles and lashings. On this a second tier was often placed, without making the draft of water more than 6 to 7 inches. A triangular bow of plank was placed in front to defense it from snags. 50 floaters carried 100 bales on 6 inches of water.[7]

Merchants in Brazoria are said to read like a "Who's Who" of early Texas history. They include John and Sterling McNeel, Robert and Andrew Mills, Walter C. White, Edmund Andrews, William T. and John Austin, Edwin Waller, James M. Westall, George Russell, George B. McKinstry, Ammon Underwood, James Perry, A. G. Reynolds, and R. Stevens. Some of these merchants also owned, or had an interest in, one or more schooners. In all at least 125 different vessels took part in the Brazoria trade between 1830 and 1836. It must be remembered that Texas merchants were dependent on wealthy New Orleans merchants to extend liberal credit to them. They handled most of the transactions for the sale of Texas cotton to England. Merchants in Brazoria had a standing relation with a New Orleans firm to receive and market their cotton. When the cotton arrived in New Orleans, the consignee would issue a bill of domestic exchange on his correspondent at the port. This usually was for an amount equal to about half the current market price. New Orleans banks purchased these bills, charging from six to eight percent interest and one to two percent exchange. The local merchant charged two to five percent for his services, and what was left, after deducting all charges, was turned over to the planter. James Walter Breedlove, New Orleans banker and cotton broker, was an important link for Brazoria. His brother, A. W. Breedlove, immigrated to Austin's colony in 1831 and remained a citizen of the community until his death in 1847. Breedlove and John Austin were business associates, with an interest in the schooner *True Blue,* which was involved in tobacco smuggling.[8]

Wealthy planters made it a practice to visit New Orleans once or twice each year to renew old business contacts and make new ones. The heart of the New Orleans business district was Levee Street, which was along the levee near the river. A man could borrow money on past or future cotton crops or on his grandfather's name. It was a gentleman's world.

In 1831 the *Majesty* made it as far as Brazoria by sending men ashore with ropes at every turn in the river to drag the ship up the river. The *Ocean* and the *Yellow Stone* worked on the river and also worked at towing sailing vessels up the river. The *Laura* worked the river for some time before being pulled out for other duty. In February of 1839 the *Laura* was back in the Brazos during a time of high water. The *Mustang* and the *Lady Byron* worked to Brazoria and above. During a period of high water in 1843, the *Mustang* went as high as Nashville; in November of the same year she went down at Jones Landing. The *Lady Byron* took the *Mustang*'s place working the Brazos River, only to sink below Richmond, losing half of a cargo and 370 bales of cotton.[9]

The *Cayuga* entered the Brazos River after pledges of 5,000 acres of land, and $800 in cash, were raised by a number of men in the Austin Colony and offered to the captain who would bring his boat to San Felipe. This small schooner made regular trips up and down the river until it finally got stuck on a sandbar on return from a voyage that had gone as far as San Felipe. There settlers had given a gala party for the crew and captain. The captain was William Plunkett Harris in 1834.[10]

The small steamer *Amite* was put into the Brazos trade because it was able to get over the bar without great difficulty. This vessel was engaged in the lower Brazos trade out of

Brazoria until it was seized for debt and sold by Capt. R. J. Calder, sheriff of Brazoria County.

The steamer ***Lafitte,*** built at Quintana in 1841, ran regularly between Columbia, Brazoria, and Velasco to Galveston and Sabine Pass.[11]

A list of merchants and cotton brokers located in Brazoria is difficult to piece together. However, early travelers told of the activity going on at the old port. One travel writer remarked that the town was one of the most important trade centers of the fertile region devoted chiefly to cotton.[12]

In 1839 the steamer ***Friend,*** which had been working the Buffalo Bayou trade, was transferred to the Brazos River and set out up the river to Washington, but had to settle on Brazoria because of low water. The trading firm of McKinney and Williams, of Velasco, hired the small steamer *Ocean* to tow sailing vessels up the Brazos. In 1836 it was headed upriver with a vessel in tow, and, when approaching the wharf at Brazoria, it ran into a snag and sank at the wharf. McKinney and Williams offered a $5,000 reward to raise the boat and apparently someone performed the job, as business went on as usual at the Brazoria wharf. Evidently, Thomas McKinney was a big dealer since, when he was told of the loss of the *Ocean,* he remarked: "I wish the loss of the *Ocean* was our greatest . . . ."[13]

Patrick McGreal was a merchant located on the waterfront in Brazoria. Once he lost a cargo of merchandise worth $40,000 when a boat went down. Another boat trying to cross the bar lost $80,000 of his merchandise. It is reported that he often took in $5,000 a day in cash. He did a big credit business.[14]

John Austin brought the first steamer, the *Ariel,* to the Brazos River in 1830. The steamer arrived at Velasco, and then at his own port of Brazoria, and later went up as high as Bolivar, where he was planning another development. After working the *Ariel* out of Brazoria for a short time, he decided to run the ship to New Orleans to get a load of supplies; however, the *Ariel* experienced difficulty crossing the bar. When they finally made it over, the vessel was in bad shape. The captain put into Galveston Bay and ran up Buffalo Bayou, where the *Ariel* was left to slowly rot in the mud.[15]

Brazoria was the seat of courts in the municipality of

Brazoria. After a short time it was moved to Columbia, but then returned to Brazoria in 1836.

Mail route No. 4 was established between San Felipe to Velasco, via Fort Bend, Orozimbo, Columbia, and Brazoria. In 1840 the Republic established route No. 19 to run from Velasco to San Felipe, via Crosby's, Brazoria, Orozimbo, and Big Creek. In 1845 the last Republic mail routes included Brazoria on Route No. 14.[16, 17]

Something of the character of Brazoria can perhaps be seen from the large number of citizens who left their mark on history.

Henry Smith is one of those outstanding individuals. He took over the job of *alcalde* of the jurisdiction of Brazoria in 1833 shortly after being wounded in the Battle of Velasco. The first American to be named to the office of political chief of the Department of Brazos, he was a delegate to the Convention of 1833 and delegate to the Consultation. After Texas' independence, he was elected provisional governor of Texas. In Texas politics he had many admirers, and equally as many detractors. He ran for the presidency but was defeated by Sam Houston, who immediately named Smith as secretary of state and treasury. In 1840 he served one term in the U.S. House of Representatives. After this term he returned home to retirement until he got California gold fever. He died in Los Angeles County in 1851. One of his daughters, Harriet, married Col. George W. Fulton, an inventor and founder of the famous Coleman, Fulton, Mathis Cattle Company.[18]

Jane Long was the widow of Dr. James Long, who was killed while following the path of a revolutionist in 1822. Mrs. Long, two children, and a slave girl finally were rescued from Galveston Island, where her husband had left her. In 1827 Austin granted her a league of land in the vicinity of Fort Bend on the Brazos, and she moved there to a cabin that Ben Milam built for her. After a marriage to Edward Winston, she moved to Brazoria in 1832 with her black maid, Kian. In Brazoria she opened a hotel and advertised that they would give "the best which the country offers to merit part of public patronage." Through the next several decades, public figures and travelers alike stayed at her tavern that became famous for the dinners and balls. Stephen F. Austin, when he was released from a Mexican prison after eighteen months, was honored with a dinner and ball at which over 1,000 paid seven dollars to hear his speech that set the moral tone for the coming revolution against Mexico. (On September 8, 1935, distinguished guests from all over Texas came to commemorate this historic event. It was the occasion for the first radio broadcast sent out from Brazoria.) Jane Long's suitors were many, including President Mirabeau Lamar. In 1837 she relocated to Richmond, where she operated a hotel and took care of her successful plantation. She died in 1880 at the age of eighty-two. The *Galveston News* of January 2, 1881, eulogized her under the headline: "Death of a Texas Heroine." She was known at various times as the "Mother" or "Sweetheart" of Texas.[19]

Carrie Nation, who gained fame when she led in the battle to outlaw liquor in the United States, was a native of Brazoria. Legends say that her first husband was a merchant in Brazoria but lost his business because he hit the bottle a bit heavily. Perhaps she took up her hatchet at this point and led a nationwide crusade against alcohol.[20]

Col. James W. Fannin, Jr., who was shot and his forces massacred at Goliad, settled on the San Bernard River near Brazoria and was well known in the community. His letters confirm that he was a slave trader. He put up slaves for his half to purchase a plantation in a partnership with Joseph Mims. Before his death, Fannin wrote to Mims and asked him to care for his family if something happened to him, which Mims did for the five-year life of the partnership. Fannin was an agitator for the Texas Revolution, member of the Committee of Safety and Correspondence, and later was named colonel of a provisional regiment of volunteers.[21]

Romance and legend are intertwined in the story of the outlaw Jesse James, who made a visit to Brazoria to drop out of sight for a while. A member of his gang, Ford Smith, fell in love with a local girl and married her, then left the gang with Jesse's permission. The couple lived a respectable life, and no doubt old-timers in the area can point out where the couple lived.[22]

William Harris Wharton and his son, John A. Wharton, left a lasting imprint on Brazoria County. Attorney William Wharton moved to Texas in 1827 and married Sarah Ann Groce, daughter of Jared Ellison Groce, and they made their home on a large plantation on Eagle Island, given to the bride by her father. William Wharton was at the forefront in the Texas Revolution, always pushing for independence from Mexico. He was named judge advocate but resigned his commission to serve with Stephen F. Austin and Branch T. Archer as commissioners to the United States to secure aid for the young nation. Later he was appointed first minister to the U.S. On a return voyage he was captured on the high seas and taken to a Mexican prison, from which he escaped.

His son, John A., read law with his cousin, Jack Harris, and E. M. Pease. Where his father had been an advocate of independence from Mexico, the son became a bearer of the cause of the Confederacy. He served in Terry's Rangers, and when Terry was killed, he was elected colonel to take his place. Eventually, he became a major general and was decorated for his actions. On April 6, 1865, in the headquarters of Maj. Gen. John Magruder, he renewed a verbal dispute with George W. Baylor. John Wharton called his critic a liar and slapped his face. Baylor drew his gun and killed the hero. The son died as the result of a bullet wound growing out of a feud; his father, William, was killed when he accidentally discharged his pistol as he was dismounting his horse. The father was buried at Eagle Island and the son in the State Cemetery at Austin. William Wharton's portrait hangs in the Texas Senate.[23]

Dr. Anson Jones established a medical practice in Brazoria in 1833 which had soon grown to be worth $5,000 per year. He counseled forbearance and peace in the dealings with Mexico. When war came, he enlisted as a surgeon and was on the field at San Jacinto. He returned to Brazoria and evicted James Collinsworth from his office by a challenge to a duel. He was elected to the Second Congress of the Republic and was opposed to annexation. President Sam Houston appointed him minister to the United States in 1839, only to be recalled by President Mirabeau B. Lamar in 1839. After marrying Mary (Smith) McCrory, he returned to politics when Houston appointed him secretary of state. In September 1844 he was elected president of Texas and took office on December 9. During his election, he did not speak out one way or another on annexation. The issue became active when he postponed calling an annexation convention to try to win recognition for

Texas from Mexico. The new Congress rejected the treaty with Mexico and approved the joint resolution of annexation. Brooding over his political reverses, he took his own life on January 9, 1858.[24]

Brazoria furnished many leaders in the post-Revolution period in Texas. Branch Tanner Archer was one. He represented the Brazoria municipality at mass meetings and demanded removal of port regulations imposed by the Mexicans in 1832. He participated in the Battle of Gonzales and left there to attend the Consultation, and was elected to head the group. A member of the first Texas Congress, he served as Speaker of the House during its second session. Archer County in North Texas was named in his honor.[25]

The Customs District of Brazos was created by the General Council on December 27, 1835, and on June 12, 1837, the organization of the customs service was finally settled.[26]

Jerimiah Brown was named the first collector for the District of Brazos. The office was originally listed in Brazos (Brazoria), but on September 20, 1837, records show that $710.15 was paid for a customshouse building in Velasco. William F. Austin was listed as the collector on March 2, 1841. During the quarter ending December 1837, a total of twenty ships arrived on the Brazos. Exports were listed as cotton and hides. During this period, 244 passengers arrived and 122 left. In the quarter ending March 31, 1838, thirty-seven passengers arrived and 226 departed. In the same period 721 bales of cotton and 228 bags of cotton seed were shipped. The report showed that in March 1839 twenty-six ships arrived with 167 passengers, and thirty-one ships departed. Cotton shipped amounted to 1,689 bales, plus hides and cotton seed. Records show that R. M. Potter was the collector in June 1844.[27]

In 1842 President Sam Houston was having a hard time trying to keep from going to war with Mexico and at the same time keeping on track to obtain statehood for Texas. Brazoria, which had produced many patriots, was not 100 percent behind Houston and his policies. Sometime in 1842, Houston's opponents sought to have a convention in Brazoria. Little about the men or the purpose of the meeting is known.[28]

In 1838 auxiliaries of the American Sunday School Union and other American Sunday school organizations were formed at Brazoria. Emily Perry, mistress of Peach Point Plantation, made it a habit of attending church services in Brazoria when no minister was available at Peach Point.[29]

In 1833 cholera moved into Brazoria, causing a great number of people to flee. John Austin was one of the many victims.[30] The exodus of people, plus deaths, left Brazoria with only five or six families. By October the scare evidently had passed.[31]

The Brazoria bar was one of the most influential in the Republic days. It was headed by the firm of John A. Wharton, John W. Harris, and E. M. Pease (who later became governor).[32]

Brazoria was beset with the rise of law violations. In 1841 Col. Willis Alston was lynched near Brazoria after killing a well-known and popular physician, Dr. John McNeill Stewart. The trouble originated with a killing in Florida and finally reached a fever pitch in December, when a mob took Alston out to be hanged. A pistol exploded in the crowd, wounding a man. In the following melee, Alston was shot down.[33]

The area around Brazoria ranked high in growing cotton and corn. Settlers claimed that anything capable of growing would grow on the Brazos bottomland.

The hazards of steamboat travel in the mid-1830s was drawn clearly by Ammon Underwood, who kept a journal of his Texas travels. Underwood had been traveling in the area and procured passage on board the schooner *Dart,* bound for New Orleans. The schooner stopped at Velasco and picked up a number of passengers, in part because the steamer *Empress* had been condemned as unseaworthy. They left Velasco at 6:30 A.M. and made a run at the bar across the mouth of the Brazos where "we remained thumping for about 4 hours when we were so unfortunate as to get over." Double trouble followed the *Dart.* The captain, attempting to drown his troubles, took to the bottle, and the crew was unable to pump water out as fast as it was coming in. Finally, the captain was put to bed and the ship was turned around. The *Dart* barely made it back to the beach, where it was grounded, and everyone got safely ashore.[34]

In *British Correspondence,* Jos. T. Crawford to O'Gormall in May of 1837, it was noted that the writer came up the river on the steamer *Miles* to Brazoria, where he wrote: "I ascended on board the Steamer thirty miles to Brasoria, a small Town on the south or right bank, where there is a good deal of business going on and several large and well assorted Stores . . . ."[35]

The population of Brazoria grew at a steady pace. At its peak it is said to have had as many as 5,000 to 6,000 residents. The population dwindled after the Civil War and the start of a new Brazoria a few miles inland from the old landing. Old Brazoria retained its beauty and charm for many years, but after the courthouse was moved to Angleton in 1897, things definitely took a turn for the worse as more and more people moved away.[36]

The plantation owner did not always have smooth sailing. During the "Panic" of 1837 (financial panic plus a hurricane), cotton was stacked on the banks of the Brazos for nearly a mile with no buyer in sight. Markets were bad and times were tight in the city of Brazoria. Everything was cheap. An unbroken cow pony would only fetch a plug of tobacco, perhaps starting the old saying: "Not worth a plug of tobacco."[37]

The first cotton gin in the county was built by John and James E. B. Austin, of Brazoria, in time to gin the 1826 cotton crop, which averaged from 2,500 to 3,000 pounds of seed cotton per acre, or about two ginned bales. The partnership also built a store and other outbuildings in Brazoria, presumably on the river in order to be able to ship and receive freight from the Brazos steamers. In 1830 Chesley Stringfellow and his mother, Susannah, moved to Brazoria and opened a hardware and mercantile building. He was a partner with Michel B. Menard, founder of Galveston, in a store in Galveston. Stringfellow expanded and owned two plantations and three steamships operating between Brazoria and Galveston. He married Sophia Ahrens. The *Texas Gazette* reported that a seventy-mile road was now staked out between San Felipe and Brazoria, and another road ran twenty-five miles from Brazoria to the mouth of the Brazos River.[38]

As more and more immigrants came into Brazoria, Messers. Brigham & Marsh, merchants of Brazoria, announced that they would act as agents of the *Texas Gazette,* which was establishing a reputation as being a spokesman for Austin and other leaders in the early 1830s. In an ad in the *Gazette* the Brazoria firm of J. B. Dickinson and Company advertised a wide selection of goods; the estate of A. B. Clark offered a law library; and David Hamilton let all horse lovers know that the fine-blooded horse Bellaire would stand in the fall season. In October 1830 the *Nelson* docked at Brazoria with a full load of merchandise to open a store at Perry's Landing. William T. Austin and his wife arrived on the same ship, and he immediately entered into the mercantile business. He also opened a new hotel in Brazoria.[39]

The commercial growth of Brazoria was disturbed in December 1831 when two ships, disregarding recent orders by customs director George Fisher, failed to stop at Brazoria, where a small Mexican guard was stationed. Shots were exchanged, and one Mexican, as well as possibly one Texan, were wounded. Fortunately, for all parties, the incident was overlooked by the Mexican authorities. However, events at

A WAY OF LIFE – Plantations on the Brazos River afforded a lifestyle that was luxurious to an extreme. The plantation owners and their wives lived in fine homes and had carriages for every need. This runabout probably awaits the lady of the house for a morning ride.

Anahuac and Velasco would find the people of Brazoria in the forefront. Capt. William J. Russell, commander of the *Brazoria,* mounted Austin's two cannons on his ship. The Texas forces won a decisive victory at Velasco, losing seven men. The open breach was healed by the visit of Col. Jose Antonio Mexia after a week of talks in Brazoria, topped by a Santa Anna ball and dinner held in the hotel of Mrs. Jane Long.[40]

Despite this turmoil, plus the flood and cholera epidemic of 1833, the growth of Brazoria continued. The era of the steamboat was beginning to be felt. J. A. R. Cleveland opened a business in Brazoria, and Meriwether Smith bought Mrs. Long's hotel. A marine insurance agency was offering insurance to planters, but a minor setback occurred when the seat of government for the municipality of Brazoria was shifted from Brazoria to Columbia. However, economic conditions were good in 1834, with an estimated 5,000 bales of cotton being shipped out of the Brazos River, chiefly from the port of Brazoria.

Brazoria, like many other areas where cattle were raised, had a problem finding a market for their beef. A packery was established on the Brazos River between Brazoria and East Columbia. Cattle were slaughtered for their hides, bones, and tallow, and all of the meat was thrown into the river. This served to get rid of the smelly waste and produced good fish stories. Fish came up the river and grew to enormous size, feeding on the waste. In descriptive language, an old-timer said: "You could not eat them. They were neither fish and neither beast!"[41]

Bell's Landing/Marion/Columbia/West Columbia

Josiah H. Bell was a mover and a doer. He was also a confidant of empresario Stephen F. Austin, having come to Texas with him in 1821, settling near Old Washington. He served as *sindico* and *alcalde* before Austin put him in charge of the colony, beginning in 1822, when Austin was imprisoned in Mexico for eighteen months. In 1823 he moved to another grant on the lower Brazos River and in a short time had created Bell's Landing, about halfway between Brazoria and Bolivar on the west bank of the river.[1]

Within a short time he had built docks, sheds, and rooms

for storing freight at the new landing. Bell wanted to call the new port Marion; however, rivermen soon noted the landing as Bell's Landing. With the landing well established, Bell decided to found a new town about two miles from the river. He proceeded to clear a road from the landing to a new town site that he called Columbia (now called West Columbia). The development of this new town was rapid, to the point that by 1836 it was for a short time the first capital of Texas.[2] A long, one-story building with a gallery running along the front was built for a hotel at the landing. J. P. Taylor had a store in 1838. Ammon Underwood established a general mercantile store and built a nice home on the river in 1833. The Underwood store was known all over the country.[3]

Business picked up in 1845 in East Columbia, with M. Pinkard advertising general merchandise "for sale cheap." Dr. John Corbin advertised his presence in East Columbia. In 1849 Henrich Jansen and wife Maria Jurgensen Jansen opened a blacksmith and carriage shop with a sideline of building furniture. Some of his pieces are on display today in the Varner-Hogg Plantation house. Thomas Dwyer opened stores in Columbia, Brazoria, and Quintana.

Evidently, Bell picked a good place for his landing. According to Mary Austin Holley, it was a beautiful spot. She wrote:

> Back from Marion about 2 miles is the town of Columbia the seat of justice for the county, contains a new hotel kept by Bell—new and spacious, the largest building there. There is besides a building or two for court house offices etc. This town is on the edge of the prairie, and the scenery is pretty about it. A broad road through the timber is cut to the landing—very muddy in wet weather .... Marion is now called Columbia, being considered a part thereof, and is the landing. They propose to connect the two settlements by a railroad .... The Landing is flourishing. It is not very healthy and last summer, which was a sickly one, more died at Marion, in proportion to the numbers, than elsewhere. Still it is growing fast and a great deal of business is doing there. March 13, 1838.[4]

Conditions in 1836, just after the Battle of San Jacinto, were unsettled as President Burnet sought to bring about a semblance of civilian government. He finally set September 5 for election day to name officials for the first administration of the Texas Republic. At the same time that he issued the order, he also designated Columbia as the site for the meeting of Congress on October 3 because "that town had the most adequate housing accommodations and because it possessed a newspaper, *The Telegraph and Texas Register.*" After the newspaper duly ran the news, a committee was immediately appointed in Columbia to prepare the necessary buildings to accommodate the first meeting of Congress.[5]

There was an air of excitement in Columbia as they prepared for the October meeting of Congress. The two buildings that would house the official Congress functions were spruced up and, no doubt, any plantation within a short distance of Columbia offered to accommodate the expected senators,

EAST COLUMBIA was laid out in a bend in the Brazos River where Varner Creek intersected. Front Street was primarily for commercial establishments.

representatives, military officers, politicians, and those seeking favors from the new government. These included soldiers wanting bounty land scrip and settlers seeking free land. Naturally, there would also be the curious and those who hoped to make a fast buck either by selling the new Republic something or gaining a coveted franchise.[6]

Francis Lubbock, Texas patriot, and an early merchant in Velasco and Houston, in his memoirs left behind some thoughts on Columbia:

> Congress was then in session [October to December, 1836], and I hastened with my goods up the river by steamboat to the capital . . . . leaving the river at Bell's Landing, where we were all put ashore. I found the town of Columbia about two miles westward on the edge of a prairie dotted with live Oaks. The Congress was occupying two frame houses, the larger one, with partition removed, for the Representative chamber, and the smaller one for the Senate [14 members], the shed rooms being used for committees . . . . I took my meals with Fitchett & Gill, the tavern-keepers . . . . the town presented a wild and romantic appearance to me.[7]

Sam Houston was inaugurated at this first session of the Texas Congress. The hero of San Jacinto had won the election with 5,119 votes to 743 for Henry Smith and 587 for Stephen F. Austin. This was also the meeting that selected the city of Houston as the permanent capital. Fifteen towns sought the honor of being designated as the capital for the new Republic. Four ballots were taken, with Houston getting eleven votes on the first ballot and Matagorda eight. On the next ballot Matagorda lost support, and New Washington took over the second spot. On the final vote Houston got twenty-one votes, Washington fourteen, and one vote was cast for Columbia.[8]

The bar at the mouth of the Brazos River was a formidable block against all types of ships trying to bring supplies upriver. Small, coastwise sailing vessels, designed to be able to sail in three feet, or less, of water, managed to get across the bar on a regular basis. Sometimes the ships would have to stand off the bar until a high tide rolled in to give a bit more depth to the channel. From the time that Bell's Landing was established, freight came into the landing in increasing amounts. Since Bell had ties with Austin, it was only natural that freight destined for San Felipe would be sent to Bell's Landing, where wagons were waiting to take the goods upriver. The first steamboat on the Brazos was the *Ariel,* owned by Henry Austin. After several runs up the river, the owner removed the *Ariel* from the trade. It was not long before William P. Harris and Robert Wilson were induced to bring the *Cayuga* from the Mississippi River to work on the Brazos in 1833. For the next two years, the little sidewheeler was one of the main carriers on the river. It has been suggested by some students of riverboats that when the ship disappeared from the manifests in 1836, its name had been changed to the *Branch T. Archer.* Whether this was true or not is debatable, but the fact remains that starting in 1830 steamboat traffic on the Brazos increased to the point that the sidewheelers were carrying more freight than the sailing ships.[9]

Bell's Landing suffered a blow in 1833, when one of the heaviest floods known on the river inundated everything that was not on a high hill. Right on the heels of the floods an epidemic of cholera swept through the colony, claiming a number of lives in Bell's Landing and West Columbia.[10]

Columbia, from its inception, was a city that prided itself on its culture, refinement, and involvement in politics. With Gen. Martín Perfecto de Cos standing ready with an army just below the Rio Grande, patriots in Columbia played host to a meeting in June 1835 to discuss the gravity of the situation. On August 15 William H. Wharton presided over a consultation in Columbia which called for a gathering of all Texas citizens. However, cooler heads prevailed and support was given to the Mexican Constitution of 1824. The upshot of this meeting was the calling of a convention at Washington-on-the-Brazos for October 15.[11]

When Santa Anna put the Alamo to the sword and headed toward East Texas in pursuit of Gen. Sam Houston and his army, the people of Columbia acted with unrestrained panic. They joined the Runaway Scrape, abandoning practically everything except the clothing on their backs, and headed for the United States border. With the news of victory at San Jacinto, the people turned around and returned to their homes. The retreating Mexicans, as well as lawless *gringos,* left a trail of wanton destruction, but order was soon returned and everyone began getting ready for the inauguration of Sam Houston as the new president of the Republic. The Columbia *Telegraph and Texas Register* began publication at this time and continued as long as the capital remained in Columbia. They reported the inauguration ceremonies held October 3, 1836, where Houston was sworn in as the first president of the Republic of Texas.[12]

The wave of prosperity that enveloped the plantations of the Brazos River Valley in the next decade swept Bell's Landing and Columbia toward rapid growth. Officially, Bell's Landing became East Columbia, probably after Mr. Bell's death in 1838. The cotton plantations remained supreme; however, Brazoria County produced 7,329 hogsheads of sugar in 1852. Most of the cotton and sugar produced in this early period, particularly on the west bank of the Brazos, found its way out of the ports of Brazoria, East Columbia, and Quintana. This period in the history of plantation life was known as the Golden Decade. In all there were forty-six plantations in Brazoria County. Sixteen raised only cotton, nineteen were exclusively for sugar, and three raised some of both. Eight plantations were not classified.[13]

Under Mexican rule, mail was carried on the Brazos River. Route No. 4 was designated from San Felipe to Velasco, via Fort Bend, Orozimbo, Columbia, and Brazoria. In all likelihood this mail route operated on the Brazos as high as Brazoria or Bell's Landing, and then it went overland as did most of the freight in 1835. In December of 1836 Congress created a route that ran from Velasco, via Brazoria, Columbia, and Washington, to Viesca. In 1840 the Republic set up Route No. 19 to run from Velasco to San Felipe, via Crosby's, Brazoria, Orozimbo, and Big Creek. In 1843 the Route was 14, running from Velasco to Washington, via Brazoria, Columbia, Richmond, San Felipe, and Burleigh. The last Republic route was in 1845 and ran from Velasco to San Felipe, via Brazoria, Columbia, Orozimbo, Big Creek, and Richmond.[14] Columbia was granted a post office in 1846 that was changed to East Columbia in 1927. West Columbia received a post office in 1905.[15]

The Columbia *Planter* published a story on July 22, 1844, about the need for a new post office in Columbia. The editor pointed out that no mail facility existed east of the Brazos, from

STERNWHEELER HIAWATHA *was used extensively in the Brazos River trade and is pictured here at the port of East Columbia. From the appearance of the family-type crowd, the old sternwheeler evidently hauled a considerable number of passengers on its runs to Galveston.* (Photo courtesy of Thomas Smith and Brazoria County Historical Museum)

Velasco to Major Bingham's. Perhaps the editor had some influence on routes announced in 1845, as noted above.

Columbia had a Presbyterian church in 1834, and by 1840 there were ten members with the Rev. William Y. Allen as pastor.[16] A Methodist circuit rider made his rounds starting in 1839 and included Columbia. The Methodist church in Columbia was founded March 7, 1840. Since there were no church buildings, groups met in the Senate chambers. The bishop of the Episcopal church held services in Columbia during a visit to the county in 1839. Catholic congregations were organized in Brazoria in 1840.

The Columbia *Planter* reported in 1845 that the Columbia Institute, Dr. J. Wilson Copes, superintendent, opened with departments of Spanish and Latin. A notice was in the same July 4 issue of the paper noting that examinations would be held at Obadiah Rowley's Brazoria Academy at Bailey's Prairie. The Columbia Female Seminary opened on September 29, 1845.

Thomas Jefferson Callihan settled in the area and soon built a boat that he called the *Fox,* which could take twelve tons of freight to Galveston. With a good southwesterly wind, he could make Galveston in thirty-six hours and return in less than six hours when the wind was from the southeast.[17]

The *Mustang,* one of the first steamboats to travel as high as Washington, was sunk at Jones Wharf above San Felipe on December 2, 1843. A week later, the newspaper *Planter* listed the steamboat *Lady Byron* as leaving Columbia for Washington with 900 barrels of freight. Between 1840 and 1855, at least nine steamboats were working the Brazos River, all calling at East Columbia.

An old scrapbook owned by J. P. Underwood of East Columbia showed that the last shipment of slaves to Texas probably landed on the San Bernard River in 1840. A slave by the name of Ned Thompson, who arrived with this group, is the source of the story.

By 1840 competition from Houston, plus increased insur-

THE ALICE BLAIR, *a Brazos River steamboat, docked at East Columbia.* (Drawing by Ethel Smith; photo courtesy of Insitute of Texan Cultures)

ance rates, caused boats like the *Laura* and *Yellow Stone* to leave the Brazos River trade for the more lucrative Buffalo Bayou trade.

In 1843 Gail Borden headed an effort to dig a canal from the lower end of the Brazos River to Galveston, and thus avoid the treacherous bar at the mouth of the Brazos. This project faded into the sunset, but in 1850 the Galveston and Brazos Navigation Company built a canal from the Brazos to West Galveston Bay. Since it was shallow, and had no maintenance, it was not successful. However, it did point the way for a successful project in the late 1880s, when Travis Smith ramrodded a better canal.

The big change in the way the Brazos Valley farmers and businessmen could get products to market came in 1856, when the Houston Tap and Brazoria Railway Company was built linking Houston and Columbia. The train made its initial run in 1859, changing forever the life of the Brazos rivermen.

A series of boats plied the Brazos after the Civil War. The 185-ton *Sellers* ran between Galveston and the Brazos from 1869 to 1871, when it suffered a mishap and sank in the Galveston harbor. The *Sellers* was repaired and refloated but did not return to the Brazos. The *Camargo* brought sugar and cotton out of the Brazos from 1868 to 1869, before her owners transferred her to the Sabine trade. The *Travis,* a small steamer with only twenty-seven tons' capacity, went down between Brazoria and Columbia in 1869. The *John Scott* made regular runs to Columbia from Galveston in 1871–73 but evidently wasn't making money, as the owners sold it to a captain in Brownsville. The *George W. Thomas* was one of the last boats to call regularly at Columbia. Its captain was William Jenkins. The *Beardstown* called on the Brazos but was put out of business by the hurricane that struck September 15, 1875. In Galveston Bay at the time, the *Beardstown* was forced by the wind into the mud flats and eventually sank. The *Kate, Storm,* and *J. L. Graham* all left the Brazos trade.[18]

By 1845 the *Planter* was reporting a full gamut of social events. A ball was held on April 5, 1846, to celebrate annexation of Texas to the United States, and in the December papers it was reported that the Juvenile Corps Dramatic of Columbia gave their first performance. A column appearing in the paper was entitled "Mrs. Caudle's Curtain Lectures."

BRAZOS RIVER STEAMERS of this size could make it over the bar better than the larger boats. This boat is shown probably taking on freight at East Columbia. (Photo courtesy of Brazos County Historical Museum)

The story of James Bailey needs to be told. He was not a ship captain, or a renowned plantation owner, but a man who came to the Brazos Valley to build a home after a lifetime of moving westward for a perfect spot. Bailey did not live long enough to enjoy his home surrounded by beautiful trees. When the end came he called in his wife and asked: "Bury me standing, facing west, with my gun by my side. All my life I have been traveling westward, and I have never looked up to any man, so I do not want it said, 'Here lies old Brit Bailey,' but 'Here stands Bailey.' "

He was buried, as instructed, and life settled back to normal for the Bailey family; that is, until Bailey's Light began to appear. Bailey's former neighbors reported seeing a great white light arise out of the darkness from Bailey's grave. Efforts to solve the mystery were futile.

Finally, an old servant said that Bailey, on his deathbed, made the servant promise to put a jug of whiskey in the coffin.

Mrs. Bailey "got mad and threw the jug out of the window." So, the theory was that Old Brit was walking out of his grave to find whoever had stolen his whiskey.[19]

Old ports and ships pass into the past, but yarns live on forever.

Richmond

"Look for the big bend in the river."

Guidelines similar to this one were probably given to William Little by Stephen F. Austin when a contingent of settlers left New Orleans headed for Texas and their new home in the Austin Colony.

The *Lively,* a thirty-ton schooner purchased by Austin, landed eighteen colonists at the mouth of the Brazos River in November 1821, with their worldly goods, and returned to New Orleans to bring another load of settlers to Texas. On the second voyage the little ship went aground on the tip of Galveston Island and the colonists lost all of their possessions and supplies.[1]

Little and several other men set about making boats to take them up the river. The remainder of the colonists were planning on walking to their new homesites. Austin had picked out the site for his first settlement when he had made a trip from New Orleans to San Antonio earlier and had crossed the Brazos at a near natural ford. He decided that this high bluff would make an ideal place to build a fort to guard the approaches to the river, as well as guard against the Indians. Capt. Randal Jones had also visited the site as an Indian trader. He and his brother, Henry, were among the early settlers.

The men started building a small log fort on the west bank of the river at the lower end of the bend. Thus, the community got its name from the bend in the Brazos River and became known originally as Fort Settlement or Fort Bend. The county later was designated Fort Bend. The early settlers selected the future home of Richmond because they thought the high bluffs would be above river overflows during times of flooding. This proved to be correct in the great flood of 1899. Later, these first settlers at Fort Bend were joined by other members of the "Old Three Hundred." In fact, forty-one of the 297 families settled eventually in the Fort Bend area. For a number of years this loose community was known as "Louisville." By water, the Fort Bend area was about ninety-five miles from the Gulf of Mexico.[2]

Families arriving to become part of the community included the two Lovelace brothers; William Morton, who had been one of the passengers on the second voyage of the *Lively* when it was shipwrecked; the Fitzgeralds and the Fraziers, who came later; and Thomas M. Borden, who established a gin in about 1830. In all, fifteen settlers had arrived by the summer of 1822, earning the name of the "Forlorn Fifteen."[3]

Robert Gillespie, a newly arrived settler, had the dubious distinction of being the first man to be buried in the new community. At the time of his death in 1825, he was living in the home of William Morton. To mark the grave, Morton, who was a brick and stone cutter, built a tomb of brick and stone inscribed with Gillespie's name and the Masonic symbol. Morton discovered that Gillespie was a member of the fraternal Masonic Order after his death. From this start the cemetery became the designated burial place. It exists today (1993) and is filled with many names that were accorded a place in Texas history, namely Mirabeau Lamar, former president of the Republic; Deaf Smith, hero of the Battle of San Jacinto for cutting down the bridge over Vince's Bayou; and Jane Long, the Mother of Texas.

Gradually, in the late 1820s and early 1830s, families began to settle in the land surrounding Fort Bend. Land was cleared and crops were planted, small acreages for the first few years. But, as more and more slaves were brought to the plantations, the acreage began to increase. Most of the bottomland was covered with cane brakes. Workers cut the cane and left it to dry, after which the fields were set on fire. When it came time for planting the first crops, the land did not need plowing. Holes were made in the mellow, alluvial soil with hand spikes and the seed dropped into the holes. Eli Fenn, who settled in Fort Bend County in 1833, made good crops of cotton and corn in 1834 and 1835. He also had the prospects of a good crop in 1836, but the invasion of the Mexican army caused a complete loss of his crop that year. Fenn had built a boat capable of holding twelve bales of cotton. When the boat was not hauling cotton down the river to Brazoria, it was used as a ferry boat at Thompson's Ferry.[4]

When word of the advance of Santa Anna's army reached Fort Bend, Fenn joined the company of Capt. Wiley Martin, who had been ordered by Gen. Sam Houston to enlist volunteers in the area to defend the ferry at Thompson's Crossing. This was the upper ferry in the bend of the river. Another ferry, run by William Morton two miles downriver, where Fenn's boat was the ferry, was ordered sunk. However, this was not done before an advance detachment of Mexican forces under Col. Juan Almonte arrived on the scene. A disgruntled slave who was making his way to the river was captured by Almonte's forces, and they soon knew the location of a small boat that allowed them to cross about fifty soldiers to the east side of the river by dawn. By morning part of the main Mexican forces arrived on the west side of the river, and women and children fled for their lives to the countryside.

The utter confusion of the pell-mell evacuation can be seen in the story of Mrs. Gil Kuykendall and her three-week-old baby. Mrs. Kuykendall was in a field that was separated from a road by a fence. Several of her neighbors were hurrying along the road. Finding that she was having a hard time running in the field, she handed the baby over the fence to her sister-in-law, Miss Jane Kuykendall, in the lane. In their fright the women got separated, and it was three weeks before Mrs. Kuykendall was reunited with her baby. The baby nearly starved, since they had nothing to feed an infant.[5]

The following morning, with Mexicans on both sides of the river, but Santa Anna's main force still camped on the west bank, the steamer *Yellow Stone* appeared from around the bend. Captain Ross had been upriver to pick up a load of cotton from Jared Groce and, warned about the possibility of running into Mexican soldiers, he had placed cotton bales on ends all the way around the decks of the ship, making it a "cotton-clad" battleship. The *Yellow Stone* had a full head of steam up, and, according to eyewitness John Fenn (a prisoner), "the *Yellow Stone* was plowing the water for all she was worth, lashing the banks with the waves on both sides as she went." No doubt the old boat was belching the blackest possible smoke out of its stacks and the captain was using his whistle to the best advantage. The soldiers fired volleys at the old steamboat as it roared down the river, but since no one could be seen behind the cotton bales, no one was injured. The cavalry, in a desperate attempt to stop the steamer, tried throwing their lariats to rope it. Hundreds of rifle balls struck the steamer, but in a few minutes the boat disappeared around the bend of the river unscathed. The *Yellow Stone* played a leading role in the remaining days before the Battle of San Jacinto on April 21, and in the months following Santa Anna's surrender.[6]

During all of the confusion, while the *Yellow Stone* was making her dash down the river through the Mexican army, John Fenn, and Cain, Jack, and Winnie (servants belonging to the Fenn family), decided to make a break for freedom. They had been taken prisoners the day before, when Mrs. Gil Kuykendall and a group of women escaped into the bushes. They got a good start before being discovered, and despite the fact that bullets cut leaves from over their heads, they managed to escape. Eventually they were able to join the Kuykendall women and continued eastward with the tide of Texans fleeing before Santa Anna's army. Before the party crossed the Sabine River, they heard about San Jacinto and started their journey home.[7]

The Mexican army, using the "un-sunk" ferry boat, finally made their crossing of the Brazos. They went due north until past the upper end of Jones Creek, where they turned east by south, passing Dr. Hunter's home on April 14, and turned northeast at Stafford's Point on April 15. Santa Anna was hoping to surprise President Burnet and the Texas government at Harrisburg.[8]

After the Battle of San Jacinto, and the surrender of Santa Anna, it was several weeks before all of the Mexican troops left the Brazos River Valley, allowing people to return to their homes. Many found their places looted, not only by the Mexican army but by Texans called Torys, who were not loyal to Texas.[9]

Things quickly returned to normal, and Fort Bend residents turned to making a living. William Lusk, a native of Virginia, and Robert Eden Handy, born in Pennsylvania, opened a mercantile business in Brazoria. But, deciding to enter the real estate promotion business, they moved to Fort Bend in 1837 and started promoting the town. It is thought that the name

"Richmond" originated from Lusk, whose hometown was Richmond, Virginia. The name Richmond was used in newspaper ads run by these two promoters in the August 1, 1837, issue of the *Telegraph and Register.*

In the spring of 1837 Moses Lapham, an engineer connected with Bordon and Company, laid out the town of Richmond in the bend of the river, at a point where the river made a slight jog to the east, or at the right-hand side of the horseshoe. In May of 1837, when the Congress of the Republic of Texas opened its deliberations in Houston, Mosely Baker submitted a bill calling for the incorporation of Richmond – and thus Fort Bend or Fort Settlement ceased to exist and Richmond took over.

Business enterprises started springing up in Richmond. Jane Long, famous for entertaining people in high places, as well as rivermen, in her hotel at Brazoria, moved to Richmond, where she had a land grant. She established a hotel and boardinghouse in 1837. Erastus "Deaf" Smith also made Richmond his home in 1837 and formed a land agency with John P. Borden. Smith died on November 27 and was buried in Richmond. The grave was lost in the passage of time. Dr. J. H. Barnard, a physician who was spared at the massacre of Goliad, moved to the city and served as county clerk for a short time. The first newspaper, the *Richmond Telescope,* published by David L. Wood, came out on April 27, 1839. In 1842 the county purchased the old Lusk house for $600 and turned it into a courthouse. A new two-story brick building was constructed in 1849.[10]

The wharves and shipping area of the city seemed to be concentrated at the northern end of the city, or along Ferry, Preston, Calhoun, and Morton streets on the river front. An item that ran in the *Galveston News,* long considered the authority on reporting marine activity along the coast and up the rivers, tells the story about Richmond and shipping:

> Steamer *Elite* at Richmond. I now redeem the promise I made last week by sending herewith an extract from the log book of the steamer *Elite,* giving the particulars of her last trip up the river to this place.
>
> It will be seen that she came to our landing on the 13th inst. It will also be seen that she encountered some difficulties

in making the trip, but the extract shows, that to a man of the energy of Capt. William Jenkins who commanded her, these difficulties readily gave way. The great fact, established beyond the possibility of a single doubt by this successful trip at this time, is that the Brazos River is at all seasons navigable to this point, for it is admitted by all the old settlers on the river, that it is as low now, as it has been for thirty years past.

To me the present trip of the *Elite* affords peculiar gratification, because I have so long believed and written that this river was navigable up to this place at all seasons, in the face of statements and assertions to the contrary, which seem to be generally received as true, that I anxiously wanted just such confirmation of the correctness of my belief and statements as this trip affords. It must be conclusive with even the most sceptical. There never was a river in my estimation whose capacity and value have been so constantly undervalued and misrepresented, from either mistakes, or interested motives, as the Brazos River. We hope there is now an end of these things and that the river will hereafter be regarded in her true character, as one of the most valuable streams for navigation in the Southwest.

The question will be asked by your readers why not have boats run all the fall, if there has been enough water?

This, Mr. Editor is a most legitimate inquiry, and one that ought in justice to a large community to be answered, but it belongs to those under whose control the boat was before Capt. Jenkins took command of her, some two weeks since, to respond to that inquiry.

One thing is certain, when the boat ceased to run in July last there was five feet more water in the river than there is now, making about seven feet at the time.

It may be, that a steamboat could not run on the Brazos River with seven feet water, but I am quite sure it would take a man with "kid gloves" on, to see any sufficient reason why!!

This community feels under great obligation to captain Jenkins and the other officer on board the *Elite* for the energy they have displayed in bringing up the Boat, at that time when so many had pronounced the thing impracticable, and just after an attempt to do the same thing had failed, even before getting out of the water.

Yours in Haste,
J. S. S.[11]

The shipping business took a step forward with the opening of a large cotton warehouse by L. E. Harper. Near the warehouse a new brick building was constructed to house three stores, one for Major Herndon and the other two for Mr. Kendall.[12]

The controversy over navigation on the middle and upper Brazos River was constantly in the public eye, both on the river and in Houston. It has been reported by a number of sources that Houston interests, trying to keep freight from going down the Brazos and then on the Galveston, went to great ends to discredit the Brazos River. There were charges that these Houston interests sent worn-out steamers into the Brazos and sank them to give credence to their claim that shipping on the Brazos was hazardous. But despite all of the shortcomings, shipping cotton and sugar down the Brazos River was more economical than sending it by wagon trains across the muddy plains to Houston.[13] This rash declaration was published in the Washington newspaper and was signed by citizens from thirteen counties, including Fort Bend. In the end it was the railroads that siphoned freight business from the sternwheelers. The 1830s, 1840s, and 1850s largely belonged to the steamboats. Sometimes they had to wait for the water to reach the right level before they charged over the rocks, shoals, and snags to gather freight at not only Richmond but much farther upstream on a regular basis.

An early river enthusiast, Mrs. Dilue Rose Harris, who lived at Stafford's Point, Houston, and Columbus, wrote about her memories. She recalled how the planters gathered their cotton at William Little's plantation to be picked up by the steamer *Yellow Stone*: "In June of 1836 my father [Dr. Pleasant W. Rose] and other men would build flat boats and raft their cotton to Brazoria to be picked up by steamboats."[14]

Representatives of a British ship, *Ironsides,* visited in Richmond in 1840 to make arrangements for their representatives to buy cotton. The newspaper told that the boat was to be made of iron and would draw only two feet of water with a cargo of 200 bales of cotton. The purpose of the representatives' visit was to sell fifteen shares in the venture for $500 per share.[15]

In 1843 the tough little riverboat, the *Mustang,* made a

trip all the way to Washington-on-the-Brazos and then continued upstream to within about seven miles above the old river town of Nashville, before sinking at Jones Landing in November.[16] In 1843 the Houston *Telescope* reported that the *Mustang* ran twice-a-month trips between Washington and Galveston, which probably stretched the number of trips a bit.[17]

Other boats calling at Richmond in the early 1830s and 1840s included the little steamer *Laura,* which made its first trip up the river in 1837 but dropped out only to return to the trade again in 1839. The *Lady Byron* also made calls at upper Brazos ports, including Richmond. Later, this ship went down just below Richmond and lost about half of her cargo of 370 bales of cotton. In 1840 the trading firm of McKinney and Williams, of Brazoria and Galveston, sent the *Constitution* up as far as Richmond. A sister ship, the *Columbia,* chose to anchor outside the bar at the mouth of the river and cotton was rafted down the river for the *Constitution.*[18]

The *Galveston Weekly News* ran a story in 1851 that underlined the fact that the water level in the Brazos did rise and fall drastically. The paper reported that the steamers *Brazos* and *Washington* were tied up at the wharves in Richmond due to a drop in the water level.[19]

The Texas legislature, reacting to public demand, appropriated $50,000 to improve navigation on the Brazos River. To back up this legislation, a petition was presented to the Fort Bend County commissioners court on November 19, 1856, signed by Thomas B. Howard and 249 other citizens, asking that the sum of $3,125 be put up by the county to assist in cleaning the snags out of the river. The court approved the request and the work started in 1858. At that time there were five ports/landings in Fort Bend County, namely Big Creek, Waters, Richmond, Gaston, and Randon.[20]

In all shipping news it must be remembered that ferries played an important part in getting cotton and other goods to the market. In Fort Bend County three licenses were issued for ferries to John V. Morton, Richmond Ferry; James N. Thompson, Thompson Crossing; and Pascal P. Borden, Bordenstown.[21] These ferries played a big part when cotton was moved overland in wagons to Houston. Sometimes trains of forty to as

MAKING SUGAR rivaled cotton, especially on the Brazos River plantations. Giant kettles were set up to cook the juice after it had been extracted from the sugar cane. Sugarland of today is an outgrowth of the sugar making that employed thousands of slaves in Brazoria and Fort Bend counties.

many as a hundred wagons would hit the road and travel together. This would keep a ferry operator working all night.

Transportation on the Brazos had reached a point of dependability in the 1850s, when the railroad finally arrived at Richmond. The Buffalo Bayou, Brazos, and Colorado Railroad was chartered in 1850, and in January of 1856 was able to provide service in Fort Bend County. Rail transportation did not immediately put an end to steamboat transportation, but it did slow it down to some extent.[22]

In 1848 shippers up and down the Brazos, led by the people at Washington, formed the Brazos Steam Association at Washington. Its sole purpose was to improve navigation on the Brazos by removing obstacles. The association then purchased two steamboats, the ***Washington*** and *Brazos,* in order to insure customers of regular service. Capt. Stephen W. Tichenor made the first run in the *Brazos* and reported that there were four major areas of shoals between Velasco and Washington that would need to be removed or a channel cut through them. Assisting this association was a group of Galveston businessmen who proposed to do something about a link between the Brazos River and Galveston Bay to bypass the mouth of the river and the bar that obstructed traffic. A ditch was completed in 1856 but had serious problems. Meetings were held in Richmond and Brazoria by groups which promoted clearing the river, but from different viewpoints. Probably some workable solution would have been found had it not been for the Civil War that effectively put all projects on hold.[23]

When Richmond was chartered by the state legislature in 1837, Sam Houston appointed Wiley Martin, a militant Texan patriot, as county judge. He was later admitted to the bar and was elected to the Senate. In the election that followed, Richmond was chosen by a narrow majority to be the county seat. John V. Morton, son of William Morton, both survivors of the *Lively* shipwreck, was named sheriff. The main street in Richmond is named after these two men who played such a large role in Richmond and Texas history. The first courthouse was a house at the end of Morton Street that the county purchased from the Lusk estate for $600.[24]

The first church in Richmond was established by the Methodists in January of 1839, when a missionary minister met with a group in the Bryant home. Their first church was on the corner of Fourth and Houston streets. A school was in the offing, according to an article in the *Galveston Weekly News* on September 2, 1851: "A fine academy is being built of brick, sixty feet long, two stories, and will have four large rooms. In 1850 there were no public supported schools in Fort Bend County. The town of Richmond now contains two stores, a new fine brick courthouse, a Methodist Church, Masonic Hall, Temperance Hall, etc."[25]

The first post office was established in Richmond in 1846. Before that time, mail was probably put off at landings by whatever steamer was making the trip. In 1840 mail Route No. 19 was established by the Republic and ran from Velasco to San

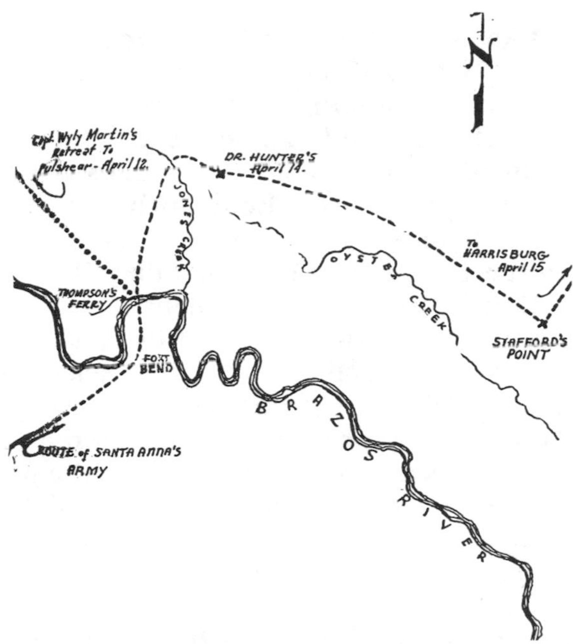

ROUTE OF SANTA ANNA – General Santa Anna brought his Mexican army into Fort Bend County on April 11, 1836, and began looking for a way to cross his troops over the Brazos River. It was at this point that the steamboat Yellow Stone *made her famous run downriver as the Mexican army lined the riverbank, firing their rifles at the "Cotton Clad."*

The YELLOW STONE *made its dash through Santa Anna's army as it lined the banks of the Brazos River near Thompson's Ferry in a prelude to the Battle of San Jacinto. The* Yellow Stone *continued to play a part in the Texas Revolution.*

Felipe. In 1843 Route No. 5 was designated to run out of Houston to Egypt, via Richmond. In 1845 the last Republic routes showed Route No. 22 running from Houston to Egypt, via Hodge's Bend, Richmond, and Damon's Mill.[26] Outside the city of Richmond, in Fort Bend County, the census taker of 1850 found eighty-six plantations. Those with a value of over $10,000 and less than $20,000 included Jane Long, Lawyer Herndon, George D. Parker, the Simontons, William Ryon, Henry Jones, David Randon, James Knight, Randolph Foster, James M. Briscoe, the Gastons, Churchill Fulshear, Joseph Kuykendall, Archie Hodge, the Pevyhouse Estate, Samuel B. Glasscock, and J. D. Waters. By the time the 1860 census was taken, it was obvious that prosperity, based on the plantation system, was in full bloom in the county. The white population had almost doubled in ten years and stood at 2,016. The rendition of property had also doubled, with land on the rolls for $3,250,000 and slaves at $3,140,000. These values were second only to those in Harris County. Improved water transportation, plus the B.B.B. & Co. Railroad, which now traversed the county from east to west, opened markets at reduced rates to plantations. Cotton was the big cash crop, but in Fort Bend County sugar was becoming an important second cash crop.[27]

Richmond is today a thriving community, but it is definitely a community with a past that is remembered fondly.

Jane Long went to Richmond in 1837 and built a hotel, but soon retired to live on her prosperous plantation. Former President Mirabeau B. Lamar retired in Richmond to continue his courtship of Jane Long but was never able to convince her to marry him. He died at his home in Richmond in 1859 and is buried in the old cemetery. The parents of Carrie Nation opened the National Hotel in Richmond in 1861. Two men who drew white beans after the ill-fated Mier Expedition, William Kinchem Davis and Col. William M. Ryo, are buried in Richmond. Thomas J. Smith, survivor of the Goliad Massacre, returned to his home in Richmond and is buried there. Benjamin F. Terry, Fort Bend plantation operator, organized Terry's Rangers and was killed while leading a charge against Union forces on December 17, 1861.

Fort Bend County was hard hit, like all plantation-oriented areas, after the Civil War. But eventually the land that had helped create wealth again allowed the people to regain their rightful place.

Few episodes in history left as deep an imprint on the land as did the regime and the newcomers who controlled the vote of the freed slaves. The tension was shattered when gunfire broke out in the streets of Richmond, leaving several dead. It was years before real peace returned to the area. As mute testimony to these days, visitors need to see the old courthouse square and the tall monument topped by a marble bird. The Jaybird Democratic Primary persisted until modern politics set new rules.[28]

Very little commerce, other than a few barges, still makes use of the Brazos River. However, the river continues to have a mystical impact on the people who live by its side. Today dams control the floodwaters, but nothing can dampen the romantic longings of a dreamer who stands on a bank overlooking the dirty, red water and lets his mind wander to the days when the sternwheeler ruled the waters and brought crowds running when the mailboat sounded its mournful whistle.

Washington-on-the-Brazos

John W. Hall probably had high hopes for the success of his ferry when he set up business on the Brazos River just below the mouth of the Navasota River. But never in his wildest dreams did he envision that his city would play a major role in the tumultuous events that swept over Texas in the next three decades.

In 1830 Hall laid out a townsite on the west side of the river. Not much happened there until 1833, when John W. Kinney built the first home. Hall initially called his new settlement La Bahia, after the old road that passed nearby.[1]

Hall's father-in-law, Andrew Robinson, had given his daughter, Patsy, a section of land in 1824 and it was surveyed and platted in 1833. For many years Robinson operated a ferry that bore his name on the Brazos River where the La Bahia road crossed.[2]

In 1819 the forces of Dr. James Long, adventurer, soldier, and dreamer, tried unsuccessfully to Americanize Texas, or establish a Republic of his own making. From his headquarters in Nacogdoches, Long issued a proclamation declaring Texas to be an independent republic. Trading houses on the Trinity River and at the Falls of the Brazos were established by Long's brother, David Long, and Captain Johnson. The site of the Brazos fort, which was supposedly garrisoned by about twenty men, was located near the present site of Washington. It was under the command of Captain Walker and Captain Johnson. Mexican forces under Colonel Perez captured Johnson and ten of the men. The others escaped and returned to the United States.[3]

By 1834 Hall, Asa Hoxey, Thomas Gray, and possibly others formed the Washington Town Company to promote the town and named it Washington, since Hoxey's home was in Washington, Georgia. Hoxey was a doctor, as well as a slave-holding plantation operator and businessman. He was well educated and represented Washington County in the Consultation of 1835.[4] The community grew, and in 1835 they petitioned the Mexican government to establish a separate municipality.[5] The petition requesting the new jurisdiction was signed by forty-six men. A second, identical petition was signed by an additional twenty-five individuals. Election places were set up July 18, 1835, in the town of Washington and six homes of individuals. Joshua Hadley won with 160 votes over B. J. Williamson, who had 147. Jno. W. Hall was named sheriff with 151 votes.[6]

The city of Washington was on a bluff; in fact, from the river there were two levels to reach the post oak grove that was cleared for the actual townsite. As with most towns, the principal street was named Main Street, and if you followed it down the bluff it went directly to the ferry that crossed the Brazos River.[7]

By 1836 Washington is reported to have had two hotels, at least fifty houses, and a population of about one hundred. The General Council of the provisional government met in Washington, and the Convention of 1836 also met in the community to draft the Declaration of Independence.[8] The city was proposed as the seat of the government for the new republic and received seven votes on the first round of balloting. On the fourth and final round of voting, Houston received twenty-one votes to fourteen for Washington.

In 1842 the old city again was host to the government of

Texas for a short time before it was moved to Austin. But conditions were on the downward trend, according to a note in Adolphus Sterne's diary: "Sunday the 9th of January 1842 warm cloudy weather, left after Breakfeast passed trough Independence a beautiful little place 18 m. passed trough Washington (where the Declaration of Independence was made) a fine Place, but all the fine Stores and dwelling Houses most all deserted . . . ."[9]

In 1842 President Sam Houston transferred his administrative headquarters from Austin to Washington due to General Santa Anna's presence. Since Washington, despite its growth, was a small town, the government was hard-pressed to find suitable quarters. Hatfield's Grocery/Saloon was the largest building in town, so the government rented the building for the House of Representatives. To remove temptation, the inside stairway leading to the second floor from the ground floor saloon was removed and put on the outside. The hole in the floor was covered with boards that were not nailed down. During the inauguration of President Anson Jones, a ball was held on the second floor. In the middle of a spirited reel, an

INDEPENDENCE HALL – Washington-on-the-Brazos was the stage where a lot of Texas' early history was made. In fact, the Declaration of Independence was signed there.

attractive but rather large woman almost fell through the loose planks. She was saved by Gen. T. J. Chambers. The capital was returned to Austin in 1845. Washington was incorporated in 1837.[10]

The Hatfield Saloon gained quite a reputation for gambling. One day three Methodist preachers came to town, Rev. Robert Alexander, Rev. Wilson, and Rev. Littleton Fowler. Mr. Alexander, who was a giant of a man at almost seven feet tall, immediately engaged the meeting room upstairs for church services the next Sunday. The gambler sent word that he could not preach there on Sunday since the building was being used for other purposes. Alexander showed up exactly on the posted hours, paid no attention to the cards that were being hastily hidden, spread his Bible on a billiard table, and announced that anyone who did not wish to hear him could leave. No one left. He then preached a fire-and-brimstone sermon. When he finished, the men made up a purse for him and told him if he ever needed more money to call on them. The Methodists went on their way, rejoicing.[11]

John W. Kenney, who built the first house in Washington, was an itinerate Methodist preacher in Kentucky and Illinois before he moved his family by covered wagon to the Brazos River and built a log cabin. Supplies, especially salt, were in short supply, so Kenney and several other men fashioned a pirogue from the trunk of a large cottonwood tree and floated down the river to get supplies and bring them back to the settlement. He delivered one of the first sermons in the area in 1834, in the home of Samuel Gates. Z. N. Morrell, an evangelistic Baptist preacher who was a friend of both Sam Houston and Davy Crockett, delivered an early sermon in Washington and is credited with helping start the Baptist churches in the area. Washington and Washington County became a center of church and education activities, part in Washington and part at nearby Independence, where the Baptists started a college that grew into Baylor University. It was at Independence that Sam Houston joined the Baptist church and was baptized by Baptist minister Rufus Burleson. Judge W. P. Ewing is said to have taught school in a log cabin just outside of town. Mrs. Jack Hall taught school in Washington in 1837, and Washington College was chartered in the same year. L. P. Tucker opened a school for boys just a short distance from Washington in 1839. In 1834 a girls' academy was operated by the two Misses Sims.[12]

Settlers came down the old La Bahia Road at a steady pace, and in a short period twenty-two lots were sold for $1,902.35. In fact, after Washington got started, the La Bahia Road branched off to cross the Brazos River at Washington rather that at Robinson's Ferry, which was a few miles upstream. Later still, another road, Goucher Trace, was laid out between Bastrop and Washington. The prestige of Washington grew after being singled out several times for important meetings. This had a positive effect on the growth of the community. Being near the center of power was a stimulant. When hostilities broke out in Gonzales on October 2, 1835, a large company of men, under Capt. James G. Swisher, offered their services. When delegates to the General Council from all over Texas gathered finally at Washington on November 1, 1835, the community had come of age.[13]

A good description of Washington was given by a newspaperman from the *Galveston News* who visited the city in the spring of 1839:

> .... the main road from Houston to Washington ran up the eastern portion of the Brazos valley until within a few miles of the ferry. It then turned nearly at right angles through the bottom until it reached the river at the ferry, which was located at the foot of Main street. In crossing the ferry you could not see any of the town on account of the high bluff on which it was situated. After ascending the second bluff, the houses were brought to view, rising gently back toward the prairie, which was nearly a mile still further to the west .... There was only one principal street, which was known as Main street. There were some cross streets with a few dwelling houses located on them, but the main business was confined to the one principal street.
>
> On Main street ... was a building in which the declaration of independence was written and signed ....
>
> There were two hotels in the place, one kept by H. R. Cartwell [Washington], the other by Esquire Roberts [Planters]. There were two or three dry goods firms in the place. E. S. Cabler kept one, Bailey, Gay & Hoxey another, and David Ayres another .... Washington then contained a population of some 250 inhabitants, about equally divided

> between a fixed resident population and a floating one. The floaters were mostly gamblers, horse racers and sports of all classes. The resident portion lived in very good houses, made of clapboards and logs . . . . there were two gambling houses, one run by Major B. M. Hatfield, a San Jacinto veteran, and the other by Mr. John Rumsey.[14]

Ranching and farming provided the bulk of the income for settlers in Washington County. Their biggest problem was in getting their products to market. Ranchers had an advantage over farmers, since they could round up their cattle and drive them overland to market. Cotton farmers, once they had produced a bale of cotton, were faced with about sixty to seventy miles of roads that became almost impassable in wet weather. Early farmers were known to have pooled their cotton and built rafts or keelboats and floated their crops down the river to ports like Brazoria, where steamboats called regularly. Very few records of such rafting exist in Washington County; however, in Brazoria shipping records mention is made of cotton coming in regularly from up the river – Washington.

Just when did steamboats start making regular runs up to Washington and above? The *Ariel,* owned by Henry Austin, was brought to the Brazos River in 1830 but never ventured above Bolivar before it was removed from the river. The *Cayuga,* a small eighty-eight-ton sidewheeler, received little mention in riverboat news on the upper Brazos River but must have been the first boat to make it as high up the river as Washington. Merchants and planters in and around Washington were anxious to get a boat to come up the river to pick up their cotton, and so in 1833 a petition was circulated by men in Washington County pledging 5,000 acres of land and $800 in cash to anyone who would bring a steamboat up the Brazos to Washington. Robert Wilson and William P. Harris, operators of several steamboats out of New Orleans, decided that they would accept the challenge, and the *Cayuga* made it to Washington and picked up a load of cotton in the fall of 1834. Henry Austin, William Barret Travis, Asa Brigham, and A. M. Breedlove each pledged 500 acres.[15]

The *Yellow Stone* entered the river trade in the mid-1830s. An early writer, Mrs. Dilue Rose Harris, wrote that the *Yellow Stone* "was to run from Brazoria on the Brazos River to San

Felipe and Washington."[16] When Gen. Sam Houston pressed the *Yellow Stone* into service to transport his troops across the Brazos River at Groce's Ferry in April of 1836, the boat was just returning from a trip up the river to pick up cotton, possibly as high as Washington. ("She was to go to Groce's ferry to a little town called Washington.") The load of cotton was used to put around the decks to make her a cotton-clad warship and immune to the rifle fire of the Mexican cavalry.[17]

The *Mustang* and its captain, J. W. McGown, probably opened the era of steamboat traffic – and prosperity – to the port city of Washington. The small boat actually did not have enough power to battle the Brazos currents, and when it finally did come into sight of the old port the entire town turned out to watch the vessel as it huffed and puffed to make it to the Washington dock. The *Mustang* did not have a whistle, only a two-inch pipe that vented steam into the air. This pipe was covered with a box, and the engineer evidently opened the valve full as the box exploded with a crashing, rasping sound followed by an immense cloud of vapor. The crowd, thinking that the ship had blown up, scattered. It was several minutes before the people returned to visit the little ship.

After unloading supplies, and loading cotton, the *Mustang* continued on up the river, going as high as Port Sullivan. Captain McGown then turned his boat around and started downriver. When he came to the mouth of the Little River he decided to do more exploring and headed up the river that was running full. One of the crew, Aquilla Jones, was standing on the wheelhouse in order to get a better view of the countryside. Distracted by the scenery, Jones did not see an overhanging limb until he was about to be swept off his perch. He quickly "seized hold of the limb and unfortunately held on too long, letting the boat pass from under him, being suspended nearly thirty feet in the air, over a raging river, on a limb that swayed so he could not climb back to the main body of the tree." The *Mustang* had to send back a yawl to rescue the crew member.[18]

The people of Washington were so fired up about the *Mustang*'s trip that they commissioned Y. M. H. Butler, president of the Brazos Steam Association, to have two boats built to ply their trade from Washington to Galveston.[19] The boats were on the river in 1849, with Captain Tichenor on the *Brazos* and Captain Haviland aboard the *Washington.* Merchant Thomas McKinney, of Brazoria and Galveston, was in Washington when Captain Haviland of the *Washington* arrived in port. He loaned $750 to Captain Haviland to make advances to the planters, and another $500 to cotton broker Basil M. Hatfield in Washington to be used for advances. By the time the boats made their second trip up the river, the word had reached plantations and cotton stacked up at most ports. More than 1,500 bales came in from the area surrounding Washington to await shipment. Both boats made the run from Velasco to Washington in five days, despite the fact that they had to stop and chop a new supply of wood often. Despite all of the enthusiasm over the Brazos boats, they did not make money and were forced into bankruptcy. The new owners removed them from the Brazos.[20]

The 1850s were kind to the paddlewheelers. There was plenty of business, and with the exception of a couple of dry years, there was enough water to allow most boats to make it up to Washington. During this decade one or more boats always made the rounds of the old ports and landings, picking up cotton and delivering merchandise. The *Jack Hays* made a single trip in 1850. Other boats that operated during this period included the *Camden, Reliance, Bell, Major A. Harris, Julia, Magnolia, Belle Sulphur, Nick Hill,* and *Fort Henry.*

With the boom in river traffic in the late 1840s and the 1850s, the city of Washington prospered and its population increased from 500 to 700. Hotels, dry good stores, livery stables, blacksmith shops, saloons, and gambling halls lined Main Street and expanded into other areas. In 1849 it was reported that as many as three steamers were tied up at Washington. One was the *Sam Williams,* a larger steamer.[21]

Washington was seldom without one or more newspapers to keep readers abreast of news in other parts of Texas. The *Washington Emigrant* appeared in 1839, the *National Vindicator* and the *Texian and Brazos Farmer* were around in 1843, the *Texas Ranger and Brazos Guard* appeared in 1845, the *Texas Ranger and Lone Star* came in 1854, and the *American* was publishing in 1856.[22]

The decline of Washington can be attributed to several

factors. In 1856 the Houston and Texas Central Railroad approached the leaders in Washington and sought $11,000 to pay for a bridge over the Brazos to Washington and also to assist in the right-of-way from Hempstead to the river crossing. Washington's leaders, who were heavily invested in river transportation, turned the offer down. As a result, the railroad went from Hempstead to Navasota, completely missing Washington. Washington County raised funds to build its own railroad from Chappel Hill to Brenham then crossed the Brazos near Lancaster to join the H.T.C.R. at Hempstead.[23]

Within three to four years, Washington's population began to decline. This was hastened by the Civil War and improvement of surface transportation. The *Sulphur Belle* called at Washington in 1859. Once the Civil War broke out, the Confederacy took over a number of river steamboats and transferred them to the Rio Grande River, which during the days of the coastal blockade was the Confederacy's only open port to European suppliers. After the Civil War, a few paddlewheelers returned to the lower Brazos, where they continued to work for many years. The upper Brazos did not hear any more steamboat whistles.

The 1850 census for Washington County shows that the port of Washington-on-the-Brazos was a live-wire town with a number of businesses in and around the city. A sampling of those listed includes P. H. Lusk, lawyer; B. Galsper, lawyer; A. P. Lipscomb, lawyer; Frank Lipscomb, student-at-law; W. L. Bishop, merchant; W. B. Lipscomb, lawyer; James T. Key, doctor; C. F. Barber, attorney; Sam Adolph, grocer; A. G. Compton, merchant; W. W. Hackworth, merchant; R. C. Barlow, attorney; A. W. Flora, tavern keeper; Charles Coungton, grocer; O. B. Eldridge, doctor; F. W. Robinson, merchant; L. B. Madden, merchant; G. I. Duncan, blacksmith; John Burlago, saddler; John Harris, tailor; Geo. Stillman, blacksmith; I. F. Crosby, attorney; I. Thompson, merchant.

Rickland Thompson, merchant; I. B. Root, merchant; Johnson, merchant; I. B. Wilkins, merchant; Mr. French, merchant; I. W. Wynne, lawyer; Noah Check, merchant; John –, physician; J. M. Wood, merchant; L. C. Baxter, printer; Hal H. Edmington, merchant; John H. Day, sheriff; Elisha D. Little, assessor-collector; Thos. Casadey, grocer; T. A. Jackson, merchant; John C. Wallace, merchant; L. M. Este, innkeeper; James Este, innkeeper; I. T. Church, shoolmaster; James Cowan, ginwright; A. B. Cowan, merchant.

J. M. Wood appeared to be the largest merchant, listing the value of his merchandise at $35,000.[24]

Port Sullivan

Sullivan Bluffs joined the community of landings on the Brazos in about 1850–51. Steamers made it to Sullivan Bluffs as early as 1843, but the town of Port Sullivan came along later. Perhaps when the *Mustang* made the initial voyage to Sullivan Bluffs it was to pick up cotton from one of the several plantations in the area. And, it is possible that the *Mustang*'s captain just wanted to be the first steamboat to establish a new "head of navigation on the Brazos."[1]

It is likely that the new city was actually established by plantation owners who simply needed a safe place to build their homes out of the wilderness, where they could establish schools and churches.[2]

Port Sullivan's desire to become a port ended in disaster in 1851, when a shipment of 144 barrels of mess pork and sixty additional barrels of foodstuffs consigned to western army outposts did not go through the port as directed. It was consigned to Hubby and Sillaven, who had just completed a Port Sullivan warehouse building, probably to handle the shipment. No record of the *Brazos* ever reaching Port Sullivan with this merchandise has ever been found. A story in the Galveston *Weekly Journal* in November of 1852 mentions only two boats as having reached Port Sullivan, and the *Brazos* was not one of them. The fact that the port was actually in business is verified in an ad that appeared in the Washington-on-the-Brazos *Texas Ranger* on April 30, 1851: "C. M. Hubby – A. W. Sillaven / STORING AND FORWARDING / The subscribers having completed their new warehouse at Sillaven's Bluff, are ready to receive and forward freight, and solicit patronage from the public. / Hubby & Sillaven."[3]

Actually, settlers started putting down roots in the Sullivan Bluffs area as early as 1835 as part of the Robertson Colony. Augustus W. Sillaven (this name is sometimes written as

Sullivan, hence the name Port Sullivan) came to Texas in October of 1835, and in December he received a quarter league of land on the Brazos that came to be known as Sillaven's or Sullivan's Bluff. Sillaven became a member of the Texas Army at San Antonio.[4] Indian trouble kept the area on guard for a number of years. As more and more settlers came into the area, the demand for cheaper and better transportation was a determining factor in the riverboats starting to make runs above Washington in the 1840s and also caused Sullivan's Bluff to become Port Sullivan, as people saw the potential of the site as a good place to live and a good port site.[5]

An unidentified reporter for the Galveston *Weekly News* visited Port Sullivan on October 14, 1852, and gave an excellent description of the new town that probably came into being sometime in 1851:

> The population is about 200 or upwards, there are 20 families in the place, four stores, and as they say, "a small chance of goods" are sold. James Ferguson leaves in a day or two for New York, to replenish his stock, and lay in a large supply so as to furnish the merchants above this place. There are two blacksmith shops, three carpenter shops, one circular saw mill, two or three large warehouses, and last but not least (for the intelligence of the place) there is a P.O. and P.M. [post office and postmaster], also a mail from "Independence" once every week, and it is likely next year the arrival will be semi-weekly. There is also several Doctors, and but one lawyer, Mr. Farley, whose acquaintance we made. He was very kind in offering us all the information we wanted in reference to the country. There is one thing very much needed in the place: A Tavern, for the accommodation of the traveling public; there is at present no place in the village where they "take in strangers." The village is filling up very fast, and is generally the opinion that it will be "some" place. Mr. S. [A. W. Sillaven] does not ask extravagant prices for his town lots, he will sell them reasonable and on twelve months time.[6]

The business section was centered in blocks one to ten. Records show that these business lots changed hands frequently. Lots numbered in the seventies appear to have been reserved for residences. Lucy Elkin bought three and operated a boardinghouse. The first postmaster was Hawthorn S. Chamberlin, appointed March 24, 1852. In 1854 mail came once each week from Independence. A Mr. Foster advertised a hotel in 1854 and called it Sullivan Hotel.

Steamboats were slow to come to Port Sullivan, even in years of plentiful rain. When they came they were not always dependable, so farmers whose livelihood depended on getting their products to market used any method available. Flatboats and keelboats filled this need. In May of 1853 a flatboat made it down the river from Port Sullivan to the mouth of the Brazos, probably Velasco or Quintana, with 250 bales of cotton.[7] In 1854 citizens of Washington were treated to the sight of seven flatboats loaded with cotton headed down the Brazos from Port Sullivan. One boat was loaded with more than 500 bales.[8]

In April 1854 a flatboat with 327 bales of cotton from Port Sullivan landed in Columbia.[9] Port Sullivan was considered the absolute head of navigation on the Brazos for steamboats because of the shoals there. Flatboats could come down through the shoals. A flatboat loaded with cotton from Marlin, which is forty miles upstream from Port Sullivan, made it down the river in 1854 to Port Sullivan.[10] It would be safe to say that the amount of cotton coming out of the upper reaches of the mid-Brazos piqued the interest of the ship owners' pocketbooks to a point that they were willing to risk running boats to Port Sullivan when the water was high.

The *Mustang* was a tough little boat that had been built for a ferry in Galveston. When the owners decided that it was unsuited for that job, they sent it to the Brazos. The boat's lack of power made steaming upriver in the swift Brazos quite a chore, but the *Mustang* made it to Washington in January 1843. A few days later it pushed on upriver as high as Sullivan's Bluff.[11]

Capt. Basil Muse Hatfield, a veteran riverboat pilot, is quoted in the Washington *Texas Ranger* as having taken both the *Washington* and the *Brazos* up the river to Port Sullivan. Rain was an everyday occurrence in 1850, and as a result the Brazos reached new heights, measuring four miles wide at Washington. J. W. McGown, a merchant in Cameron, saw this as his big chance to get a steamboat to come up the Little River to Cameron. He went to Washington and offered Captain Hatfield $500, plus a certain amount of freight, to take the *Washington* to Cameron. Since the captain liked a challenge, he fired up the *Washington*'s boilers and headed her up the Little River. On numerous occasions overhanging trees had to be cut. But finally, with the goal just two miles distant, he had to stop due to a heavy concentration of shoals. He eased his ship near an overhanging bank, and for two days the ship was the scene of a big celebration, with food and dancing for all.[12]

After having conquered the upper Brazos once, Captain Hatfield did not hesitate to head the *Brazos* upriver to Port Sullivan in 1854, when the water was high. When they arrived the captain and the crew were given a rousing welcome and a ball. Captain Hatfield greeted guests as they arrived. Despite the big party and speeches, the *Brazos* left port with only 140 bales of cotton aboard. The short notice of the arrival of the ship did not give the farmers enough time to bring their cotton to the port. This was the last appearance of the *Brazos* and *Washington* on the river.[13]

With business picking up on the Brazos, more and more boats were sent to take care of the added shipping. In 1852 Capt. William Smith removed the steamer *Camden* from the East Texas lumber trade and took it to the Brazos. The owners wanted to sell the little boat, and they urged the captain to push hard for business. The company's agent, D. S. B. Bennett, was a passenger on the *Camden*'s first trip, which went to Washington and then on to Sullivan's Bluff. At Moseley's Landing the captain became embroiled in a bitter fight with local merchants. Evidently, the fight came about because Smith charged different rates on freight to different people. The *Camden*'s call at Port Sullivan was its last, after hitting a snag near San Felipe and going to the bottom with a cargo of 200 bales of cotton, all of which were saved.[14] People at Port Sullivan felt that with the visit of the *Camden* their port was now established as a regular steamship stop and the head of navigation on the Brazos.[15]

In May 1852 the *Reliance* called at Washington. After unloading cargo, it headed upriver for Port Sullivan with a load of merchandise. When the ship was just below Munson's Shoals the river fell dramatically, trapping the ship so that it couldn't go up or down. After a short wait, the water level rose and the captain was able to continue to Port Sullivan, where he discharged freight. He then returned to Washington on May 26,

1852, with 500 bales of cotton picked up at landings above Washington.[16]

An ad in the Washington newspaper in 1852 announced that the steamboat *William Penn* would go to Sillaven's Bluff as soon as the water permitted. Within a few days the water level rose enough for the boat to make the trip, and it picked up a load of cotton, pecans, and hides. On December 1, 1852, it headed down the river, only to see the water level drop six feet in a few hours. The *Penn* was left high and dry. It was near the end of January of 1853 that the water level improved enough for the *Penn* to finish her voyage that ended at Quintana. The captain of the *Penn* must have had a stout heart because he advertised that he planned to run his ship regularly to Washington and Silliven's Bluff, water level permitting. Another ad, run just a few weeks later, indicated that the *Penn* boasted of comfortable accommodations for passengers. Insurance was available to merchants, with the rate depending upon the destination. For instance, rates above Munson's Shoals (meaning Port Sullivan) cost the shippers one-half percent of the value of the goods shipped.[17]

The steamer *Major A. Harris* began calling regularly at Washington starting in 1852, with Capt. William Jenkins at the helm. The *Harris*' agent ran advertisements saying that the ship would make regular calls to Washington and would ascend to Sullivan's Bluff when the water level was right.

The *Fort Henry* entered the trade on a regular basis in the mid-1850s. After taking a load of cargo to Washington in January of 1858, the boat went on upriver to Port Sullivan to discharge cargo and to take on 200 bales of cotton.[18]

After 1854, which seemed to have been the high mark of steamboat traffic to Port Sullivan, only one other steamboat – the *Fort Henry* in 1858 – ever called on the old port.[19]

Despite the lack of steamboat traffic, it appears that for a few years Port Sullivan continued to serve as the center of trading in the area. The town was well established and the ferry immediately below the town proved to be a commercial asset. A number of ox-drawn wagon caravans came through the Port Sullivan ferry, adding business to the community. The towns and counties to the west of Port Sullivan traded with Houston, and it appeared that the bulk of trade went overland, or down to Washington, since steamboat traffic was not always dependable at Port Sullivan. The port was a major stop on the road between Belton and Houston. One old-timer remembered seeing six to eight ox wagons at a time coming down the main street loaded with cotton headed for Houston. Another traveler told how, during low-water periods, water came to the hub of his buggy at the crossing at Port Sullivan. An 1858 map of Texas shows a road from Port Sullivan to Cameron and Belton on the west. A railroad promotional pamphlet published in 1869 pointed out that the trade from at least twelve counties crossed the Brazos at Port Sullivan. Of course, the railroad was pointing out that they could serve this territory.

Augustus W. Sillaven, owner of the townsite, benefited with increased commercial activity in the city. In 1858 he had sold one-third of his 1,107 acres of land for a total of $6,140, plus the money he got from the sale of quite a few lots. Before the town was built, he was sheriff. Afterwards he became county commissioner and served as a notary public. In 1851 he purchased Hubby's interest in their joint warehouse and continued its operation for about one year. He attested to the fact that he had a great attachment to Port Sullivan, but he sold out and moved to Arkansas, ending an early chapter of the port.[20]

Despite limited successes getting cotton to market on the Brazos, the hazards and undependable water level of the river were unacceptable. A conference was held in 1854 to devise means and methods of clearing the Brazos. Before this could be implemented, the water level in the river was bad for three straight years. This set plantation owners, businessmen, and ordinary people on the path to seek new and better methods of transportation. Railroads appeared to be the answer to all their problems. Before the Civil War, the Houston and Texas Central started out of Houston headed for Austin. The war halted its westward movement at Millican in Brazos County, with a branch to Brenham in Washington County. After the war, the main line stayed east of the Brazos, missing Washington and Port Sullivan. Port Sullivan was still viable in 1871, but the decline was steady.[21]

Census figures tell the story of peak and decline: 1860, 960; 1870, 1,423; 1880, 123. Businesses closed and moved to other towns like nearby Hearne, which was growing. By 1875 the Methodist church was gone; not even a circuit rider served the area. The college, which had been Port Sullivan's pride, burned in 1878. The school had been served by three teachers and had an enrollment of about eighty. James Archie Peel, a pioneer of Port Sullivan, remembered the college as being located on the outskirts of the town in a grove of trees. The two-story building had large rooms with large hallways. The building was heated by fireplaces. The boys' dormitory was called Steward's Hall. Peel's description of the town was glowing:

> When I moved here it was the finest community I ever saw .... It was the only town accessible to the people in the early days and was the largest town in all of this section of the country. The leading citizens were Tom Anderson, William Anderson, C. G. Wilcox, A. Harlan, Alf Harlan, H. A. Foster, J. A. Foster, R. J. Davis, R. A. Smith, Dr. F. Hall, Dr. Hightower, William Easterwood, William Duncan, Charles Duncan, and Pastor Whippie. W. T. Watt was the saddle shop man and ran a hardware. Later he established the Provident National Bank of Waco and was president. Colonel W. H. White was the only lawyer and John Sailors was in real estate. Mrs. Duncan ran the hotel and Dr. H. Gent and Dr. Wilson opened a drug store and brought their drugs from Galveston by ox wagon.[22]

The Masonic Lodge, which had been extremely active, peaked in 1871 and finally moved to Maysfield in Milam County in 1885. By 1894 the town was completely gone and fences had been put across the Cameron and Port Sullivan road. Early in 1900, a store and gin were built near the site of the old town. A bit of growth took place, but no port activity.[23]

In 1985 an Austin Metal Club spent some time combing the old town site without finding anything of consequence other than bottles and junk.[24]

In 1916, prior to World War I, the federal government attempted to build locks at Port Sullivan to control the water and make navigation once again possible. The war caused this project to be abandoned.

One of Port Sullivan's residents who became renowned was Charles Goodnight, who moved to the port as a lad of fifteen and worked for several ranchers for the handsome wage of ten to twelve dollars per month, plus good advice. He also hired out to a racing outfit at Port Sullivan as a jockey, since he weighed only ninety pounds with saddle. He became famous as a Ranger and Indian scout, and established the Goodnight-Loving Trail.[25]

Probably Port Sullivan's fate was not sealed entirely by the railroad failing to bring their line to the old port, nor to the steamboats that quit running. The people were weary of pioneer life and chose to move to some city where their needs could be satisfied. The railroad and steamboats gave the old city a nudge downward, but it was a desire for a better life that hastened the end.

Plantation Landings

Bolivar

Henry Austin, cousin of Stephen F. Austin, had great plans for Bolivar, a city on the Brazos that he envisioned would become a leading port. His grant of land was on the west side of the Brazos upriver from Brazoria. Mary Austin Holley, an early writer, located his grant as being above Bell's Landing, which was fifteen miles above Brazoria. Austin planned to develop this location into a city; however, his plans never materialized. During the early period of settlement on the Brazos, Bolivar was considered the head of navigation on the river. In 1830 Austin brought his steamship, the *Ariel,* from the Rio Grande to the Brazos and on up to Bolivar, where the boat remained for some time before being removed to Galveston Bay.[1]

Austin built a home for his wife and children at Bolivar. It was described by Mary Holley as being furnished with "New York furniture in its puncheon-floored rooms, its fine china spread upon white board tables, its chairs of rawhide and deer skins."[2] At one time there was a ferry across the river at Bolivar and evidently a road that led to the Galveston Bay area.[3] Henry Austin was convinced of the wisdom of opening communication between Bolivar and a ship anchorage on Galveston Bay. A good prairie road to Brazoria, Columbia, and Bolivar was also envisioned by the planners.[4]

When steamboat captains found that they could run their

boats much farther upriver than Bolivar, it is believed that Austin gave up his idea of a town and the would-be-port as just another dream. An advertisement announced that the lots in the townsite would be sold by Chas. D. Sayre of Marion; Edmund Andrews and F. A. Sawyer of Brazoria; and J. H. Polly, Bailey's Prairie. Notes in the *Austin Papers* indicate that the town failed to generate any interest and was abandoned in 1839. Henry Austin was made postmaster in 1838. The office closed sometime before 1843.[5]

Orozimbo

The Orozimbo Plantation belonged to James Aeneas E. Phelps, a settler who came to Texas as a member of Stephen F. Austin's famous Old Three Hundred families. His plantation was located on the west side of the Brazos River about twelve miles north of Columbia, or Bell's Landing as it was called when it was first founded. The plantation, a large producer of cotton, apparently shipped from their own landing.[6]

In 1840 Orozimbo was listed on a mail route out of Velasco. It was discontinued in 1843 but reappeared in 1845 on postal route No. 14, running from Velasco to San Felipe, via Brazoria, Columbia, Orozimbo, Big Creek, and Richmond.[7] A post office was established at the plantation in 1846, with J. A. E. Phelps as the postmaster. It is known to have lasted until 1847 and possibly longer.[8]

On July 30, 1836, Gen. Antonio López de Santa Anna was held prisoner at the plantation for a period of time. He had been held at the plantation of Maj. William H. Patton, two miles northwest of Columbia, until a plot for the general to escape or kill himself was discovered. Santa Anna's life was saved by Dr. Phelps, who pumped poison out of his stomach. Later this act of compassion was rewarded when Santa Anna, who had returned to power in 1842, ordered the release of Orlando Phelps, who had been captured as a member of the ill-fated Mier Expedition. Orozimbo also had the distinction of being nominated as a site of the capital of Texas; however, in the voting that followed the plantation did not get any votes.

A town never developed despite an offering of lots for sale. Mary Austin Holley noted that there were two houses, one belonging to Dr. Phelps and one other.[9]

Escher's Landing

Casper Escher and his wife, Mary, moved to New Orleans from Switzerland in 1820 and in 1837 took up residency on a headright about four miles up the Brazos River from Velasco. The couple had fourteen children, which included four sets of twins. Yellow fever and other diseases left them with only three to live to maturity (Mrs. Peter Stewart, Mrs. Hanson, and Mrs. Seaburn). Mr. Escher died at an early age and his wife managed the farm, with the aid of slaves, and also took care of Escher's Landing, handling all of the cotton contracts with the agents and ship captains. The nearby Wharton and Herndon plantations used the landing, which was equipped with a wharf and a large, clapboard-covered shed for storage.

Mrs. Escher managed the affairs of the landing with ease, keeping rough rivermen or plantation owners at arm's length with her commanding presence. Produce from the Wharton, Herndon, and Escher plantations were sold to riverboats that supplied stores up and down the river. Cotton and sugar were the big crops for all of the plantations. Mrs. Escher was buried in 1870 in a family plot on the plantation that has been lost through the years.[10] Today it would be located in the extreme southwestern corner of Dow Chemical's Plant B.[11]

Gaston's Landing

This old landing was on the plantation of Hudson Gaston and was located above the plantation of Col. David Randon. San Felipe was above the landing, which was located in what is now Fort Bend County.[12]

Groce's Landing

Groce's Landing, or Groce's Ferry, was located on the Brazos River in the present county of Waller. Jared E. Groce operated a large plantation there, and his home, Bernardo, was as well known in early days in Texas as is the Menger Hotel in San Antonio today. Groce came to Texas in 1821 in a caravan of at least fifty covered wagons, bringing his family and an undetermined number of slaves. He brought a quantity of cotton seed with him and established the first cotton gin in Texas. Some of his early cotton was carried by ox wagons as far as

Harrisburg for shipment. Later it was taken down the river to Brazoria, but then steamboats began to call at his landing regularly to pick up his cotton. No doubt cotton from the surrounding area was brought into his landing for shipment. The steamer *Yellow Stone* came up the Brazos in early March of 1836 and started loading the cotton that had been brought to the landing.[13]

Perhaps the entire United States was introduced to Bernardo and Groce's Landing when Gen. Sam Houston brought his weary soldiers to the landing on March 31, 1836. Groce played host to the entire army. Dozens of beeves were slaughtered. A field hospital was set up near Bernardo, and all types of supplies were turned over to Houston's army. The army had reached San Felipe and paused long enough to put the torch to the town. At this point word was brought to Houston that the *Yellow Stone* was at Groce's Landing taking on cotton. He immediately moved down the river to the landing.

Houston waited and rested his men. When the Mexican army was reported near, he began to move. General Houston reported the successful ferry operation to David Thomas, his acting secretary of war, the next day:

> At 10 o'clock yesterday (April 12), I commenced crossing the river, and from that time till the present (noon) the steamboat and yawl (having no ferry-boat) have been engaged. We have eight or ten wagons, ox-teams, and about two hundred horses, belonging to the army; and these have to pass on board the steamboat, besides the troops, baggage, &c. This requires time; but I hope in one hour to be enabled to be in preparation [to march].

With Houston's army safely across the river, Captain Ross turned his attention to the *Yellow Stone*, rigging her as a cotton-clad with cotton bales lining the decks. He then headed his boat downriver and made a successful "run" of the gauntlet of Mexican troops assembled at the two fords in Fort Bend County.[14]

San Felipe

San Felipe was built on a high plain overlooking the Brazos River at a point that the Atascosito Road crossed. The site was chosen by Stephen F. Austin as the capital of his colony and later became the unofficial capital of all of the settlements of the Austin Colony. The Conventions of 1832 and 1833 met in San Felipe, and the Consultation in 1835 made it the capital of the provisional government until 1836, when Washington-on-the-Brazos took over. The city was burned to the ground by Sam Houston in his retreat into East Texas to keep it from being of aid to the advancing army of General Santa Anna.[15]

When the *Cayuga* made an exploratory trip up the Brazos River in December of 1834, it stopped at San Felipe while on its way downriver and a welcoming party was given for the ship's crew at a local tavern. Captain Harris was the skipper of the ship.[16]

There are few records of steamboats stopping at San Felipe; however, it is likely that incoming freight was dropped off by boats traveling upriver past the old Atascosito Ferry.

Tenoxtitlan

Gen. Mier Teran, commandant of Coahuila, ordered the establishment of a fort where the El Camino Real crossed the Brazos River. Lt. Col. Francisco Ruiz was sent from San Antonio with a company of soldier-convicts to build the fort, which was on the west bank of the river. While a ferry operated at this spot in later years, there is no record of steamboats ever calling on the landing. A fight that broke out between Mexican soldiers and local settlers gave rise to a saying: "The first shot of the Revolution may have been fired at Gonzales, but the first fist fight between a Mexican soldier and a Texan occurred at Tenoxtitlan."[17]

Nashville

Nashville was located on the west bank of the Brazos River six miles north of Fort Tenoxtitlan, two miles south of the mouth of Little River in present Milam County. It dates back to the beginning of Austin's Colony and was probably established as a town by Sterling C. Robertson in 1834. Nashville was a frontier trading post and served as a bastion against Indian raids. One shocking attack by the Indians occurred after Z. N. Morrell, a Baptist preacher, had just finished a service. They killed two men in the congregation. An avenging group of men were immediately mounted to chase and kill the Indians.

While Nashville was on the Brazos, and was a trading post, there are no records of steamboats stopping on a regular basis. It is likely that goods may have been off-loaded when boats were running up the river as high as Port Sullivan.[18]

Warren

Warren was a small landing in present-day Washington County that was established as early as 1839. Several warehouses were located near the river to store and hold cotton from the Chappel Hill area until a riverboat called. There was an inn and a blacksmith shop. No record exists of a general merchandise store, but more than likely there was one.

Lancaster

A ferry operated by Samuel A. Bogart was in operation on the Brazos in Washington County as early as 1845. Later a town was laid off and called Ralston, then Newport, and finally Lancaster. Cotton was brought into the port for shipment. It was located two miles upriver from Warren.[19]

San Luis

San Luis, Texas: A promoter's dream city!

George Hammeken flooded cold northern cities with promotional literature about San Luis, pictured as paradise on earth. He focused on its beaches, climate, and best of all, the opportunity to make a bundle.

Even the street names were designed to give someone in the cold north a vision of a tropical paradise: Palm, Grape, Lime, Nopal, Centre, Orange, Cherry, Olive, Date, Plum, Peach. If the promoter could have peeked into the future and seen ads of Galveston Beach today, with its bathing beauties, perhaps he could have filled his ads with the Queens of 1838 and watched his city overflow even faster than it actually did.[1]

Hammeken, a native of Philadelphia, became aware of the fact that surveyors had discovered that the water was fourteen to eighteen feet deep at the Big Pass, or San Luis Pass, leading into West Galveston Island. He immediately sensed that this might be his opportunity to develop the great deepwater port on the coast.[2]

Within a short time Hammeken had interested the Austin family, owners of most of San Luis Island, as well as a group of Philadelphia businessmen, other eastern businessmen, and some European capital to look with favor on his dream to build

THE CITY OF SAN LUIS was laid out by promoters that envisioned ships of the world calling at their deepwater port. For a short time the city boomed, but a series of unforeseen happenings left the promoters with many lots to sell.

a new port city. His new port would open onto the Gulf of Mexico with enough depth to take care of any ship on the high seas with a protected harbor that would afford cover in case of a storm. Within a few months of conceiving the idea, the money had been assembled and work started on the project sometime in 1839. Settlers began to arrive from all over the world.[3]

The San Luis Stock Company, proprietors of the City of San Luis, was organized with the following listed as participants. Besides Hammeken, there were three other primary promoters: Tod Robinson, Matthew Hopkins, and S. J. Durnett. Others involved were F. A. Sawyer, W. B. P. Gaines, Ferdinand Pinkard, James Love, James R. Jennings, James F. Perry, William H. Jack, Judge J.R. Morris, J. Templeton, and D.R. Mills. Perry was the representative of Stephen F. Austin.[4]

A must for all towns that were sold by promoters was a fine hotel where guests could live in luxury while they signed up for lots in the new town. Not only did the new town have its hotel, it also boasted of the *San Luis Advocate,* which ran the following ad in late November of 1840:

> BENNETT'S HOTEL
> San Luis, Brazoria County, the subscriber has opened his house for the accommodation of travelers and boarders.
> CHARLES H. BENNETT[5]

It did not take Mary Holley long to make it to San Luis to see and write about the new town. Mrs. Holley was Stephen F. Austin's cousin and was known in Texas as a writer to invite to new towns. In writing about San Luis, Mrs. Holley had a bit of conflict of interest since the Austin family owned the bulk of San Luis Island and she would benefit from sale of land. But, of course, conflict of interest was an unknown concept in Texas in 1840. Mrs. Holley traveled to Galveston in November 1840 and wrote:

> Col. Love met me . . . & took me to his house, while James [her cousin] got ashore the baggage . . . . I found Hammeken here – the same obliging creature as ever . . . . I will get Chinn to survey my land . . . in small tracts to suit purchasers.

After a few days in Galveston, Mrs. Holley traveled to San Luis to see for herself the new town that she hoped would enable her to sell some of her inherited land. It is not known whether she went by buggy down the island or by boat.

> I did not find in San Luis, Calypso & her nymphs, but I am instantly reminded of old Telamaque – especially in the town of Idomeneus, where they were all happy because so busy. It is a lovely spot by nature, & the houses, about 20 of them, are in every stage of progression, from the skeleton frame to the neatly finished edifice. Carpenters, surveyors, wharf-builders, & boatmen are all active. There are no idlers here . . . . My room is in the second story – has four windows, all looking on the sea. I sit with them open that I may drink in the delicious view & soft fresh air . . . . 2 or 3 piers to connect the island to the main done. When the whole is completed & the causeway, there will be a good prairie road to Brazoria, Columbia, & Bolivar, each about 15 miles . . . . Mr. Hammeken had his piano brought into the parlor below & last evening we had a concert of the household around it. He and I performed with the aid of Mr. Allen, a Methodist preacher from Shelby, Virg. . . . He preached in the long dining-room twice Sunday . . . .[6]

Glowing accounts of the new project received wide publicity. Promoters pointed out that it would rival New Orleans and would become one of the most important ports in the world. Special attention was called to the fact that the new port would tap one of the richest plantations along the Brazos River Valley. People came from France and England, no doubt influenced by the foreign capital that was invested.

Since there was no source of fresh drinking water, work was started immediately on several community cisterns, each thirty feet in diameter and constructed of bricks imported from Philadelphia. These cisterns were located where they would catch the rain from the huge cotton warehouses put up in connection with the cotton compress, which was one of the first businesses to go into operation. The press was of the old screw-type that was powered by a mule. The compress was vital to the entire scheme to bring cotton to the port for shipment to foreign markets. Historians are divided on who owned the press. Some credit a Mr. Brown, while others say E. D. John was the owner. Historian Hays, in his writings, said that Robert Mills, one of the largest merchants in Galveston, was the owner. In all probability there is truth to all reports. Records show that 5,000 bales were compressed in San Luis in 1841 for foreign shipment.[7]

New residents of the town included two doctors, Dr. Smith, who had written medical books in France, and Dr. Richardson, who was reputed to be an excellent physician. In the eighth issue of the *San Luis Advocate* the editor had a few words about the medical outlook of the community:

> Doct's Richardson and Smith propose to edit a medical and surgical journal to be published in the office of the *San Luis Advocate* at the city of San Luis. It is intended to present to the reader, in a condensed form, not only the improvements of the science but a faithful portrait of the prevailing endemicks of Texas, their treatment and medical topography. The first number will appear in January Next. It will be published quarterly.[8]

Chief attraction of the new city was a wharf that was 1,000 feet long. Warehouses were built at the wharf and were managed by Andrews and Hammeken. Plans were announced to build a windmill for grinding corn, but it is believed that this gristmill was never built.

Shortly after Charles H. Bennett built the Bennett Hotel, where Mrs. Holley stayed, Mrs. Matthews opened the Central House and started serving meals. Two of the first merchants were J.F. Woodhull and Mr. Hopkins. Woodhull advertised in the *San Luis Advocate* that he had just received a shipment of "20,000 fine Havana segars."

James R. Jennings ran the land office that handled all of the land sales. Opposite the Bennett Hotel, J. J. Tucker added to the cultural life of the city by opening a studio to paint portraits.

Alonzo G. Follett was assigned to San Luis as the deputy customs collector, since ship arrivals and departures were daily occurrences. At times as many as ten ships were in the harbor at once. The secretary of navy for the Republic of Texas ordered the removal of the navy yard from Galveston to San Luis, but there is no record of this ever happening. A notice carried in the *San Luis Advocate* September 14, 1840, shows the heavy movement of ships:

PORT OF SAN LUIS

Arrived

Sept. 4 – Schr *Delaware*, Brookfield, master, from N. Orleans
5 – Sloop *Brazoria*, Lombart, master, from Galveston
6 – Sloop *San Domingo*, Johnson, from Galveston
6 – Sloop *Burrows*, Haskins, from Galveston
7 – Sloop *Tom Jack*, Matison, from Columbia
8 – Steamer *Rodney*, Bogart, master, Galveston
11 – Sloop *Brazoria*, Lombart, from the Brazos
11 – Sloop *Champion*, Leetch, from Brazos
12 – Sloop *Tom Jack*, Matison, from Galveston

Cleared

Sept. 6 – Sloop *Burrows*, Velasco
8 – Sloop *San Domingo*, Velasco
8 – Sloop *Tom Jack*, Galveston
8 – Sloop *Brazoria*, Velasco
8 – Steamer *Rodney*, Columbia

Immediately below this ad was another:

> FOR NEW YORK: The fast sailing Schooner *Delaware* having all her cargo engaged will positively leave on the 23 inst. for the above port. For passage only having good accommodations, apply on board or to – ANDREWS & HAMMEKEN

From the tone of the news and the ads it was evident that the people in other cities looked at San Luis as a place where things were happening. The Everett & Co. of Houston ran this classified ad:

> For Sale or Trade – 300,000 acres valuable improved, unimproved, located and unlocated lands in desirable parts of Texas. FOR SALE OR TRADE, DAILY – Droves of Cattle and Wild Horses, Mules, Oxen, Cows &c, and other live stock. FOR SALE OR TRADE – Building lots, business stands, family residences, &c, in flourishing cities and towns in Texas. WANTED – $20,000 on Bond and Mortgage on valuable property, worth $150,000, and daily increasing in value.[9]

The bulk of the vessels entering the port of San Luis were from the United States; however, ships from England and Germany were listed in old records as having called at the port during its brief life. A lot of the ships that called at the old port brought new settlers, especially in the first few years when the promoters were running ads in a number of newspapers. At the end of five years the population was estimated at 2,000.

The *San Luis Advocate* was owned by S. J. Durnett, with Tod Robinson as editor. W. Y. Allen was a correspondent paid at the rate of $5 per column. He worked until he had earned $50 and asked for his wages. Later he was quoted as saying: "I didn't get a red cent." The *Advocate* folded in 1841, and the *San Luis Times* was started by F.B. Neal on January 5, 1842. However, by October 1842 it moved to Galveston and was known as the *Texas Times.* When Neal moved the plant from San Luis to Galveston the boat turned over, dumping his equipment into the water. The Washington hand press and most of the equipment was fished out of the water and used.[10]

Although San Luis was not officially chartered until 1841, people were living in the area as early as 1836. The Follett family built and operated the Halfway House, an inn, supply store, and convenient place for sea captains, mail carriers, or travelers to meet. The colonial-style home was two and one-half stories and had fifteen rooms. Travelers remembered the planting around the grounds, especially the oleanders that could be picked from the second-floor windows. The Follett family continued to operate this inn until it was destroyed by a storm in 1875.

Another member of the Follett family, Bradbury Follett, was a steamboat builder. He built the *Lafitte* in a yard at Quintana.

Between 1834 and 1838, A. M. Clopper ran a mail route from San Luis Island to Velasco and back. From the 1840s to after the Civil War, a stage line operated between Galveston and San Luis to an inn that was operated in 1850 by Julius Lobenstein, who was also the driver of the stage. Passengers wishing to proceed would cross San Luis Pass on the ferry that was operated by A.B. Follett. A. Burr Follett also operated an inn on the Brazoria side of the pass. The stage continued to Velasco, Brazoria, and Houston.[11]

San Luis earned a nitch in the history of the Civil War in April of 1865, when the steamer *Arcadia*, a sidewheeler, tried to outrun a Union picket gunboat. Captain Sterrett had been running close to the coast, hoping to be able to make it to the protection of the guns at the Mud Fort that was located near San Luis Pass, when the picket boat spotted him and gave chase. Just four miles short of his goal, the captain decided that he would run his ship aground and try to save the cargo. With a full head of steam he drove his boat close to shore, and the crew was able to make it to shore despite gunfire shattering the bow of their boat. The picket gunboat blasted the *Arcadia* and set her on fire, and the ship and cargo were consumed by flames. After the fire, all that was left of boat and cargo were the two boilers, which remained there for more than a hundred years. Beachcombers for years would pick up pieces of the old boiler that washed ashore.[12]

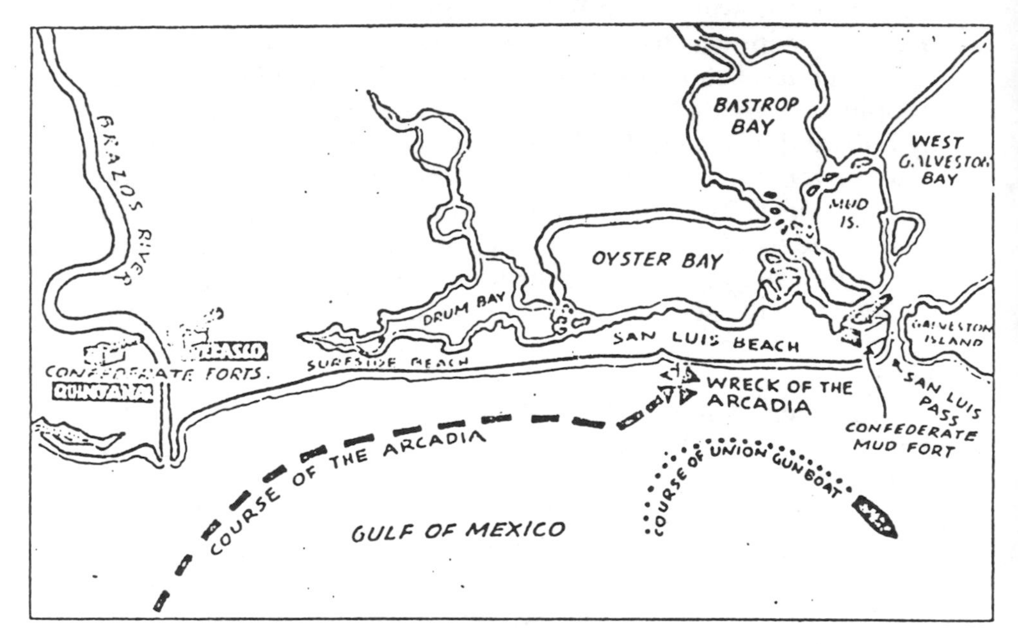

BLOCKADE RUNNER – During the Civil War, gun emplacements on both sides of the Brazos River and the Mud Fort at San Luis Pass kept Union ships at bay, giving rise to captains with a flare for danger to run the blockade. The Arcadia *was making a run with cotton cloth and trade goods when it was spotted by a Union gunboat. The* Arcadia *made a run for protection of the shore batteries, but just four miles short of safety the captain took hits and tried to beach his boat and save the cargo, only to have the gunboat finish the job.*

It appears that no one thing caused the demise of San Luis. A depression in the early 1840s affected a number of businesses and probably caused some of the backers of the town to draw down their money. A change in tides evidently caused sand to fill in the harbor, reducing it from depths that any ship could use to eight to ten feet. The kingpin of the industrial base, the compress, was not as efficient as some of the newer presses in Brazoria County and other cotton-growing areas, and as a result cotton was not being sent to San Luis. The combination of all of these factors caused people to start leaving. Within a short time, the population had been cut to less than 500.

Ten years after its founding, San Luis was almost deserted. The fine homes that had been built were deserted, the freshwater cisterns were invaded by salt water, and hurricanes played havoc with warehouses and wharves. Some houses were moved to other locations, leaving just a few people who chose to make the ghost town their home.

If those early developers could revisit their dream city today, they would find that a bridge now arches over all obstacles to join Brazoria County with San Luis Island. Vacation cottages fill the empty lots.

Houston

Great cities are created because the imagination of man knows no bounds.

But, even in their most fantastic projections, it is doubtful that the Allen brothers, Augustus C. and John K., could have conceived of a city that would grow, divide, and multiply like Houston. In all likelihood, a great city would have grown up somewhere in the Galveston Bay area, but to have enough faith to plant the seeds of greatness at the end of a fifty-mile, twisting, muddy bayou was a wager that few people would have taken.

The business careers of the Allen brothers were as bold and brash as that of the city of Houston. Leaving promising careers in the East, the brothers arrived in San Augustine in 1832 and in a short time moved to Nacogdoches, where they engaged in the volatile but highly profitable business of trafficking in Texas land certificates.

When the Texas Revolution broke out, the Allen brothers bought the *Brutus* and equipped it as a privateer, later selling the ship to the Republic at their cost. During this period, they made many friends who would bring fruit in later business transactions.

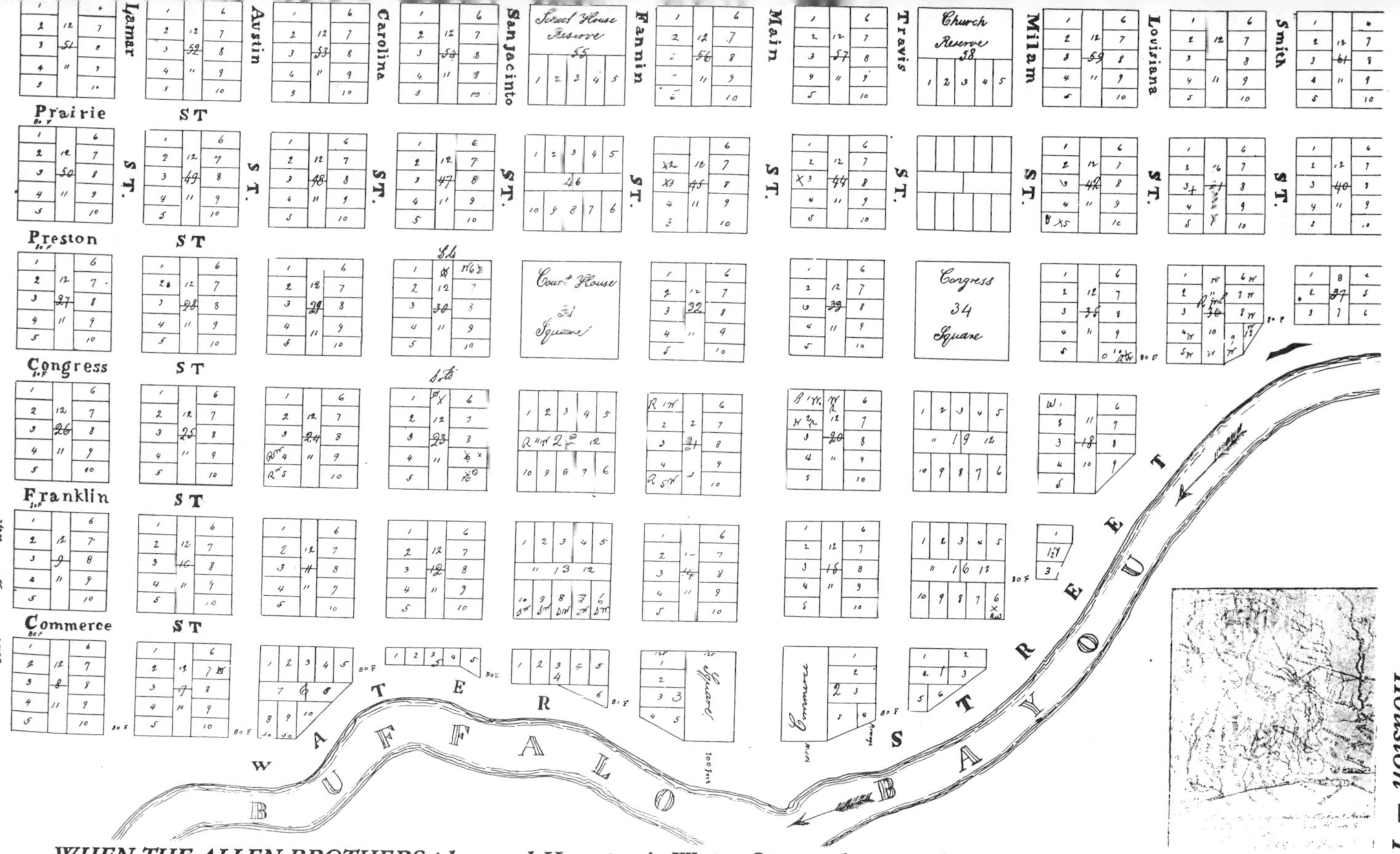

WHEN THE ALLEN BROTHERS planned Houston's Water Street, they made sure that there was ample space for a large number of wharves and commercial houses. Their foresight paid off, as the city at the end of the bayou grew to be a major port.

In 1836 they purchased a half-league of land, known as the John Austin grant, near Harrisburg on Buffalo Bayou. Their keen sense of the potential of a great seaport sold them on the site, and in a short time they hired Gail Borden and Thomas H. Borden to map and survey the site. Houston was on its way.

John's experience as a representative from Nacogdoches in the Texas Congress helped the Allens pull off their biggest deal. They convinced Congress that Houston was an ideal spot to locate the new capital. To sweeten the deal, they offered to build a suitable capitol out of their own funds and to rent other buildings to the state. The deal was closed, and Houston became the capital of the Republic of Texas. This was the jump-start that the new city needed.

Actually, the Allens did not live to see the full fruition of their dream of Houston becoming a great cotton export facility, nor the establishment of a cotton exchange recognized worldwide. John died in 1838 of congestive fever. Augustus took part in the planning that saw the Allen business enterprise grow and prosper. Unfortunately, the fact that John died without a will planted seeds that eventually broke up the business association with the four other brothers. It also caused the estrangement of Augustus and his wife, who was unhappy over the use of her money in family projects. Augustus left Texas and went to Mexico, where he established new business relationships and was appointed United States consul for the port of Tehuantepec on the Pacific Ocean.[1]

The great potential of Buffalo Bayou as a waterway on which to build a city was underscored in an ad that was placed by John Allen in the Columbia *Telegraph and Texas Register* on August 30, 1836:

> The town of Houston is located at a point on the river which must command the trade of the largest and richest portion of Texas . . . . The town of Houston is distant 15 miles from the Brazos river, 30 miles, a little North of East, from San Felipe, 60 miles from Washington, 40 miles from Lake Creek, 30 miles South West from New Kentucky, and 15 miles by water and 8 or 10 by land above Harrisburg . . . . The proprietors offer the lots for sale on moderate terms to those who desire to improve them, and invite the public to examine for themselves.[2]

Not only did the Allens advertise their new town locally, but they sent the same ad to the *Commercial Bulletin* of New Orleans, *Mobile Advertiser, the Globe of Washington, Morning Courier* and *New York Enquirer, New York Herald,* and *Louisville Public Advertiser.*[3]

The success of Houston in 1836 was aided and abetted by the Allens, but it was the availability of Buffalo Bayou as a viable route of transportation that gave the promoters the clay with which to work. As early as 1825, John R. Harris' Harrisburg was a well-established port with schooners plying between the Buffalo Bayou port and New Orleans on a regular basis. The first steamboat to come into Harrisburg was the *Cayuga,* a small sidewheeler that specialized in coastal traffic. The Harris brothers also owned the *Rights of Man, Machauna,* and *Ohio*

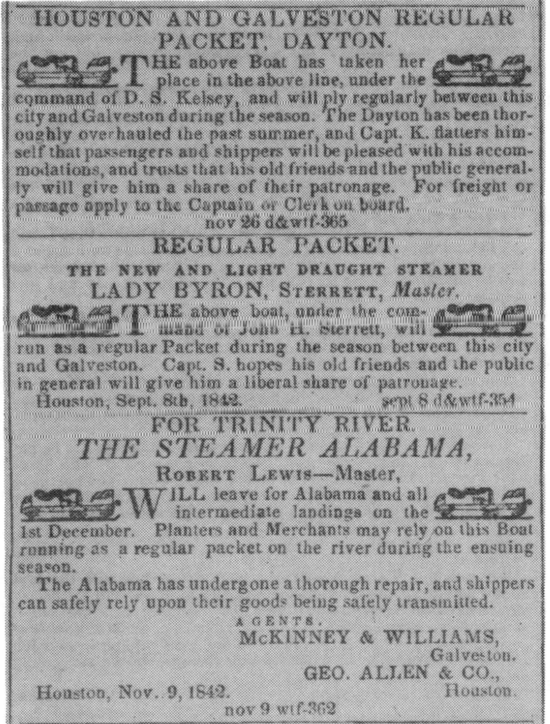

HOUSTON AND GALVESTON REGULAR PACKET, DAYTON.

THE above Boat has taken her place in the above line, under the command of D. S. Kelsey, and will ply regularly between this city and Galveston during the season. The Dayton has been thoroughly overhauled the past summer, and Capt. K. flatters himself that passengers and shippers will be pleased with his accommodations, and trusts that his old friends and the public generally will give him a share of their patronage. For freight or passage apply to the Captain or Clerk on board.

nov 26 d&wtf-365

REGULAR PACKET.

THE NEW AND LIGHT DRAUGHT STEAMER

LADY BYRON, Sterrett, *Master.*

THE above boat, under the command of John H. Sterrett, will run as a regular Packet during the season between this city and Galveston. Capt. S. hopes his old friends and the public in general will give him a liberal share of patronage.

Houston, Sept. 8th, 1842. sept 8 d&wtf-354

FOR TRINITY RIVER.

THE STEAMER ALABAMA,

Robert Lewis—Master,

WILL leave for Alabama and all intermediate landings on the 1st December. Planters and Merchants may rely on this Boat running as a regular packet on the river during the ensuing season.

The Alabama has undergone a thorough repair, and shippers can safely rely upon their goods being safely transmitted.

AGENTS.

McKINNEY & WILLIAMS, Galveston.

GEO. ALLEN & CO., Houston.

Houston, Nov. 9, 1842.

nov 9 wtf-362

STEAMBOAT ads were a regular feature of all newspapers during the days of river steamboats. This ad appeared in the Telegraph and Texas Register *on January 18, 1843, in Galveston.* (Courtesy of Institute of Texan Cultures) that operated on the Bayou. The *Ariel,* first steamboat operated in Texas, was brought up Buffalo Bayou to the mouth of the San Jacinto River, where it rotted. The *Yellow Stone* was probably the most famous boat that was brought into use on the bayou to move cotton to New Orleans. During the revolution the *Yellow Stone* played a major role in defeating the Mexican army.[4]

The Allens chartered the *Laura,* a small, eighty-five-foot sidewheeler, to make the initial voyage to Houston in January 1837. The boat reached Harrisburg with no difficulty, but it took three days to go the next fifteen miles, as the twisting channel had to be cleared of logs, and trees with limbs extending over the water had to be cut back. All of the crew and passengers pitched in with the work, and they finally reached their goal.[5] Among the prominent Texans who were on board the *Laura* on that path-finding day were John Kirby Allen, the proprietor; Moseley Baker, a hero of San Jacinto; Benjamin C. Franklin, a distinguished lawyer; and Francis Richard Lub-

FOR THE CITY OF HOUSTON.

THE REGULAR

PACKET  **STEAMER**

LAURA,

T. W. GRAYSON, MASTER.

WILL leave Marion, on Tuesday, the 21st February, at 4 o'clock, P. M. for the above city, and all intermediate ports. For freight or passage apply on board; or to Aldridge and Davis, Marion, or to Thomas H. Borden. Columbia.

N. B.—The Laura, this trip, will touch at Anahuac.

Columbia, Feb. 20, 1837. 59-1

SEEKS BUSINESS – The packet Laura, *working out of Marion on the Angelina River, was billed as the first steamboat to reach Houston with cargo. This ad ran in the Houston* Telegraph and Texas Register *before the boat was purchased by Andrew Smyth.*

bock, a young merchant and later a Civil War governor of Texas. Lubbock wrote about the trip:

> We had to rig what were called Spanish windlasses on the shore to heave the logs and snags out of our way, the passengers all working faithfully. All hands on board would get out on shore, and cutting down a tree would make of it a windlass by boring holes in it and placing it upon a support and throwing a bight of rope around it, secure one end to a tree in the rear and the other to the snags or fallen trees in the water. Then by means of the capstan bars we could turn the improvised capstan on land, and draw from the track of our steamer the obstructions. Capitalists, dignified judges, military heroes, young merchants in fine clothes from the dressiest city in the United States, all lent a helping hand.

Actually, the trip was more like a huge party, with the boat tying up at night and the passengers going ashore to dance and frolic with the settlers. However, Lubbock became impatient with the pace and took a small yawl and pushed ahead of the *Laura* to see the new townsite for himself. Ironically, the yawl went past the townsite and had to back up before sighting the stakes marking out the streets at the water's edge. The *Laura* reached its destination on January 27, 1837, thus proving to a few doubters that the new city of Houston was the true head of navigation on Buffalo Bayou.[6]

But critics of the new city at the end of the twisting bayou persisted. Francis Moore, Jr., editor of the new Houston *Telegraph and Texas Register,* was still a skeptic. He wrote: ". . . the bayou above Harrisburg being so narrow, so serpentine and blocked up with snags and overhanging trees that immense improvements will be required to render the navigation convenient for large steamboats."

No doubt John Allen felt as if he had been bitten by the man he had fed. He had promised Moore a building for his presses. But, to put the matter to rest once and for all, he arranged for the 262-ton, 150-foot-long steamboat *Constitution* to visit Houston. The editor evidently became a believer when the "giant" ship docked a couple of days later in Houston. Probably the editor had the last word, since the *Constitution* was too large to turn around in Houston's turning basin and was forced to back down the channel to a large bend just above

Harrisburg.[7] This bend in the bayou was known thereafter as Constitution Bend, until it was made into the Turning Basin for the modern-day Houston Ship Channel.[8]

Early travelers were impressed with the beauty of the spot, especially the sandy bar at the foot of Main Street. "Everything around the landing place was in a state of nature except the portion of the steep bluff which had been scraped off sufficiently for a roadway to enable drays and carts to get to the sand bar, which had been converted into a wharf," according to John Lockhart in his writings years later.[9] But perhaps it takes more than one perspective. Editor Bartholomew wrote:

> The first attempt at public improvement in Houston was the construction of a board walk up the slippery bayou bank from the water at Allens' Landing. Another bit of civic improvement was accomplished—the dragging of logs along the streets which flattened the weeds and brush and smoothed out the sea of mud .... All this despite the fact that there was no lodging house, no eating establishment, no public houses of any sort except the two saloons in tents which utilized wood shavings and pine needles for floors ... important men, financially, began arriving in numbers, bringing money, equipment, supplies and workmen. They came by small-boat, on horseback over the sodden prairie and even on foot. Wagons arrived too, following a few sunny, drying days.[10]

A frontier Baptist preacher high up on the Brazos River read about the young city of Houston and determined to make a trip to the new port to get much needed supplies and lead and powder to fight off the Indians. It took him two weeks to make the trip from near present-day Hearne in a wagon pulled by eight oxen. He got his powder, a few supplies, and directions to find lead. He wrote: "... it was a city of tents. A large round tent, resembling the enclosure of a circus, served as a drinking saloon and there was plenty of whiskey and cigars." He loaded his wagon, and after preaching a sermon, headed back to the Brazos River Valley with his supplies.[11]

The first session of Congress in Texas at Columbia adjourned in 1836 after naming Houston the capital. Before Congress reconvened on May 5, 1837, great changes had been made in Houston, despite all of the stories from critics. Frame buildings were built almost overnight, stores opened, a lodging house opened, and the saloons multiplied, along with promoters and hustlers. The promised two-story courthouse was not ready in time for the first term of court in March of 1837, but the contract was let to Thomas W. Ward and, using lumber from Maine, the building took shape on the corner of Main and Texas. The State of Texas paid Allen $5,000 per year for rent on the building. His agreement with the state provided that the building revert to him, provided that the capital was moved out of Houston. In later years it was turned into the Capitol Hotel.[12]

A small steamer, trying to make it upriver to Houston in time for the opening session of Congress, had a rough trip, hitting a number of submerged logs. In fact, when within sight of Allen's Landing, the valiant craft settled into the mud bottom. Fortunately, it was shallow and the decks were above the bayou waters. Seeking to make the best of a bad situation, the boat was turned into a hotel and was immediately besieged by men desiring to rent quarters. Sleeping was done in two shifts, both day and night.

With the first anniversary of San Jacinto fast approaching, carpenters worked day and night to get something suitable built for the grand affair. The big celebration was planned for a two-story building to go up on Main Street between Preston and Prairie that would house the Carlos Saloon. With no floor and no roof, and the gala day at hand, an improvised 25 x 50 floor was built for dancing, and the festivities proceeded. Gen. Sam Houston, still not completely recovered from the wound he received at San Jacinto, led off the dance with Mrs. Moseley Baker as his partner.[13]

Houston was a raw frontier port city, but change was in the air from the beginning. A Philosophical Society was founded before the close of the first year, and other societies were also being organized. The love of horse racing caused the Jockey Club to be founded in October of 1838. Several churches were formed in 1838, including the Christ Church (Episcopal) on the corner of Texas and Fannin. Rev. Littleton Fowler, a Methodist who was chaplain of the Senate (1837–38), preached to the citizens and obtained from Allen a deed to half a block on Texas Avenue, where the First Methodist Church was built. Rev. W.Y. Allen arrived in March of 1838 to bring enlightenment to Presbyterians. The Baptists held regular meetings as early as August of 1838. The Roman Catholics, with Father Timon and Father Odin, met regularly. The Senate chambers doubled for years as a meeting place for churches. Houston was on the move with saloons on one corner and temperance lectures on another. A board of health was organized, as was a waltzing academy. The Houston City School was functioning with a tuition of three dollars for the rich; the poor were admitted free.[14]

With the capital as the driving force, Houston made rapid gains. The population set at 2,073 – 1,620 males and 453 females – to make it the largest city in Texas. When Congress decreed in 1839 that the capital would be moved to Austin, things went slack in Houston, but quickly the focus shifted to the commercial potential of Buffalo Bayou. Talk of a railroad to connect Harrisburg and the Brazos Valley was projected, and work was actually started until the project fizzled in 1840. Not to be upstaged, Houston put up plans to run a line to the Brazos Valley and eventually to Austin. This first idea did not materialize. Congress returned briefly to Houston in 1842, but businessmen continued to recognize that Houston's future depended upon trade with the Brazos Valley and increasing trade over Buffalo Bayou. The boat landing at the foot of Main Street was the center of commercial activity. Long trains of wagons brought an ever-increasing amount of cotton, hides, and other products into the port.[15]

The drag put on business activity by the menacing attitude of the Mexicans during the Republic years was shattered when Gen. Zachary Taylor marched south with an army to instigate the Mexican War. Annexation to the United States came in 1845, and business prospects looked up. It appears that no one had taken a census during these years, but in 1850 Houston had a population of 2,396, so they had fully recovered from the loss of the state government and were firmly committed to a future depending on Buffalo Bayou.[16]

Actually, Houston owes its initial sustained growth to the wagon trains that flowed into the new port city in an almost continual caravan, but especially after the fall harvest and in early spring. It was commonplace to see a train of a hundred or more wagons drawn by four to six yoke of oxen approaching the city from the south, west, and north. Oxen were used primarily because of their endurance, wide hoofs that did not sink into wet soil, and because they could forage for their food. Since there was no bridge across the bayou when the city was first established, all of the wagons had to be ferried across the stream at the foot of Main Street. There were two main campgrounds, Vinegar Hill, located where the Southern Pacific Depot was later built, and the Old Indian Campground, at the intersection of Houston and White Oak Bayou. Merchants provided these campgrounds free of charge. The loads were commonly cotton, wool, hides, beeswax, cured meats, hogsheads of molasses, ripened sugar cane, melons, grain, or other produce from the farm or dairy.

Since these trips involved shopping, the women and children were usually included. After supper each night social gatherings took place, and old-fashioned barn dances were held for all ages. The trips were six months apart, so the shopping had to be done with care in order to make sure that the staple goods that they took home, such as flour, lard, salt, etc., would last. Large household purchases were made with care because they had to be transported home in the wagon. Clothing and bolts of cloth were bought with an eye toward style and durability. Magic lantern shows, minstrel shows, or occasionally a traveling stock company were events looked forward to by the pioneers. These camping yards were always interesting places at night. As soon as campfires were lit, guitars, banjos, harmonicas, fiddles, and accordions were brought out, and singing and laughter filled the air. The Virginia reel was the favorite of the dancers.

Houston's trading and warehouse district was along Buffalo Bayou. Samuel Allen's warehouse was an immense, rambling structure that covered an entire block. The warehouse of Tom Whitmarsh, built about 1850 on the banks of the bayou, was near Allen's business. Wagons could be unloaded in front of the store and the goods moved into the warehouse while men and women shopped for needed supplies. When it came time to ship the products, a long, wooden chute was connected with the steamboat below for ease of loading. The Macatee warehouse and store covered an entire block across from Vinegar Hill and was popular for customers coming in from the Brazos and Colorado river valleys. It was not uncommon for as many as 200 wagons to unload at Macatee's in a single day. The Louis Pless warehouse was a two-story structure near Samuel Allen's huge galvanized iron warehouse. H. D. Taylor was another leading commission merchant and forwarding agent. He was located at Commerce and Travis. Later, in 1889, the warehouse and cotton gin of J. Ziegler and Company was located on the bayou near a railroad bridge. They were allowed to flag a train to a stop when cotton barges passed underneath the bridge so that a spark from the wood-burning engines would not set fire to the bales of cotton.[17]

The length of most wagon trips was from three to four weeks, depending on the distance from Houston. The pioneer family would usually tarry from several days to a week. Sometimes, if there was a little extra cash, they would treat themselves to a steamboat trip to Galveston before hitting the long road home. Supply wagons working out of Houston commission houses ranged as far south as Brownsville, north to Fort Sill, Oklahoma, and west to New Mexico.[18]

The wagoners and their camps provided Houston with a chapter in history. So did the plantation owners, who came to the forefront in the days before the Civil War when Southern plantations were in full bloom in the Brazos River Valley. Called plantation barons, they came to Houston riding on their own railroad – the Columbia Tap Railroad. The plantation owners on the Brazos bought Houston's interest in this short line in the early days of railroading. In later years it was often referred to as "Joe Bonney's Road" after their general manager, superintendent, baggage master, freight agent, ticket agent, and even chief engineer. The town of Bonney was named for this genial railroad "baron." The cotton baron would usually be dressed in long-tailed coat and pantaloons of the period, topped off with the customary large sombrero with a Mexican blanket over his shoulder. His wife was dressed in the fashion of the day: large hoop-skirts, a huge poke-bonnet, with a cashmere shawl or lace mantilla to grace her shoulder. The children were dressed in the latest fashion. Since the Hutchins House, or the Barnes House, had been forewarned of the coming of the baron and his family, a coach drawn by four fine horses, driven by a Rocky Mountain Express driver, was standing by at the station to greet the Bonney Express and to whisk the guests off in style to the hotel, where they proceeded to hold court. Also forewarned, the cotton factors, bankers, and wholesale merchants would be on hand to vie for the favor of the plantation owner. After all, in a good year his plantation might produce several thousand bales of cotton. Quite a striking contrast between the baron and the wagoner—but it took both to make Houston what it is today. [19]

It was obvious to Houston's leaders that its future was tied to the bayou. Local legislators got an act through the Texas Congress in 1840 authorizing Houston to build and maintain wharves. The Houston Chamber of Commerce took the lead to solve clearing of the channel, and in January of 1842 the Texas Congress passed a law that allowed the removal of sunken vessels within twenty days if the owners failed to act. The Port of Houston was established in June of 1841, thus giving more authority to keep the channel open for steamboat traffic.[20]

The Allens furnished the early push to get Houston

BAYOU CITY Cotton Compress, located on Buffalo Bayou, played a big role in the development of Houston. This picture, taken sometime before 1890, shows a barge loaded with compressed bales.
(Photo by Wm. Fritz; Courtesy of Institute of Texan Cultures)

started, but soon other men began to make their presence felt in the business world. In 1839 William Marsh Rice arrived in Houston. He worked at various merchandising endeavors before making his mark as a cotton broker and in real estate. In 1845 Houston received 14,000 bales of cotton, and in 1861, due in large part to Rice, 70,854 bales went through the port. Another successful merchant was Thomas W. House, who came to Texas in 1838. He was a money lender, merchant, cotton factor, banker, and investor in railroads. It was natural that Rice and House were identified as businessmen who were good at pushing projects, such as better roads leading into Houston and the introduction of railroads. Their individual and collective efforts made things happen in Houston. Rice's fortune multiplied as his business enterprises grew. He was murdered in New York in 1896 by his valet, and the bulk of his estate went to the William Marsh Rice Institute. House's business interests ranged from establishing fleets of wagons in the early days, to helping organize the Board of Trade and Cotton Exchange and railroads. He died in 1880. One of his sons, Edward Mandell House, became famous as an adviser to President Woodrow Wilson.[21]

Roads and then railroads played important parts in Houston's battle to become the trade center in Texas. Most of the cotton and other raw products from the Trinity, Neches, and Sabine ended up at Sabine Pass or Galveston for shipment. Houston, from the beginning, fought to bring the Brazos River Valley trade into Houston overland, as well as that of Central Texas. At least two large wagon yards were established in Houston to take care of the men and oxen while they were in town. During dry weather, the freight could move with relative ease. But during long spells of rain, the roads became long stretches of mud holes, making it necessary to unload wagons several times a day. Despite the drawbacks, large amounts of cotton and other products were moved into Houston by the trains of wagons. The number of oxen pulling a wagon depended upon the load they were pulling. For instance, five yokes of oxen could pull a wagon loaded with five bales of cotton or six yokes could manage a wagon with six bales. The sheer weight limited the number of bales, especially in wet weather, since the wheels would cut too deeply into the soil. Several plank roads were planned to solve the mud situation, but none were successful.[22]

It soon became apparent that railroads were the key to building the port of Houston. As the counties in the Gulf Coast area began to develop, the need for transportation became acute. By the time the Civil War was ready to explode, Houston had five railroads leading into the countryside bringing raw products into the port for shipment. Prosperity was evidenced in the bankrolls of the wealthiest merchants. William Marsh Rice was reported to be worth $750,000; William J. Hutchins, $700,000; Thomas William House, $500,000; and Cornelius Ennis and Paul Bremond, $400,000 each. These fortunes were made largely because Buffalo Bayou offered an ever increasing avenue for Houston to enter the world trade market.[23]

One of the lines that was featured in the early railroading (1853) was the Buffalo Bayou, Brazos and Colorado Railroad, owned by a group of Boston capitalists headed by Sidney Sherman. They hired W. J. Kyle and B. F. Terry to run the job. Wagoners argued against the line, saying it would destroy life along the line. Houston saw the line as a threat to their well-being and a boost to Harrisburg. Rather than fight, Houston decided to join and conquer. The city built a railway to tap the Buffalo Bayou, Brazos and Colorado in order to divert traffic and thus prevent the resurgence of Harrisburg as a port. The editor of the weekly *Telegraph* headlined the story: "Every Man for Himself and the Devil Take the Hindmost . . . . The construction of the Tap Road will secure to Houston the lion's share of the benefits resulting from the entire cost of the Harrisburg road." Later Houston sold the tap to a group of Brazoria planters for $172,000, more than recovering their $130,000. The planters extended the line into the sugar cane growing area to the south, and when the first shipment of sugar and molasses came to Houston it was labeled the "Sugar Road."[24]

Perhaps no tale about the development of Houston and Buffalo Bayou would be complete without a word about Charles Morgan. As founder of Morgan Steamship Line, he was a man to be reckoned with when any planning about ports and facilities was being considered in the Galveston Bay area. Work to improve navigation in Buffalo Bayou had been minimal until 1866, when the Houston Direct Navigation Company was founded and started on a program of dredging and deepening an area known as Morgan's Point. At this time Morgan was in the midst of trying to get Galveston to improve facilities that his line used and at the same time forestall a proposed rate increase. Galveston turned a deaf ear, and Morgan chose to go his separate way. Morgan immediately purchased Houston's interest in the Houston Direct Navigation Company and put his crews to work cutting through Morgan's Point and dredging a channel across the bay to get rid of two bottlenecks that had troubled ships trying to reach Houston. Once the cut was completed, Morgan put a chain across the new canal and demanded toll payment for all ships passing. Eventually, Galveston saw the error of its ways and relented. Morgan discontinued steamer service into Houston and returned to Galveston with his business. Houston later got the Corps of Engineers involved in the project, and while it was years in final fulfillment, the federal government did take over a part of the responsibility for Buffalo Bayou. The Harris County Houston Ship Channel Navigation District was given life in 1911 to assure Houston of deep water for their inland port.[25]

Houston's place among world ports is maintained by the giant tankers, steamships that can hold the cargo of dozens of the early-day paddlewheelers. But it was these paddlewheelers, as well as a goodly number of windjammers who sailed the Seven Seas, that brought Houston to the point where these supercargo carriers could take over.

The *Ariel,* the first paddleboat to sail up Buffalo Bayou, never returned and now lies in her resting place near the mouth of the San Jacinto River. The *Cayuga* started on Buffalo Bayou but moved to the Brazos before returning during the Revolution to take men and timber to Galveston, refugees to Anahuac, and supplies to Harrisburg. The vessel was joined by the *Laura* and the *Yellow Stone,* in moving supplies and troops. The *Cayuga* took President Burnet to visit the victors of San Jacinto and later moved the wounded, plus Gen. Sam Houston, to New Orleans. The schooners *Flash* and *Kosciusko* brought in merchandise to Morgan and New Washington. The *Shenandoah* got caught in the bay with a load of slaves during the Revolution. The *Independence* and the *Brutus* were resting in bays after pursuing Mexican ships in the open seas. The

Invincible brought a prize ship into Galveston, welcome, indeed, because of her load of food that went to the Texan army. The *Pennsylvania* brought the Twin Sisters cannons, a gift from the people of Cincinnati (labeled as hollow ware because officially the United States was neutral). The *Pocket* brought supplies to Harrisburg. John Allen chose the *Laura* to make the first voyage up the bayou all the way to Houston, soon to be followed by the *Cayuga,* the *Yellow Stone,* and then the *Constitution* to show the world that Houston was indeed the head of navigation on Buffalo Bayou. Four boats, the *Branch T. Archer,* the *Sam Houston, Friendship,* and *Laura* made regular trips into Houston. On a less regular schedule were: *Emblem, Rodney, Rugus, Putnam, Correo, Trinity, Patrick Henry,* and *Dayton*. The first steamers to go down were the *Emblem,* on February 6, 1840, and four days later the *Rodney* was caught in a rise and damaged. The *Brighton* hit a snag and went down, causing an investigation of the flurry of sinkings. Gradually the snags were removed, sandbars done away with, and bottlenecks widened.[26] Accidents happened, and boats went down, but the spirit of the riverman was one of adventure – and even racing. The *Sam Houston* and the *Courier* decided one day to liven up the trip along the bayou, and so the safety valves were tied down and the pine knots and pitch were poured into the boilers. It was a thrilling race until the *Sam Houston*'s boilers got so hot that the boat "trembled like a man with a violent ague."[27]

The Allens of the 1830s built a firm base for the Jesse Joneses of the 1900s to fashion a city that now plays host to space flight. Perhaps Houston's slogan should be "A city where wagons made space ships possible."

Buffalo Bayou/ Trinity, Galveston Bay Landings

New Washington

Nicholas Clopper, like so many of the early Texas pioneers, was a man who looked at Texas as a place to make a lot of money in land and trading. He bought a half-league of land on the north side of Buffalo Bayou near Harrisburg in 1826 and then picked a spit of land between Galveston and San Jacinto bays for his future city, to be known as Clopper's Point. He rushed home, bought merchandise to sell, and returned with his sons, Edward, Andrew, and Joseph, aboard the *Little Zoe.* The Cloppers unloaded their merchandise in Harrisburg, set up a store with Andrew in charge, and loaded the rest of the merchandise in wagons and headed west toward San Antonio. They sold their merchandise, but along the way Edward died of the fever. Probably this disenchanted Clopper, and when James Morgan offered Clopper a good price for his land he sold out in 1834 before his dream was fulfilled.[1]

Morgan had high hopes for the new town that he planned for Clopper's Point. It would be called New Washington. He signed on with Lorenzo de Zavala, who had the backing of New York financiers to develop Texas real estate. They brought a group of Scottish highlanders and free blacks from New York.

General Santa Anna destroyed New Washington, and the settlers scattered to the winds. After San Jacinto, Morgan built a home for himself at the point and it became a showplace. He remained active in promoting Texas real estate, including the Trinity landing known as Swartwout.[2]

Lynchburg

An 1831 traveler in Texas, who stopped at Lynchburg overnight, described the ferry/port in this manner: "We stopped for the night at Mr. Lynch's on the western banks of the river San Jacinto, at the mouth of Buffalo Bayou. The land is very low and marshy, and the sallow countenances of the children indicate the unhealthiness of the situation. Mr. Lynch had a store, containing quite an assortment of goods, and was about erecting salt works on the opposite side of the river, where there is good salt water. His house is an inn, and he keeps a ferry boat on the stream for the convenience of travelers."[3]

During the Runaway Scrape, Lynchburg was overrun by people fleeing in front of Santa Anna's army. President David Burnet appointed men to provide timber and food and to construct temporary shelters for the fugitives. Colonel Gray described the scene: "The prairie near Lynchburg resembled a camp-meeting ground, being covered with carts, tents, mules, women, children, baggage, slaves, and cattle."[4]

Nathaniel Lynch was one of Austin's Old Three Hundred colonists, receiving his land on the San Jacinto River in 1824. John D. Taylor settled on the opposite bank at a point known as Midway, the meeting place of Baron de Bastrop and Stephen F. Austin in 1824 to issue land titles. In 1831 David G. Burnet located a steam sawmill at Lynchburg. The mill was built by Norman Hurd and Gilbert Brooks, who came with the machinery and operated the mill. Burnet built his home just a few miles above the ferry, and a family cemetery is of historical interest there. Zavala Point, named after its famous founder, Lorenzo de Zavala, was nearby. Lynch was appointed the second judge of the municipality of Harrisburg. He was listed as postmaster in 1836. Evidently, the post office lapsed for a few years but was reinstated in 1852 and not closed until 1927. He died in 1837. A ferry operating across the Houston Ship Channel in 1949 was called Lynchburg Ferry.[5]

San Leon/Edwards' Point

Ritson Morris brought his family to the west side of Galveston Bay in 1825 and settled on the bluff called Edward's Point, opposite Red Fish reefs. Later the place was called San Leon, and in 1838 an attempt to found a town brought settlers to the area. Later the name was changed to North Galveston, but shortly it was being called San Leon again. The community's claim to fame comes from the fact that in February of 1834 the first load of Africans from Cuba landed at San Leon. They were the property of Col. Ben Fort Smith for his plantation near Stafford's Point. They lost their way and stopped at the house of Dr. P. W. Rose, as reported later by his daughter, Mrs. Dilue Harris, in her writings.[6] A post office was granted in 1910 and exists today.[7]

Stafford's Point

Located about fifteen miles downstream from Harrisburg, Stafford's Point was near Oyster Creek. The community had a school, with Davis Henson as the teacher. The schoolhouse was built of logs and was about halfway between the homes of Dr. Rose and Mr. Dyer. The building, previously a blacksmith shop, was without windows, had an open doorway, and a floor made of split logs with the face smoothed. After the Battle of San Jacinto, when most settlers had returned to their homes, a Mr. Bennet was hired and the school reopened. Dr. Pleasant W. Rose, with his wife and children, settled there after moving from Harrisburg. In addition to practicing medicine, Dr. Rose operated a store. The community must have had some sort of meeting place, as holidays such as July Fourth drew settlers from all over the area. A Mr. Choate furnished music with his violin.[8]

San Jacinto

A small settlement located on the south bank of Buffalo Bayou and the west bank of the San Jacinto River across the river from Lynch's Ferry bore the famous name of San Jacinto. Very little is known about this community, except that it did exist. An ad in the *Galveston Daily Civilian,* May 19, 1858, listed the advertiser's address as San Jacinto, Texas. Apparently it did exist as a recognized community, at least until 1858 and possibly later.

An ad in the *Texas Gazette* dated July 10, 1830, carries this message: "Enoch Brinson of San Jacinto Bay has opened a house of private entertainment, also a blacksmith shop." It appears that there was a settlement in the area where the San Jacinto River ran into San Jacinto Bay, which must have been the town of San Jacinto.[9]

In a speech that Gen. Sam Houston delivered in the Senate of the United States on May 24, 1859, he said:

> The army rested for perhaps two hours, when, at the tap of the drum given by the General, they were again on their feet, and took up the line of march *for San Jacinto* for the purpose of cutting off Santa Anna below the junction of *the* San Jacinto and Buffalo Bayou [emphasis added].

It is obvious that General Houston was headed for a place – San Jacinto – that was known to him. It is also obvious that he was not referring to the San Jacinto River, as he identified it in the next phrase.

George W. Grover, who moved to Texas in 1824 with his parents, and who took part in the Plum Creek Fight, the Santa Fe Expedition in 1841, and other engagements during this period, settled in Galveston and became a business and civic leader and history buff. His papers in the Rosenberg Library, Galveston, give many insights into early Texas history, including these observations about the settlement of San Jacinto. He died in 1901.[10]

Harrisburg

Harrisburg is a city of "what ifs."

What if General Santa Anna had not burned the city to the ground? Would Harrisburg, instead of Houston, have become one of the greatest ports in the world?

What if the Allen brothers had not appeared on the scene at the exact right moment? Would Harrisburg have been able to rebuild and expand?

What if the Harris brothers had been as good at politics as the Allen brothers?

Nothing will change the fact that Harrisburg is today a "no city" swallowed up as Houston grew and spread to include more than 100 square miles of territory in Harris County. Still, "what ifs" are always interesting for the historian to tamper with.

John Richardson Harris, a native of the state of New York, was a man of foresight, and when he met Moses Austin and heard his story of opportunity in Texas, he became a convert. Evidently a man of some means, Harris came to Texas in his own vessel, possibly the *Rights of Man,* in 1824. He chose land at the junction of Bray's and Buffalo Bayous as his 4,425-acre grant, which he received through the Austin Colony from the Mexican government. He built his home on the peninsula between the bayous in 1824 and then built a store and warehouse on Buffalo Bayou. Apparently he had an agreement with the Austin Colony to receive their freight and forward it to them overland. In 1826 he employed Francis W. Johnson, who later featured in the ill-fated Battle of San Patricio, to lay out the town of Harrisburg. In 1828 Harris shipped eighty-four bales of cotton to New Orleans on the *Rights of Man* – probably the first shipment of cotton out of Texas. According to old records, it is assumed that the cotton was grown by Jared E. Groce on his plantation near the present city of Hempstead.[1] Seeing the need for a sawmill in Harrisburg, John Richardson laid plans for a steam mill and went to New Orleans to buy part of the machinery. While there he contracted yellow fever and died.[2]

David Harris was appointed administrator of his brother's estate. It is not clear whether David came to Texas with John R. Harris, or arrived later. Records show that he and his brother operated a store at Bell's Landing on the Brazos River in 1827.

As one of Austin's colonists, David received his grant of land on the San Jacinto River. He took over the operation of the new sawmill and other Harris business interests. In 1830 another brother, William Plunkett Harris, who operated a successful shipping business on the Mississippi with Robert Wilson, showed up in Texas and made large claims against the estate of John Richardson Harris. In 1833 Jane Birdsall Harris, John's wife, moved to Texas with her son, Dewitt Clinton. The other two children came later.[3]

An interesting description of Harrisburg in 1833 was given by Mrs. Dilue Harris, daughter of Dr. Pleasant W. Rose. Dr. Rose was stranded on Galveston Island after a gale. After the storm he opted to settle in Harrisburg rather than proceed to Matagorda, his original destination. She listed at least eleven families with homes in Harrisburg, as well as a dozen or more unmarried men. At that time John W. Moore was the Mexican *alcalde.* Moore was an active revolutionary at Anahuac, a delegate from Harrisburg to the Consultation, and a representative to the Convention of 1836. He went on to serve as a member of the First Congress of the Republic as a delegate from Harrisburg. In addition to the Harris store and sawmill, there was a landing and a warehouse where the Harris ships were anchored when not working. The list of customers of the Harris store reads like a list of Austin's colonists, plus just about every plantation in the Brazos. After leaving the Cartwright farm near Harrisburg, Dr. Rose moved his family to Stafford's Point.[4]

The steam sawmill, planned by John Harris and put into operation by his brother, David, evidently was filling the community's need for lumber. The *Texas Gazette* reported on July 22, 1830, that "The steam Saw Mill at Harrisburg of Messrs Wilson and Harris is in operation and works very well." (Wilson was the partner of William Harris and a party to the suit filed against the estate of John Richardson Harris.) On July 31, 1830, the newspaper reported: "Sloop *Alabama,* Captain Lovejoy, arrived at Harrisburg from New Orleans, will leave for Matamoras with cargo of plank from the saw mill."

DeWitt Harris, son of John R. Harris, had arrived at Harrisburg with his mother in 1833 and, with Mrs. Harris, opened a store that was patronized by Indians who came to sell their buffalo, bear, and deer skins, as well as blankets and beadwork. At one time two to three hundred Indians were camped near town. The population of Harrisburg had increased considerably during the past year.

The Kleberg family were residents at that time, and Mrs. Rosa Kleberg, a recent arrival from Germany, had an experience that jarred her into the awareness of the frontier. She was alone in the house that they had just rented, trying to bring order to the stack of baggage. Without warning, a half-naked Indian, the first she had ever seen, appeared in the middle of the kitchen. Spying a loaf of bread on the table he picked it up, and in the same motion he deposited two large venison hams on the table, calling out: "Swap! Swap!" Without another word he disappeared with the loaf of bread, leaving the speechless woman somehow pleased over the swap.[5]

Not all Indian contacts were peaceful. In the summer of 1829 a group of about thirty settlers met in Harrisburg and organized an expedition against a band of predatory Indians. Once on the march, they picked up another eighty men from the vicinity of Groce's Plantation, and then proceeded on to within twelve miles of the Waco village, where they defeated about 200 Indians. The party returned home with the loss of two men. When trouble with the Mexicans came to a head in Anahuac in 1832, many Harrisburg citizens marched with Col. Frank Johnson to the aid of the Texans held at Anahuac.[6]

The years of 1834 and 1835 were especially profitable for the Harris enterprises. At the same time, disagreements with the Mexican government were growing. On December 30, 1835, the General Council created the Harrisburg municipality and designated the town as the seat of its government. Edward Wray, *alcalde,* and H. H. League and Nathaniel Lynch, judges, transacted business of the Republic until April 16, 1836, when Gen. Antonio López de Santa Anna burned the entire town to the ground, with the exception of the home of John W. Moore.[7]

A military company was organized in Harrisburg in the fall of 1835, with Capt. Andrew Robinson in command. The first lieutenant was Archelaus Bynum Dodson. A flag made of blue, red, and white calico of equally sized pieces, with a single white star in the field of blue, was put together by the wife of the first lieutenant, Sarah Rudolph Dodson. A descendant of the maker wrote later that the single star was like Texas, alone in her opposition to the autocratic government that had been established in Mexico by Santa Anna. The flag was carried by James Ferguson, second lieutenant. Due to opposition by Stephen Austin, the flag was not used. When the Alamo fell, the flag was found in the old fort. Sometime in March of 1836 the printing press of the *Telegraph and Texas Register* was moved from San Felipe to Harrisburg. They were in the process of getting out an edition when the Mexican army arrived. The press was dumped into the bayou and was later recovered.[8]

After the fall of the Alamo, General Santa Anna began his sweep toward East Texas, trying to catch the elusive Texan army under Gen. Sam Houston. Cries of "The Mexicans are Coming" became all too familiar to Texans, and the Runaway Scrape took on an ever-increasing urgency. President David Burnet, Vice-president Zavala, and other members of the cabinet of the provisional government were guests in the homes of Mrs. Jane Harris, and others, from March 22 until April 13, 1836, when they departed hastily for New Washington to the home of Col. James Morgan. Everyone remaining in Harrisburg left just before the Mexican army arrived. When the Mexicans left, the entire town, as well as the countryside, had been sacked and burned.

It is hard to imagine the feeling of despair that the residents of the once prosperous Harrisburg must have felt when they straggled back to their homesites after San Jacinto. All that remained were the charred skeletons of their homes and businesses. To make matters worse, insofar as the Harris family was concerned, was the cloud over the title of property once held by John Richardson Harris. When he died his brother, David, who had been in partnership with him in several deals, took over the business. Another brother, William Plunkett, arrived on the scene in 1830 with his partner, Robert Wilson. Before long Wilson was listed as the owner of the sawmill, along with David Harris. Together, and collectively, the group operated several steamboats, namely, the *Mecana, Cayuga, Rights of Man, Nelson,* and *Ohio,* all of which made it through the war and were evidently put back to work or sold in the area. The fact that the Harris property was involved in litigation immediately after the war kept several individuals from investing in the future of Harrisburg. The city was incorporated in 1837 and consolidated with Hamilton on the opposite bank of the bayou, under the name of Harrisburg Town Company, which functioned until 1849.

Jane Harris, John's wife, fled Harrisburg as the Mexicans approached, going first to Anahuac and then to Galveston, where she remained until after the Battle of San Jacinto. She returned to Harrisburg, and with the aid of Mexican prisoners-of-war she built a new home. She was a stockholder in the newly organized Harrisburg Town Company from 1839 to 1849. The company had hired Frederick Jacob Rothhass to make a new plat of Harrisburg to reflect its union with Hamilton. Until her death in 1869, Jane Harris operated an inn.[9]

Andrew Briscoe, merchant, patriot, judge, promoter and banker, acquired an interest in the Harrisburg Town Company and was instrumental in bringing new businesses and residents to the area. In 1836 he was appointed chief justice of Harrisburg, Harris County. He was instrumental in promoting a railroad from Harrisburg to the Brazos River. Legends say that at least two miles of the roadbed were in place in 1840 before the dream faded. In 1847 Sidney Sherman acquired the Harrisburg Town Company and promoted the Buffalo Bayou, Brazos, and Colorado Railway Co., the first railroad in Texas, to run from Harrisburg to Stafford's Point, in Fort Bend County on the Brazos River. It was completed on September 7, 1853, and reached as far as Alleytown before the Civil War.[10]

Harrisburg was granted a post office in 1853. It stayed in existence until 1892, when it was consolidated with Houston, operating as a separate unit until 1927. Under the Republic, Route No. 1 ran from Houston to Galveston, via Harrisburg.[11]

For a few years Harrisburg was the rail terminal in the area and a busy shipping port. It retained its importance as a railroad center until the railroad yards were destroyed by fire and rebuilt in Houston in the 1870s. While Harrisburg was making small development gains, Houston was making giant leaps. In December of 1926 Harrisburg was annexed to Houston.[12]

Galveston

"A man is judged by the company he keeps."

Michel Brindamour Menard started hanging around in the early 1800s with the likes of Davy Crockett, James Bowie, Anson Jones, Sam Houston, John and Augustus Allen, and Thomas McKinney – all land promoters waiting for a chance to settle in Texas and make it big.

Menard was an illiterate Canadian immigrant who had taught himself to read, and with the words of wisdom that he gained from these land promoters he went to work. Actually, he was ahead of most of the promoters of his day in that he had the backing of a rich and powerful uncle, Lieutenant Governor Pierre Menard of Kaskaskia, Illinois. Being a fast learner, he quickly moved into big-time deals by acquiring a foothold in Galveston in 1836 (league and labor in Seguin grant on east end of Galveston Island), and later he secured a clear title from the financially broke Republic of Texas that was glad to get $50,000 for the former home of pirates and freebooters.

IN THE BEGINNING – Galveston's port district in 1845 looked a great deal different from the way it does now. In this drawing, labeled "cotton docks," it appears that the season is just getting started. The hulk of the old sailing vessel underlines the dangers that can befall a ship even in harbor. (This copy of a document in the Rosenberg Library, Galveston, printed with permission)

Evidently aware that he needed additional help, he enlisted other men to join him in forming the Galveston City Company: Gail Borden, Jr. (secretary and agent 1839–1851), publisher of the *Telegraph and Texas Register*; Samuel May Williams, former secretary to Stephen F. Austin and successful merchant; Thomas F. McKinney, Williams' mercantile partner and an early cotton trader; William H. Jack, Texas patriot and distinguished statesman; A. J. Yates, loan commissioner for the Republic of Texas; John K. Allen, co-founder of Houston; Augustus Allen, co-founder of Houston; Mosley Baker, lawyer and patriot; David White, investor from Mobile, Alabama; James Love, jurist and planter; and Judge William Hardin, patriot and early jurist in charge of Mexican prisoners at Galveston.[1]

Actually, Menard settled in Nacogdoches in 1829. After a time he went back to Illinois but returned to Texas in 1832 and developed a trading post and sawmill on Menard Creek in southern Polk County. He was a delegate from the municipality of Liberty and signed the Declaration of Independence. Having moved to Galveston to protect his interests, he began the founding of the city in 1837. After serving in the Congress of the Republic in 1838, Menard devoted the rest of his life to his business interests, which were many.[2]

Between the time that Lafitte and his men left Galveston Island, and the time that Menard began the modern city of Galveston, the wind-swept island harbor had a number of transient guests. Gen. James Long, who sought to establish his own Republic of Texas, occupied the island and rebuilt Lafitte's Fort. Leaving his pregnant wife, Long rushed off to La Bahia, where a rebellion was supposedly under way. Long never returned, eventually meeting his death in Mexico. Troops that remained in Galveston gradually left Long's widow alone in the fort. On December 21, 1821, she gave birth to Mary James, presumably the first white child born in Texas. She left the island in March 1822 with James Smith and his family, and lived with them on the San Jacinto River for a short time before she went on to make a page in Texas history for herself. Her ordeal in the fort was shared by her six-year-old daughter Ann, a twelve-year-old slave girl, and a dog named Galveston.[3]

Probably at no time during the next decade did Galveston Island remain deserted. Colonists heading to Austin's Colony,

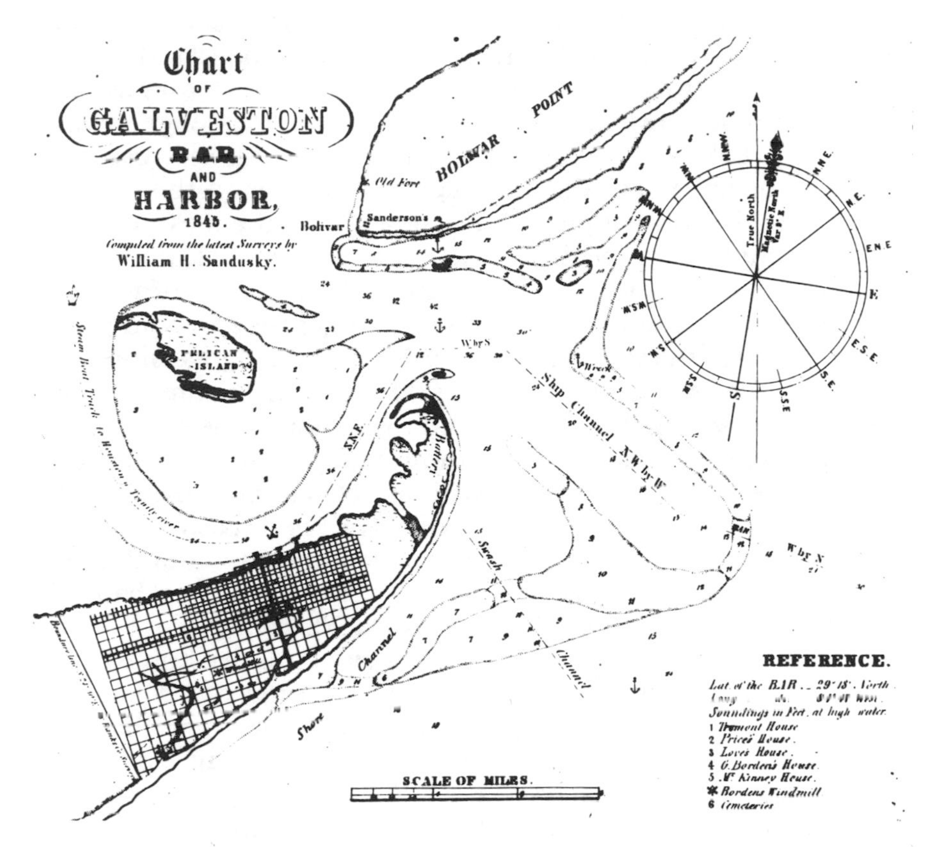

GALVESTON Bar and Harbor in 1845. This drawing, by William Sandusky in 1845, shows the layout of the harbor and Bolivar Point. (Courtesy Barker Texas History Center and Institute of Texan Cultures)

as well as other settlers, came by sea and land, and many stopped at Galveston Island. The Mexican government designated the harbor as a port of entry in 1825 and built a small customshouse in 1830. The Texas Navy made full use of the harbor, and during the final days of the Texas Revolution President David G. Burnet and other government officials took refuge in whatever shelter was left on the island. Burnet and the other officials set up shop for a while at Harrisburg. However, when General Santa Anna began approaching they made a hasty retreat to Morgan's Point, where they boarded the schooner of war *Flash* for the trip to Galveston. Thus, Galveston became the seat of Texas government for a short period of time.[4] A number of other refugees were on the island when four men, sent by Gen. Sam Houston to tell of the victory at San Jacinto, arrived several days later. One of the messengers was Capt. R. J. Calder, who volunteered because of his interest in a young woman, Mary Walker Douglas, who was on the island. Evidently, she was happy with the news – and the messenger – as the couple were wed and moved to a farm at Richmond. Burnet, who was the last to hear the news, became infuriated and even threatened to arrest the messenger for spreading the news before giving it to the president. The "government" moved to Velasco. Later, about 2,000 Mexican prisoners from San Jacinto were held on the island for a short time.[5]

The city of Galveston was now ready to move. John D. Groesbeck laid out the town, with streets running parallel to the bay labeled in alphabetical order and the crossing streets numbered in sequence. Levi Jones, a land promoter and merchant, was appointed general agent after purchasing half of White's interest. The first sale was April 20, 1838.[6]

Little was done toward building a city on Galveston Island until the spring and summer of 1837. In June the customshouse of the Republic of Texas was authorized, with Gail Borden as collector. He occupied the first floor of an old Mexican house. Amasa Turner's family had the second floor. In August the contract was let for a customs building to be built on the northwest corner of Strand and Tremont streets. Since Houston was the capital of the state, vessels began to arrive with merchandise for the new seat of government. There were from twenty to twenty-five vessels of foreign tonnage at anchorage in Galveston harbor when the hurricane of October 10, 1837, a gale of terrific magnitude, struck the island, inflicting damage to anything that was standing. All of the ships, with the exception of a schooner from Mobile, were washed ashore. Most were refloated. A large brig called the *Perseverance* was used for a customshouse by Mr. Borden for nearly a year after the storm. One called the *Elbe* was never launched again, being converted into a hotel and later a jail.

In January 1838 less than a score of houses were standing. Most of the estimated population of 250 were housed in tents. There were no wharves at this time, and any freight that was

STEAMBOAT DAYS – Some of the first docks built in Galveston were designed to take care of the paddlewheelers that ruled the river cotton trade in the days before the railroads entered the picture. (Drawing reproduced with permission of Rosenberg Library, Galveston)

moved in or out was done by lightering or by flats. Flats were temporary barges that could be moved to a ship for loading and unloading.[7]

Col. Amasa Turner, active participant in the Texas Revolution, was in charge of an army detachment in Galveston during the storm and is responsible for the detailed story of how people packed into his two-story house, with the ballast probably keeping it from blowing away. He built one of the city's first wharves in 1838, which proved to be in a bad place, and the pilings were destroyed in two years. E. McLean built a wharf just west of the Turner wharf, which also failed. The pilings for Turner's wharf were of pine, driven without removing the bark, which resulted in worms destroying it in two years. Turner also built the Galveston Hotel on the south side of A street. Menard's, or Central Wharf, had a 100-foot "T" at the end.[8]

An ad in the Houston *Telegraph and Texas Register* marked the beginning of trade:

> The steamer *Leonidas,* Capt. Hanna, will ply regularly between this city and Galveston, and will leave for the latter

place on Sunday morning the 6th inst. For freight or passage apply to the captain on board, or to Dowsell and Adams, agents. Passenger fare $7.

Captain Hanna was an old-timer with a small shell island, long since removed, named after him, as well as a chain of shell and oyster reefs in East Galveston Bay.

In April of 1837 William Bryan of New Orleans announced that he had instigated a line of steamers that would ply between New Orleans and Galveston and Matagorda bays, sailing on the first, tenth, and twentieth of each month. The *Constitution,* the *Conroy,* and the *Crusader* were evidently aimed at bringing products from the Brazos River Valley and Galveston Bay into New Orleans harbor. There is a note in the *Civilian and Galveston* on October 5, 1838, that the *Crusader* foundered in the Gulf sixty miles off Brazos Santiago. All hands were lost except Captain Mitchell, who managed to reach shore after great hardships.

On September 28, 1838, the Van Winkle Brothers advertised in the Galveston newspapers that the *Sam Houston,* Capt. O'Brien, master, would enter the Houston and Galveston trade on a twice weekly basis. In December 1839 the *Emblem,* Capt. J. Bryan, and the *Rufus Putnam,* Capt. John H. Sterrett, were also listed in ads soliciting business between Galveston and Houston.[9]

Thomas F. McKinney and Samuel May Williams had a mercantile business at the mouth of the Brazos River, and in the summer of 1837 they opened a store and warehouse in Galveston. It was destroyed in a hurricane that hit in October but was quickly rebuilt, as well as adding a wharf and the Tremont Hotel. This hotel became the *in* place in Galveston and continued to be the festive center of social life until it was destroyed by fire during the military occupation after the Civil War by "unknown causes." The commission part of the business was taken over by Henry H. Williams, Samuel's brother. Samuel continued as a banker under the name of McKinney and Williams. The bank ended in failure, a victim of the "paper money" wave that swept Texas in the late 1830s.[10]

The Republic built a new customshouse on the site of the old one and in a short time trade was on the increase. Due to the failure of the Turner and McLean wharves, other businesses and wharves began to locate on the Strand. John N. Reed was elected justice of the peace and John Sellers constable in the first election on the island. The JP got to try his skills when Col. N. B. Yard arrived with lumber for a new home, as well as a small stock of goods. He also had a cooking stove, which suffered a broken hearth due to the carelessness of the crew. The captain refused to pay damages, and the colonel brought suit before Esquire Reed for damages in the amount of ten dollars. He won.

As more and more people arrived, Galveston started to grow. But not everyone was happy. A passenger aboard the *Columbia* hired a sturdy young sailor to bring him ashore on his shoulders, since there were no wharves. The sailor planted the new arrival firmly on the beach and pointed out to the visitor the solitary hotel. The passenger struck out, but, unacquainted with the conditions, found himself mired. He called out to the sailor: "Here, you rascal; come and help me out, and carry me back to the ship. I have seen enough of Texas, and don't want to stop in such a damned place." The sailor obliged and the unnamed visitor sailed away with the *Columbia.*

But, despite its shortcomings, Galveston's early settlers realized that their city was unique for business as well as a place for visitors. Probably the first "convention" was held in May of 1838. After the adjournment of the Third Congress of the Republic in Houston, the president, vice-president, cabinet and many senators and members of the Lower House, accompanied by the renowned Chief Bowles and several of his warriors, boarded the steamboat *Friendship* for an excursion to Galveston Island. Also included on the guest list was the chargé d'affaires and secretary of legation from the United States. One of the guests remarked:

> The steamer had on board the Executive, the Legislative and Judicial Departments of the Government of Texas, and a Branch of the Government of the United States, Alcee Louis La Branch first chargé d'affaires to Texas.

The trip was sponsored by Messrs. Jones and Allen, enterprising citizens of Houston. By this time Colonel Turner had completed the Galveston Hotel, where sumptuous meals were prepared in handsome style.

The *Telegraph* of May 12, 1838, contained an account of the all-expense paid trip:

> . . . . we started at Houston and slowly made our way down Buffalo Bayou which was shaded all the way with the rich foliage of the Magnolia and other forest trees on either bank. Passed the beautiful sites of the towns of Harrisburg and Hamilton . . . . In the course of the evening, we arrived within full view of the consecrated spot on which the signal victory of San Jacinto was achieved . . . . one member of the Lower House of Congress remarked – "All of which I saw, and part of which I was.–"[11]

William L. Moody, who came to Texas in 1852, became a positive force in the business world of Galveston upon his arrival. He centered his interests in cotton and banking and helped establish the Galveston Cotton Exchange. The Moody banking empire became one of the largest in Texas. Deep water was his driving passion. He believed that his, and Galveston's, interests lay in that direction.[12]

Trading was the name of the game, and to accomplish this it was necessary to have some sort of facility for ships to load and unload. Dr. Levi Jones advertised in a Houston newspaper (none in Galveston) on February 1, 1838, for bids on a wharf. This first wharf was built at the foot of Twenty-fourth Street. After this first wharf was built, others followed as the need arose until the harbor frontage from Ninth to Fortieth streets had been filled, resulting in the consolidation of interests and finally to the formation of the Galveston Wharf Company in 1854.[13] Port-related activities provided the main thrust of Galveston's economy starting in the days before the Republic. Merchants sought Texas agricultural products and vied to sell the same producers imported supplies.

This initial construction of wharves, warehouses, and mercantile stores took place on the "Strand" from Center to Twenty-seventh and was immediately on the bayshore. The western end of this street was submerged and only reclaimed "within the comparatively recent past when the great wharf and levee works of the Galveston Wharf Company and the Southern Pacific system were completed, a giant undertaking only made possible by the improved appliances for dredging."[14]

A partial list of the wharves is as follows: Merchants, 16th

Street; Kuhn's, 18th Street, built 1839; Brick, 20th Street; Parson's, 20–21st Street; Central, 21st Street; Williams or Palmetto, 24th Street; St. Cyrs, 25th–26th streets; Labadies, 26th Street, built 1850; Beans, 29th Street, built 1859; Galveston-Houston, 29th Street, built 1866; Government Wharf; Small Wharf, next to Government; Heidenheimer's, 28th or 29th streets; Barragh's, 16th Street, built 1838; McLeans, 18th Street, built 1840; Lufkin's, 25th Street, built 1847; Western, 33rd Street, built 1876; 15th Street Wharf. The Dries map of 1871 shows wharves at 18th, 20th, 21st, 24th, and 26th streets. The 20th, 21st, 24th, and 26th street wharves were connected by T heads along the channel.[15]

William Bollaert, an Englishman who had visited and sampled many parts of the world, probably was drawn to Texas in the late 1830s after reading Kennedy's *History of Texas.* He also had an eye for gathering information about business opportunities in Texas. In 1842 he made this entry into his daily log:

> February, 1842: there appears to be a more fixed population than formerly [he had visited Galveston in 1836], the building of houses, moving and removing them continually going on. Vessels from various parts of the world continually arriving. The steamers from N. Orleans bring passengers, emigrants, and goods, returning laden with cotton and other produce. What is known as the Market Place – Strand and Tremont St., Church St., and Customshouse – shew a scene of comparative bustle. The greater number of inhabitants are from the U. States, with a sprinkling from every part of the world.[16]

As was to be expected, a number of men opened on the Strand businesses that survived for a number of years. One of the earlier merchants was Col. J. M. Brown. A brickmason by trade, he arrived at Galveston in 1842–43 and had a hand in building and contracting a number of the early brick buildings on the island. In partnership with Stephen Kirkland, he entered the hardware business. He was president of the Galveston, Houston, and Henderson Railroad and president of the First National Bank. The firm of Brown and Kirkland was located on the Strand between Twenty-first and Twenty-second streets.[17]

Col. Ashley W. Spaight was one of the first cotton factors

and was a member of the firm of Riggs & Spaight that was doing business in the mid-1850s. At that time two cotton compresses were located on the Strand. Robert Mills, the largest plantation owner and businessman on the Brazos River, moved to Galveston in 1841 and is credited with establishing the first cotton compress in Texas. His business consolidated and was known as Mills, McDowell Company of New York and McDowell and Mills of New Orleans. The Merchants' Press occupied the entire block bounded by Strand and Mechanic and Eighteenth and Nineteenth streets and was operated for many years by Capt. A. P. Lufkin. Another prominent compress man was James Sorley, who kept all cotton statistics used in Galveston starting in 1850 until his job was taken over by the Galveston Cotton Exchange. The other ante-bellum press was known as Shippers Press and was located at Strand and Twenty-ninth Street. Later, with the arrival of the railroads, the compresses gradually left the Strand. In the early days it was necessary that they be near the docks for ease of shipment.[18]

John Sealy moved to Galveston in 1846 and formed a partnership with John H. Hutchings to establish a mercantile store in Sabine Pass. In 1854 a third partner, John Ball, joined the firm, and they returned to Galveston to set up a commission and banking business. In 1858 Sealy was president of the Galveston Wharf Company. He and his associates bought the Buffalo Bayou, Brazos, and Colorado Railroad in 1870 and the Houston Tap and Brazoria in 1873. In 1879 he became president of the Gulf, Colorado, and Santa Fe Railroad. His impact on Galveston has been long-lasting. Before his death in 1884, he set up the Sealy Foundation, which built the Sealy Hospital in 1887 and has continued to this day as a presence in financial foundations.[19]

Amid all of the commercial activity, it should be noted that newspapers made their appearance on Galveston Island from the beginning. The first was a sheet gotten out by Samuel Bangs, who was connected with the Mina, Aury, and Perry Expedition. After the war he returned to Galveston and put out an assortment of printed papers, including the *Daily Galvestonian* on March 20, 1841. However, the honor of the first newspaper has always been extended to the *Commercial Intelligencer* and the second to the *Civilian and Galveston*

City Gazette. Literally scores of newspapers have been issued from Galveston presses, but most folded after a short time. The *Galveston News* was established in 1842 and is the only one that has survived to present day. A great deal of Galveston's early history is to be found in these early newspapers.[20]

Galveston's leaders recognized early that their future lay in water-borne trade. One of their first efforts to improve channels was the formation of the Galveston and Brazos Navigation Company to dredge a channel across West Bay to Quintana, giving access to the Brazos River.[21]

The next effort to improve navigation came after it was noted that the sandbar that formed a semicircle pointed toward the Gulf between Galveston Island and Bolivar Peninsula was gradually rising, until in 1869 the water over the bar was only eight feet. Finally, the city set up a Board of Harbor Improvements, which adopted a plan put forward by Capt. Charles Fowler. This called for the sinking of a series of piles to focus the force of the current to rake the sandbar. Finally, with some federal help, the plan worked and the water over the bar was at least twelve feet in 1873. Galveston's first effort to bring truly deep water over the bar ended in failure when the project was blocked in the U.S. Congress. Learning of the failure, the Galveston forces, still led by William Moody, gained support from a broad base, including Colorado. In 1890 Congress approved the Galveston Harbor Bill. To celebrate, the Galveston Artillery Company set up its cannons on the beach and boomed a 100-gun salute. Success was evident when the British steamer *Algoa,* which drew twenty-one feet of water, tied up at the Galveston docks. While other navigation improvements were made from time to time, deep water was assured for Galveston.[22]

Probably the Morgan Steamship Line, owned by Charles Morgan of New York, did more to set the pace for transportation rates and to control ship movements than any other company during this period of early development. In fact, early steamship traffic between the Texas ports of Galveston, Indianola, Corpus Christi, and Brazos Santiago was dominated by Morgan's company. For a short time in the mid-1850s, Cornelius Vanderbilt's steamboats out of New Orleans challenged the Morgan line, and, as a result, the fare between New

Orleans and Galveston dropped to five dollars. The two titans got together, with Morgan buying Vanderbilt's ships, and rates immediately jumped. In the late 1860s another squeeze was put on Houston and Galveston. Morgan acquired the Buffalo Bayou Ship Channel Company and the Houston Direct Navigation Company, and as a result a short-cut channel was cut through Morgan's Point, belonging to Morgan. He promptly put a chain across the channel and extracted a toll for boats to use the new channel. Morgan, at that time, had an interest in the port of Clinton, a few miles below Houston. During this same time Morgan's ships shunned Galveston, supposedly due to high wharf fees. Once differences were ironed out, the chain came down and Morgan's ships returned to Galveston. He was a powerful force to deal with, especially since his interests were co-mingled with railroads.[23]

The Trinity River was one of the best sources of trade for Galveston. The *Friend* ran up as high as Liberty in January of 1840. In April 1840 the *Galveston Weekly Times* reported that the steamer *Trinity* was running from the upriver landing of Alabama to Galveston. A month earlier, the mercantile firm of Howell, Myers and Company of Galveston had commissioned Captain Gould to take the *Trinity* upriver. On his return he reported:

> .... The steamboat Trinity has just returned from a trip up the river. She went as far as Alabama, about 500 miles, and found the navigation uninterrupted, and could have gone much farther if it had been desired. The upper Trinity country is rapidly settling, and some neighborhoods are already pretty densely populated, embracing a good variety of substantial farmers, many of whom will plant cotton upon a pretty extensive scale the coming year.

By 1843 the cotton being grown in the Trinity River Valley had increased to the point that at least two steamers were engaged full-time in the trade between Galveston and the Trinity River. The *Ellen Frankland* and *Vesta* were kept busy until the *Vesta* sank for the second time and the *Frankland* foundered on Redfish Bar, loaded with cotton and freight. In May 1844 the *Scioto Belle* was withdrawn from other trade and put on the Trinity and Galveston run.[24]

During the 1844–45 season, four boats – *Oriole, Scioto*

Belle, Sparta, and *Vesta* – were making their rounds from Galveston to the Trinity River ports. The Mexican War had an adverse affect on the Trinity River steamers, as a good number of boats were impressed by the army and transferred to service in the Rio Grande River. During the 1847–48 shipping season, four boats were necessary to keep the cotton moving to Galveston. Evidently, this was not enough, as Polk County farmers complained about insufficient space for shipping cotton. Ships like the *Reliance* and the *McKinney* began to take on larger and larger loads.[25]

With the growth of East Texas, cotton production continued to rise each year. While some went directly to New Orleans, the bulk from the Trinity River Valley ended up in Galveston. By 1877 cotton exports from Galveston reached a half-million bales.[26] Naturally, all of this cotton did not come from the Trinity, but by 1877 Houston was receiving an increasing amount of cotton by rail and was shipping directly and not through Galveston. By the same token, most of the cotton from the Brazos River was also finding its way into the export trade through Houston.

The era of the steamboats is painted by historians as a romantic period where the mournful whistle brought young and old alike to the landing to marvel as bales of cotton were put aboard and all sorts of merchandise unloaded. But steamboating also had its violent side, and many rivermen went down with their ships.

The *Albert Gallatin* exploded within six miles of Galveston on December 19, 1841, as it was coming down from Houston. Five were killed and nine wounded. Capt. J. N. Sterrett of the *Dayton* brought the survivors to Galveston. The *Sara Barnes* left Galveston with thirty-one persons aboard, headed for New Orleans. After hitting a severe storm, the ship began to take on water faster than the pumps could pump it out. When the ship showed signs of foundering, rafts were made of baled cotton – four bales in one and three in the other. Finally, the ship's only yawl was loaded with seven people and the remainder boarded the rafts. The yawl was driven ashore and capsized in the surf, with three of the crew drowning. One raft with five was driven ashore. Captain Frankland and seventeen persons drowned. During the night of March 26, 1853, the boats *Neptune* and *Farmer* were engaged in one of the favorite pastimes – steamboat racing. The *Farmer*'s boilers exploded, and, despite immediate assistance by the *Neptune,* Captain Webb and a number of passengers and crew members lost their lives. The *Nautilus* left New Orleans headed for Galveston in August of 1856, loaded with thirty passengers, $30,000 in specie, one hundred horses, and fifty beeves. The boat went down in a gale, and only one man floated to shore (on a bale of cotton).

In the winter of 1859-60 the *Bayou City* exploded at Lynchburg, and several people were killed. After the damage was repaired, the boat was converted into a cotton-clad gunboat by the Confederacy. On October 3, 1871, the *C. K. Hall* went down in a gale off Cedar Point, and all hands perished except a Swedish sailor. Twenty were lost when the *Henry A. Jones,* loaded with 442 bales of cotton, caught fire and burned to the water line. Only two were saved out of twenty-two. The *City of Waco* anchored in the outer roadstead of Galveston to wait until morning to cross the bar. About one o'clock a fire broke out and in a few moments appeared to be a seething mass of flame. It is supposed that lightning struck the ship and ignited the 2,000 cases of oil stored on deck. The captain and sixty crew and passengers perished.

There was no romance in these stories.[27]

While the captains of industry were building their shipping, trade and banking empires, the education of the youth of Galveston was not neglected. It just took several years to get survival matters under control. Levi Jones, merchant and agent of the Galveston City Company, contracted with William R. Ware in 1839 to build a two-story frame building for a school at the intersection of Church and Nineteenth streets; however, in the spring of 1838 a Miss Robbins opened a female school in Galveston. When the new building was completed, Prof. E. Walbridge was the first principal. Inadequate funding caused the venture to be abandoned and the building sold. It was in the early 1840s that James P. Nash opened a boys' school on Tremont Street near Avenue H, which lasted for more than thirty years. A Mr. Smart ran a school near the intersection of Tremont and Avenue H, and the Rev. James Huckins, a pioneer Baptist preacher, and his wife taught a school at the intersection of Avenue K and Twenty-seventh Street. These were all private schools that charged tuition.

In 1846 the Texas legislature passed a law empowering the board of aldermen of a city to levy and collect a special tax for public schools. This was in the administration of Mayor John S. Sydnor. The program got off to a good start but soon got bogged down in politics. After several years, it was abandoned. Public education remained dormant until 1870.

In 1854 the Rev. J. M. Odin, bishop of the Galveston Diocese, accepted a block of land set aside by the City Company for educational purposes and promptly began construction of a brick building that was completed in November of 1854. When completed, it was opened under the name of St. Mary's University. Later Bishop Odin founded the Ursuline Convent, which was the oldest educational organization in Galveston until it was destroyed by Hurricane Carla in 1961. A number of private and church schools were started in the next several decades; some lasted while others faded away.

With new school legislation passed by the state in 1869, public schools returned to Galveston. The scholastic population at that time was 2,478 white and 631 black, served by six white and two black schools. Acceptance of public schools was slow in Galveston, as the patrons seemed to prefer their private schools. In September 1881 the citizens voted to impose a twenty-cent tax on each $100 of assessed values to support schools. Gradually, the system worked out the problems.[28]

Churches seemed to get off to a better start in Galveston. Since the Mexican government did not allow other churches during its tenure, it followed that the Catholic church took the lead in Galveston's early religious life.

Rev. John Timon was probably the first priest to visit Galveston, coming in 1838 for a short stay. Father Steely was the next and held religious services in Menard's warehouse. On May 29, 1841, Rev. J. M. Odin arrived in Galveston after a trip through South Texas. Shortly after his arrival a small mission church was built. The wooden church was replaced in 1847 with St. Mary's Cathedral. The Rt. Rev. C. M. duBuors followed Bishop Odin, who was succeeded by Rt. Rev. N. A. Gallagher. The first St. Patricks was started in 1871, but when it was half-built a storm in 1871 destroyed it completely. It was rebuilt, but in 1900 another hurricane badly damaged the building and it was repaired again. This same hurricane completely destroyed the Sacred Heart Church, which had been dedicated on January 17, 1892, but it too was replaced.

Early in 1840 Jacob L. Briggs, Joseph W. Rice, and John B. Jones called a meeting of all Methodists in Galveston. In 1841 the City Company donated two lots to the group, and in 1842 a frame church was built. It was known as the Ryland Chapel in honor of Reverend Ryland, of Washington City, who contributed $1,800. St. John's Chapel was dedicated in 1870 by Bishop Marvin. The second Methodist church, St. James Church, was built in 1872 and operated until 1901, when the two churches consolidated.

The first Presbyterian services were held in 1836 or 1837 by the Reverend Reid at the old navy yard just west of the Santa Fe station. The congregation met there and in the City Company-owned school. A 60 x 40 frame building was built on two lots donated by the City Company in 1843. This building was given to a black congregation and was moved to another location, where it was destroyed by fire a few years later. A new 60 x 120 building was built in 1876.

Baptist missionaries organized the first Baptist church in 1840. The City Company gave the group three lots at the intersection of Twenty-second and Avenue I, where a church was built and dedicated in 1847. This building served until a brick building was built, only to be destroyed by the Hurricane of 1900.

Episcopalians began forming when Rev. Leonidas Polk visited the city and held services in a private home. Rev. Benjamin Eaton preached in the residence of Stephen Southwick in 1841. A wooden church was built in 1842 on the southeast corner of Tremont and Avenue G. In 1867 a brick building was built, known as Trinity Church. The Reverend Eaton remained as the pastor until 1871. During that year, while in the pulpit reading a hymn, "Nearer, My God, to Thee," he was stricken and died in a few minutes.

Hebrew services were held in rented buildings until 1870–71, when a synagogue was built on the northeast corner of Twenty-second Street. Rabbi Henry Cohen served the group for over twenty years.

A German Lutheran church was organized in the late 1840s and later occupied the Galveston Lyceum, which stood at the intersection of Avenue G and Twenty-fourth Street.[29]

The Civil War in Galveston was fought mainly in the harbor. On October 4, 1862, Cmdr. William B. Renshaw brought a Union squadron of ships into the harbor and demanded surrender. The Confederate commander, Col. Joseph J. Cook, asked for a four-day truce, which was granted. He used this time to move men and supplies out of the area. The Federals landed on December 25 and barricaded themselves on Kuhn's Wharf. Confederate Maj. Gen. John B. Magruder waited until December 31 to counterattack. The initial attack failed because scaling ladders were too short for their job to land troops behind the Yanks on Kuhn's Wharf. Two Yankee gunboats, the *Harriet Lane* and *Owasco,* silenced the Rebel artillery.

The second half opened when the Confederate cotton clads, the *Bayou City* and the *Neptune,* came in from the west and attacked the *Harriet Lane,* inflicting serious damage in a ramming attack. The *Harriet Lane* withdrew to shallow water and sank. The Union *Westfield* ran aground on Pelican Spit and was scuttled by her crew. The battle ended with 117 Confederate soldiers killed and wounded. The control of Galveston Harbor was returned to the Confederacy for the remainder of the war.[30]

Galveston has attained many firsts, including seeing Galveston Bay frozen solid three times. The first is attested to by Mrs. Jane Long, who was stranded in the old fort in 1821 awaiting her husband, who never returned. She tells that the bay was frozen to the point that she saw Indians chasing a bear from Smith's Point to Pelican Island – all water. The second was January 1, 1886, and the third was February 1, 1895. In the winter of 1930 Galveston experienced a freakish snowstorm. A howling northwester struck, sending the mercury down to 13 degrees above zero. The frigid wind striking the warmer water of the Gulf caused an ugly black vapor to rise in the air to possibly a hundred feet, where it froze into snow.

Galveston has seen it all, from pirates, slave traders, patriots, merchants, builders, and soldiers to promoters. It has withstood hurricanes by the score, invaders from the sea, and smooth-talkers from the boardwalks. It played host to mariners who sailed the square-rigged ocean-going vessels, to the rivermen who brought romance to commerce with the paddle-wheelers. Then it welcomed the modern steamers of today which can carry more cargo than a fleet of paddlewheelers. The city has embraced untold thousands of immigrants, and given them a helping hand as they flowed into the hinterland. Through it all, Galveston developed into a city that appreciated beauty and whose tycoons left legacies to inspire all ages.

Freebooters/ Buccaneers

Oh, what a set of vagabundos;
Sons of Neptune, sons of Mars,
Raked from todus otros mundos,
Greeks and Lascars, Portsmouth tars.[1]

Tales of buccaneers that sailed the seas with wreckless abandon in years gone by have a mystic appeal. We cringe at their "plank walking" but listen with rapt attention to tales of buried treasure. Perhaps the limerick writer of long ago painted them with the proper brush: "raked from all mankind."

Since Galveston Island played host to the full gamut of mankind, a few of its tales should be entertaining.

Louis-Michel Aury made the island his base of operations in about 1816. A true, unprincipled privateer, Aury mixed looting ships with international revolution, teaming up at one time or another with Henry Perry, Jose Manuel de Herrera, and Francisco Xavier Mina. Aury's ships evidently made sizable hauls, with one cargo of specie and Indigo worth about $778,000. Aury lost his foothold on the island and decided to convoy the Mina expedition to the Santander River on April 7, 1817.[2]

Enter Jean Lafitte.

Lafitte, whose mother was Spanish and father French, was born in Bayonne, France. The family was caught up in the turmoil of rebellion, eventually ending up in New Orleans. One of the few positively known facts about Lafitte is that he and his brother operated a blacksmith shop in New Orleans in 1809 or 1810. The connection of Jean Lafitte with the Barataria establishment outside of New Orleans seems to stem from the fact that he was useful on shore as a commercial agent and not because of previous piratical exploits. He was not a sailor but was a shrewd trader. At this time in history, the Gulf of Mexico and the West Indian waters were swarming with privateers, in many instances financed by capitalists in New Orleans. Their prizes were brought into Grande Terre Island, Louisiana, to the settlement known as Barataria. It appears that Lafitte first served as a middleman, and then as a lobbyist working to prevent uncomfortable vigilance on the part of authorities. As his personal influence extended, and his gains from the lucrative traffic accumulated, he became the proprietor of ships and an employer of captains and crews.[3]

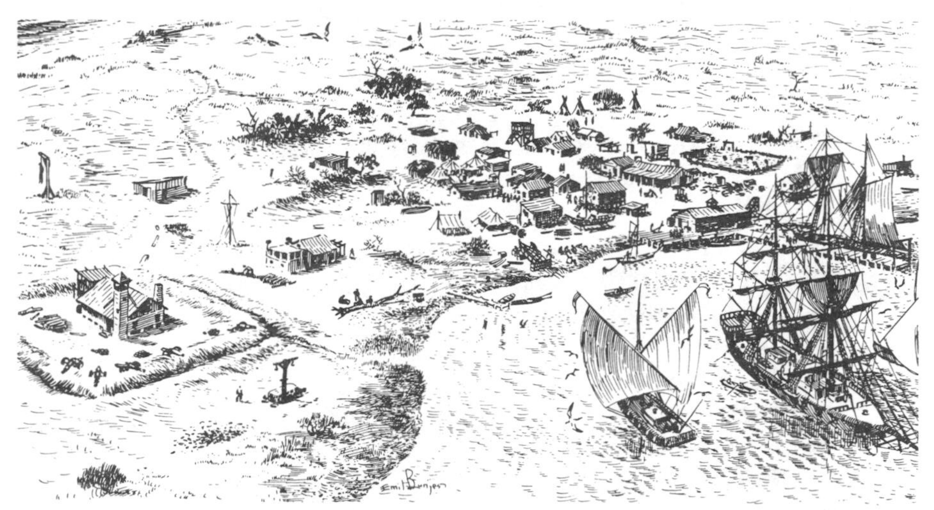

LAFITTE'S FORT — Pirate Jean Lafitte maintained a fleet of about twenty ships that operated out of headquarters on Galveston Island. The shanty town that grew up around his fort is thought to have had as many as 1,000 residents. Present-day Galveston is located where the old pirate city ruled in the 1820s. (Drawing courtesy of Rosenberg Library, Galveston)

Lafitte had probably reached mature standing in the "trade" when the War of 1812 with the British spilled over into Louisiana, which was a territory and not a state until 1812. Lafitte offered his services to the Americans but was rebuffed. The British sought his services, but it was not until Gen. Andrew Jackson was made commander of the American forces at New Orleans, and declared martial law, that the offer of the pirate was accepted. Lafitte's men received a full pardon for their crimes for their part in the victory over the British.[4]

After the War of 1812, Lafitte soon secured another fleet and obtained a commission from one of the struggling South American republics. He then resumed his attacks on Spanish commerce. Not having a base, since Barataria had been completely destroyed, he looked with favor on a revolutionary plan hatched up by Francisco Xavier Mina, with Louis-Michel Aury also as a player. As it so happened, Aury vacated his base on Galveston Island on May 18, 1817, and on June 3 Lafitte's fleet left New Orleans and took over the Galveston base.[5] Among Lafitte's trusted lieutenants at this time were James Campbell, Stephen Churchill, Lambert, Franks, Roach, Dominic You, Marotte, Pluche, Giral, Felix, Lopez, and Brown. As it turned out, Brown was not to be trusted. He captured and plundered an American vessel on the Sabine, and as soon as Lafitte heard the news he ordered Brown hanged. He also hanged another man for attempting to rob and murder an American who had visited the island for the purpose of purchasing slaves.[6]

Campeachy, as Lafitte's city was known, was built on the burned ruins of Aury's old camp on the bay side overlooking Pelican Island, where the pirate Brown was hanged. The town contained about a hundred crudely built huts, sometimes with glass windows but usually with sailcloth over the window openings. When the camp was first set up, the population was about 100; by the year's end it had increased to 800. The accommodations included boardinghouses for visiting buyers, a shipyard, saloons, pool halls, and gambling houses.[7] It had a mixed population of whites and mulattos, of many nationalities and a multitude of languages. Lafitte's women included two wives and many mistresses.

Lafitte lived in what was known as Maison Rouge (Red House), which was well provisioned and fortified and served as his headquarters. During bad weather he would turn his house over to the women and children, as in the hurricane that hit in September of 1818. This killer wind left a number dead, fourteen ships destroyed, and many houses blown away.[8]

Lafitte kept law and order in his community with a tribunal to hear cases for lawbreakers. It was sometimes referred to as his admiralty court. James Campbell, one of his captains, was placed in charge of the court, as well as the Bolivar Port Depot. Campeachy developed rapidly into a big slave market as more and more ships began to bring back loads of slaves. Lafitte was forced to build barracoons, or slave pens, capable of holding 1,000 slaves. Captain Campbell once brought in 308 slaves, of which 200 were bought by a single planter, Guy Champlain, of Mississippi. In 1853 John Bowie told that he and his brothers, James and Rezin, had made a $65,000 profit from the sale of 1,500 illegal Africans bought from Lafitte at Galveston between 1818 and 1820. The crush of slaves was so great that Lafitte built a slave barracks on the lower Sabine River, north of present-day Orange, in order to get them closer to the Louisiana plantations.[9]

The scope of the business can be seen from a report of Captain Campbell as he returned from a six-week voyage. He captured five Spanish prizes, along with $100,000 in gold doubloons and silver and cargo, hardware, and other dry goods of equal value. His ship, the *Concord,* was 120 tons with five guns and a crew of seventy-five. He became one of the leading captains in amount of booty brought back to Campeachy. He had a reputation of treating his Spanish captives mercifully and put them ashore at the first available port. Charles Croenea, who sailed as cabin boy on his last cruise in 1820, once said that he had "never seed a single man murdered" while aboard Campbell's ship.[10]

But, quite naturally, there was little honor among thieves—at least some of them. After the *Concord* was lost, Lafitte sent Campbell to sea with Capt. John Marotte, a man he mistrusted. The privateers captured three prizes: the *Cuba,* a slave ship loaded with Africans, and two galleons with dry goods, plate, coins, and merchandise equal to $200,000. Returning to base, the captain unloaded the slaves and some of the merchandise, but claimed that the silver, coins, and other valuables had been lost overboard. Campbell informed Lafitte that the valuables were hidden in secret compartments aboard the ship. Lafitte confronted Marotte, who challenged Lafitte to a duel, but backed down at the last minute. Ten days later, while Lafitte was aboard Marotte's ship, the disgruntled captain attempted to assassinate him but was shot by Campbell. Lafitte's bodyguards finished off the other seven plotters. Pirate justice was a bit rough.[11]

The pirates' stay on Galveston Island was finally put to an end by the United States government when Lieutenant Kearney was dispatched with orders for Lafitte to pack up and leave. After putting the torch to the island, Lafitte boarded the *Pride* and sailed away, leaving a chapter in the history of Galveston Island that will continue to grow as long as writers spin tales of buried pirate treasure and adventurers continue to seek the loot left behind by the pirates. The ships sailed away from the smoking ruins on May 12, 1820.[12]

Rio Grande River

When Juan de Onate first saw the Rio Grande River near El Paso in April of 1598, he paused long enough to give it a name: Rio Grande, or the Great River. In a 300-year period, it was first a Spanish river and then a Mexican river. It wasn't until the first session of the Texas Republic Congress that the boundaries of the new state dipped to the Rio Grande, thus giving the river an international flavor. But it took the Mexican War of 1846–48 before the river was recognized by both the United States and Mexico as an international boundary.

The Rio Grande is a mountain stream when it starts at the foot of the Continental Divide north of the San Juan Mountains in southern Colorado. It flows in a generally southeast direction through New Mexico until it comes to El Paso County, Texas, where it becomes the boundary between the United States and Mexico. The spring-fed character of the river changes when it breaks out of the mountains of New Mexico and enters a semi-dry area that continues on into Texas, where it meanders through the foothills of the Rockies and finally flows into the semi-arid area. In New Mexico the river is known as the Rio Del Norte. In the middle area it has always been the Rio Grande, while in the lower reaches it is still sometimes called Rio Bravo. The Pecos and Devil's rivers are the last major contributors of water to the Rio Grande from the Texas side of the border. More than three-fourths of the flow of the river in Texas comes from the Mexican side.

Texas counties that use 900 miles of the Rio Grande as their southern border include El Paso, Hudspeth, Presidio, Brewster, Terrell, Val Verde, Kinney, Maverick, Webb, Zapata, Starr, Hidalgo, and Cameron. All of these counties depend upon the waters of the Rio Grande for their survival in one way or another.

In the lower end of the Rio Grande lies the Magic Valley of the Rio Grande, where irrigation has brought great wealth and a completely different way of life. Irrigation has been practiced on the Rio Grande since the late part of the seventeenth century, when Spanish missionaries showed the Pueblo Indians how to build canals. Some of the ditches built in 1680 near Ysleta were used regularly into the 1940s.

It is doubtful whether the Rio Grande would have been used as extensively for steamboats had it not been for the Mexican War of 1846–48 and the Civil War. Gen. Zachary Taylor brought scores of paddlewheelers into the Rio Grande to move men and supplies into position to carry the war to the Mexicans. Steamboats were not new in the Rio Grande before 1845, but they were few in number.

The first steamboat on the Rio Grande, or in Texas, was the *Ariel* that Henry Austin introduced to the river in June 1829. In October the *Texas Gazette* reported that the *Ariel* had ranged as high as Revilla, which was about 300 miles from the mouth of the river, and was making regular runs between Matamoros and Camargo. Austin evidently wasn't satisfied with the monetary returns from the *Ariel,* so he removed her to the Brazos in August 1830.[1] Legends tell that Austin couldn't get used to the *"manana"* attitude of the Mexicans. He wasn't a great politician either and was rankled when several Mexican communities would not allow his steamboat to land because of the smoke from the ship's boilers.

Steamboats to the Rio Grande

General Taylor had commissioned Maj. John Saunders, an army engineer, to select and purchase enough steamboats to carry out the job of moving and supplying the army once they arrived at the Rio Grande. The first boat secured was the *Corvette,* a luxury liner taken off the Ohio River. That was followed by the *Grampus,* a 500-ton side wheeler; the *Comanche,* a sternwheeler of 200 tons; and the *Rancher,* a ship that was the star of the "Cortina War," as it carried $300,000 in bullion and mounted a cannon that helped "Rip" Ford's Rangers defeat a Mexican force. The *Rancher* later became a mail packet. Other steamers that joined the party on the Rio Grande included the *Globe, Colonel Cross, Major Brown, Bessie, Alamo, Matamoros I & II,* and others.[2]

It should be noted at this point that when General Taylor arrived with his army in 1846, there were no cities or towns on the Texas side of the Rio Grande. Communities existed only at Brownsville, Rio Grande City, and Hidalgo. In 1847 Henry Clay Davis, a trader and soldier of fortune, decided that he needed a home base and became the first American colonizer on the Rio Grande. Looking to the future, he constructed a wharf of sorts on the river and a couple of stores were built. The importance of his outpost was insignificant until General Taylor established Fort Ringgold within sight of Davis' port of Rio Grande City, which, as the head of navigation on the Rio Grande, became a trade center. When the army pulled out at the end of the war, the town slumped but stayed in business.[3]

Brownsville came into being when General Taylor decided to build a fort opposite the Mexican city of Matamoros. Fort Brown (first called Fort Texas) was named for Maj. Jacob Brown, who died during an artillery bombardment from across the river at Matamoros shortly after construction on the fort had started. Brownsville developed into a city in a short time and became the county seat of Cameron County in December 1848; in January 1850 it was incorporated. While Rio Grande City hesitated in growth, Brownsville went ahead at a rapid rate.[4]

During the opening years of the Mexican War, General Taylor won two outstanding battles on Texas soil (Palo Alto and Resaca de la Palma) near Brownsville, and then began regrouping and reorganizing for a push into the interior. It was at this point that the steamboats came into play, especially those being run by Capts. Richard King, Mifflin Kenedy, and Charles Stillman, all working for the government. It took about four days to make a round-trip from Boca del Rio, mouth of the Rio Grande, to Camargo, about 260 miles up the river, where Taylor was building up a staging point. Not all steamboats working the river at this time were under contract to the government. Quite a few were independents, and others would charter to the government for a specified time or trip.[5]

Steamboats Take Over

The *American Flag*, a newspaper of the day, carried notices of the increase in commerce on the Rio Grande. The steamer *Tom Kirkman* ran an ad announcing that their company had built warehouses at Rio Grande City (Davis Landing) and Camargo.

Owners of the steamer *Laurel* set a new schedule that called for semiweekly runs between Matamoros and ports upriver. Freight rates lower than those of other private boats on the river were advertised.

Bodman & Clarke advertised that the hotel-steamer *Frankland* was operating from the mouth of the Rio Grande.[6]

Peace was declared on February 2, 1848, between the United States and Mexico in what was to be known as the Treaty of Guadalupe Hidalgo. One of the most important clauses in the treaty, insofar as the countless steamboatmen on the Rio Grande were concerned, was that the Rio Grande, not the Nueces, was the boundary line between the United States and Mexico.

The delayed auction of the government's steamers was finally held on April 2, 1849. All interested rivermen were present and bidding on the six boats that were to be sold. Charles Stillman and his merchant partner, Samuel A. Belden, bought the *Hatchee Eagle* and the *Troy* at the public sale. Richard King purchased the *Colonel Cross* for $750, a boat that had cost the government $14,000 in Pittsburgh only three years before. This was the boat that King had operated while he worked for the government, so he knew its good points and what had to be done. He left his job as a bedmaker and bartender at Boca del Rio, hired a crew, and went into business for himself hauling freight up and down the Rio Grande.[7]

During the Mexican War the concentration of steamboats on the Rio Grande was impressive, but once the Treaty of

Guadalupe Hidalgo was signed on February 2, 1848, these ships became surplus.[8] A company was formed on March 1, 1850, composed of Mifflin Kenedy, Richard King, Charles Stillman, and Stillman's steamboater, James O'Donnell, known as M. Kenedy and Co. of Brownsville. In a short time they had a virtual monopoly on shipping up and down the Rio Grande River once they purchased a smaller rival company run by Jose San Roman and John Young, both former partners of Stillman. In the purchase King, Kenedy and Company received the steamers *Swan* and *Guadalupe*. By the 1850s, no fewer than twenty riverboats could be seen meandering up and down the river running between the mouth of the river and Camargo and Mier upriver.[9]

Steamboats Develop Area

M. Kenedy and Co. was in a good position to take advantage of a golden opportunity. They had a fleet of river steamboats ready to transport goods up the river and a series of offices and landings to take care of the business. During the Spanish rule, and later under Mexican leadership, import trade into the area south of the Rio Grande had been strictly controlled. All imports were compelled by law to enter through Vera Cruz, thus the people living in a wide band south of the Rio Grande had been starved for imports from the outside world. In 1823 Don Martín DeLeon made contact in New Orleans with two traders, a Spaniard by the name of Carlos Lazo and a Frenchman named Ramon Lafon, who knew of an unused harbor – Brazos Santiago – at the mouth of the Rio Grande. Martin chartered a schooner, loaded it with luxury goods that he thought would sell to the people south of the Rio Grande, and sailed to the secret harbor. The trip was a huge success, thus opening a window for merchandise from the United States to get into Mexico.[10]

Historians have concluded that the real reason for the Mexican War was not the land lying between the Nueces and Rio Grande rivers, but control over the rich trade with the towns below the Rio Grande. Mexicans felt that the key to this trade was the little port of Brazos Santiago.

It has been estimated that merchandise arriving at the Rio Grande River on ocean-going vessels and transshipped up the river on M. Kenedy and Co. boats amounted to $10–14 million annually. Fortunes were made by men in the trading business, and those controlling the freight business on the Rio Grande did not do badly themselves. However, they were faced with a big problem: Their old boats were not altogether suited for the Rio Grande. Richard King was named as the man to update the steamboat fleet. His idea was to build a heavy boat to lighter loads from the ocean-going vessels at Brazos Santiago and to run them over the bar at the mouth of the Rio Grande and possibly as high as Brownsville. A large warehouse would receive the goods and ship them upriver on smaller, specially constructed sternwheelers that could breast the swift current of the river in rounding bends without going aground. By 1857, the *Grampus II, Comanche,* and the *Ranchero* were on the river. They took the load off of the old boats.[11]

Brownsville

When it became obvious in 1846 that a war was going to be fought on the Rio Grande, the Anglo-Mexicans moved quickly to Matamoros. After the Treaty of Guadalupe Hidalgo was signed on February 2, 1848, most of the Anglos living on the south side of the river moved to the north side, possibly hoping to be able to influence the formation of the new city of Brownsville.

Cameron County, with Sta Rita as the county seat, was named for Capt. Ewen Cameron, leader of the failed escape of prisioners from the Mier Expedition. In the first election of officers, Israel Bigelow was named chief justice. In the years of 1847–49, a number of real estate developments sprang up in the vicinity of Brownsville, each hoping to make money for the promoters. Mansfield was the promotion of Asa Wheeler, who also ran the Washington House Restaurant and Grocery Store on Market Square. Freeport was the promotion of Capt. Patrick Shannon, who landed there in 1846 and operated a ferry with a warehouse and lumberyard at Shannon's Crossing. The old road from San Patricio and Port Isabel ended at this crossing.

It remained for Charles Stillman to organize the Brownsville Town Company and to promote its growth. Stillman's success was due to the fact that he had inside information that

BROWNSVILLE FERRY steamboat landing. This photo shows a steamboat at the Levee St. landing. The large building in center is company offices at the corner of 12th Street in Brownsville. (Photo courtesy Barker Texas History Center and Institute of Texan Cultures)

Fort Brown would move into a new area to seek protection from floods that beset the fort at its old location. Stillman built an impressive brick building to inspire confidence and laid out streets and set aside land for a public park. A disputed land title caused others to promote the same area. The difficulties were finally settled and the county seat was moved from Sta Rita to Brownsville. In its first two years, Brownsville grew to have a population of 3,000.

Brownsville grew much in the same format as Matamoros, with Mexican-style brick buildings flush with the edge of the street and Anglo-style frame houses. The first public school was started on April 17, 1854. Growth in the business world was along two fronts. The old Matamoros merchants opened stores in Brownsville, and a number of men who came to Mexico with Taylor's army stayed and opened businesses, namely, Charles Stillman, businessman; H.E. Woodhouse, merchant and packing house owner; Richard King, young riverboat captain; Mifflin Kenedy, a riverboat owner; William Clark, founder of Clarksville; Henry Miller; and John Webb. Miller helped develop Brownsville, and John Butler brought supplies to Taylor's army and then worked for Lloyds of London and was a prosperous merchant. Add to this list a host of the men who served with Taylor and chose to remain in Brownsville and make their homes. James G. Browne, an Irishman, settled first in San Patricio then moved to Brownsville, where he contracted to construct barracks at Fort Polk and Fort Brown. He became a successful merchant and his brother, William, an undertaker.[12]

Brownsville and the Civil War

Brownsville grew into a commercial center. Mifflin Kenedy and Richard King emerged as giants on the river, and were just as big ashore. As the federal blockade of eastern ports of the Confederacy began to take hold, business in Brownsville increased. When the Port of New Orleans was taken, the Cotton Road from the Old South ran cotton to the Rio Grande. The road ran through East Texas to Goliad and San Patricio on the Nueces River. From the Nueces River the road funneled through the King Ranch and also on the old Matamoros road. When the cotton reached Brownsville, it was lightered out to foreign ships at Brazos Santiago or at Bagdad, a Gulfside port at the mouth of the river on the Mexican side of the Rio Grande. Bagdad turned into a city of hastily built shacks almost overnight.

During the fall of 1863, King, Kenedy, and Stillman joined forces to move cotton to overseas markets. Captain King's job was to keep the wagon trains running from San Patricio to King Ranch and on to Brownsville. Kenedy worked to move the cotton across the river, while Stillman's job was overseeing the transportation of the cotton by land or river to Bagdad. Proof that the cotton was moving can be seen from official reports on the number of foreign ships anchored outside at Bagdad: 1862, 20 ships; 1863, 60 to 70; late 1864, 200 to 300; 1865, no report.[13]

When the Union forces finally did occupy Brownsville in late November of 1863, the flow of cotton did not stop. It was merely directed above Brownsville, even as high as Rio Grande

City to be taken across the river. Union forces held Brownsville until July of 1864. That, of course, meant a long overland trip by ox carts to Bagdad. By the end of the war the blockade was still leaking, but the cotton passing through had been reduced to a trickle.[14]

On July 25, 1864, Col. Rip Ford's forces moved toward Brownsville from their staging area at Rio Grande City. There were some minor skirmishes before the forces of the Cavalry of the West moved toward the town. On July 29 the Union forces moved out of Brownsville and down the river to Brazos Santiago, where they threw up fortifications. The Confederate forces rode into Fort Brown on July 30, 1864, and found it in better shape than when they had abandoned it. Colonel Ford found himself in a difficult position. French forces occupied Bagdad. The Union forces were menacing from their camp at Brazos Santiago and the Mexican General Cortina was making trouble from Matamoros.

The last shot that was fired in the Rio Grande in the Civil War, on May 13, 1865, was supposedly fired by a fourteen-year-old drummer boy who fired his rifle at a flash of an exploding shell.

"Boys," Rip Ford said, "we have done finely. We will let well enough alone, and retire."[15]

Colonel Ford's men decided that the cause of the Confederacy was lost and it was time for them to go home. Sometime near the end of May, most of Ford's men rode to the north and home. On May 26, 1865, Colonel Ford took his family to Matamoros, Mexico, where they stayed until Gen. Frederick Steele, commander of the United States forces on the Rio Grande (the Confederacy had surrendered) arrived in Brownsville. Ford presented himself to the general and was paroled. Later Ford, despite being a sick man, was appointed commissioner of paroles for the Confederate troops in the area. Ford is credited for the lack of malice during the takeover by Federal officials in the Valley. Richard King appeared before General Steele to plead for Ford when he turned himself over to the Federals. Later it is believed that Ford made it easier for King to have his citizenship restored.[16]

In many ways the affairs of Colonel Ford in Brownsville closely parallel those of the people of Brownsville. During the struggle a large number of Confederate troops deserted and went to Mexico. Ford convinced a number to return and accept parole and go on with their lives, which is what Ford did.

The period after the war in Brownsville, and on the Rio Grande, saw an increase in lawlessness. Soldiers without work turned to smuggling and cattle rustling. The "duty free" zone created along the border by Porfirio Diaz, president of Mexico, encouraged all sorts of banditry.[17]

King and Kenedy went about reestablishing their steamboats on the Rio Grande as fast as possible. All of their boats had been transferred to Mexican ownership, and this had to be reversed. The job of restoring the old boats, and buying new ones, was a formidable task. One of the first acts of Union authorities was the seizure of the *Matamoros, Mustang, James Hale,* and the *Senorita.* However, it appears that they were able to buy back their old boats and to operate them. Four new boats, made to the captains' specifications, were on the river by the summer of 1865. These boats were the *Antonio, Eugenia, Tamaulipas,* and *Camargo.* Early in 1866 the *Enterprise* and *El Primero* appeared on the river. It was obvious that M. Kenedy and Co. had come through the war with a great deal of their financial wealth intact. King and Kenedy were able to keep their boats busy by establishing lines to Federal officials. Soon they were submitting the low bids and were carrying all government freight. Stillman, who had been a part of the development of transportation on the Rio Grande, sold out and moved to New York, taking with him enough money that he was able to develop the National City Bank of New York. Along with the withdrawal of Stillman, James Walworth, another partner, died. After these changes the company took on a new name: King, Kenedy & Co.[18]

In 1867 a hurricane with destructive winds crushed the Rio Grande Valley, destroying Bagdad and Clarksville and knocking down most of the buildings at Brazos Santiago and Point Isabel. King & Kenedy lost four steamboats, and this had an adverse affect on business on the river. Within a short time both King and Kenedy left the river to devote full time to their ranching interests. King eventually turned the King Ranch into one of the largest and most profitable ranches in the world. Kenedy's holdings became the basis of the dynasty of the

Kenedys of South Texas. On May 5, 1874, King and Kenedy sold their steamboat enterprise to Capt. William Kelly, a captain of one of the company's boats. Before this sale Richard King and Mifflin Kenedy had reached an agreement that had divided their other interests so that when the steamboat interests were dissolved, each was free to go his separate way. With the signing of the final agreement in 1868, the two men began fencing their respective lands. Not only had an era ended on the river, but an era of unfenced range land in South Texas had also ended.[19]

The end of the King-Kenedy dynasty was not necessarily deplored by everyone in Brownsville. Most of the exponents of free trade were encouraged and looked to the purchase of the King, Kenedy & Co. steamboats by Capt. William Kelly as a good omen for business. Brownsville interests were also encouraged when the Mexican government ended free trade agreements; thus Matamoros lost its edge over Brownsville.[20]

Brownsville, as it faced the future, had excellent prospects for growth – but not from steamboats. When Capt. William Kelly had purchased King, Kenedy & Co.'s fleet of sixteen riverboats, business conditions on the river still looked good. With the opening of the Rio Grande Railroad, things went steadily downhill for the steamboats until by 1893 only one small boat was left in the trade. Steamboat days on the mighty Rio Grande River were gone forever.[21]

Rio Grande City/Fort Ringgold

Rancho Davis was established on the Rio Grande River's north side in 1847, and shortly it was known as Rio Grande City. The trading post consisting of several stores, warehouses, and wharves to take care of the regular steamboat traffic were in place in a few years. Merchandise destined for the interior of Mexico was brought up the river by paddleboats to Rio Grande City and then ferried across the river to be loaded on ox carts for transportation to interior communities.

Col. Henry Clay Davis was introduced to Mexico, and the Rio Grande River, in 1839 when he entered the area with the Army of the Republic of the Rio Grande. The scheme to set up an independent republic failed, but Davis liked the country and stayed behind and married a daughter of the well-known de la

Garza family of Camargo. He became well respected in the area. During the Mexican War, he gave valuable assistance to General Taylor's forces.

Rio Grande City became of age in 1848, when Zachary Taylor established Fort Ringgold just outside the town. This not only brought more traffic up the river, but a number of permanent settlers and business houses followed the establishment of the army post. A post office was established in 1849.[22]

Since Rio Grande City was at the head of navigation on the Rio Grande for many years, Davis was in a good position to carry on trade on both sides of the border. An active smuggling base grew up just across the river.

The owners of the steamer *Tom Kirkman* maintained a warehouse at Rio Grande City and regularly ran a ship upriver to service the area.

A port city sixteen miles upriver from Rio Grande City was developed in 1848 by interests trying to offset the strangle hold that Davis had on upriver trade through the control of all shipping at his port. Mifflin Kenedy was a part of this group.

At one time Gen. Jose Marie Jesus Carbajal moblized his Mexican followers on the Texas side of the river near Rio Grande City before moving across the river to do battle. On more than one occasion this distant trading post was the scene of meetings between freebooters, members of forces opposed to the current Mexican government, as well as other malcontents.

Rio Grande City for a time was the terminus of the Cotton Road. The primary road ran from San Patricio on the Nueces River through the King Ranch to Brownsville and then across the river to Bagdad. When Union forces began to interfere at Brownsville, the wagon trains turned north and unloaded their goods at Rio Grande City. Fort Ringgold stood as a guardian there to keep local bandits from looting the wagon trains. On their return trip the wagoners carried loads of leather goods, clothing, blankets, guns, ammunition, and medical supplies that were badly needed by the Confederate forces.

In November of 1863 Federal forces captured Brownsville, and units of the First Texas Union Cavalry occupied Rio Grande City for a short time. They also captured a supply of cotton that was awaiting shipment down the river on the Mexican side by wagons to Bagdad.[23]

After considerable delay, the Cavalry of the West, under the command of Col. Rip Ford, moved back into the area, first at Captain King's Ranch, which had been raided by Federal forces. The splintered Confederate command finally got together, and the headquarters for the expeditionary forces was established at Fort Ringgold, now in Confederate hands, in July 1864. It was from here that Ford and about 200 men circled to the south side of a troop of about 250 Union soldiers at an outpost about twenty-four miles above Brownsville. He drove the Union forces out of their positions and pulled off a victory that helped the Union commander at Brownsville decide to pull his forces back to the coast.[24] When Colonel Ford's forces reached Laredo on April 17, 1864, there were a number of commands in the area, including Lieutenant Colonel Showalter, Captain Cater, Colonel Giddings, and Major Nolan. These forces were made a part of the Cavalry of the West.[25]

Life on the Rio Grande was dicey at the best. The area was subject to raids of Mexican guerrillas, paid by the Union to stir up trouble; deserters from the Confederate forces, who were not eager to be identified; and Union sympathizers and others who were trying to stay out of harm's way. Smuggling operations also split border towns like Rio Grande City. Independent operators were constantly trying to get into the cotton operation carried on by the Confederacy.[26] Rio Grande City was the western terminus of the Rio Grande City Railroad.[27]

Port Isabel

While not a port on the Rio Grande, Point Isabel or Port Isabel was featured in early plans of explorers, traders, and soldiers seeking a way to enter Mexico and the Lower Rio Grande River.

The area was first settled by Mexican ranchers as early as 1770. In 1820 Fray Nicolas Balli took his herds of cattle from Point Isabel across to Padre Island to save them from raiding parties during the Mexican Revolution. Zachary Taylor used the town for a base of supplies brought into the harbor of Brazos Santiago. In the California gold rush of 1849, prospectors would enter at Brazos Santiago and gather their supplies and transportation at Port Isabel for their push westward to California. A railroad was built from Port Isabel to Brownsville in 1871, but it was put out of action by storms of 1873 and 1875.[28]

Hidalgo

Probably Hidalgo was never a major stopping point for the river steamboats because it was just a collection of Mexican huts during the early 1800s. When empresario José de Escandon made an effort to establish communities on the north bank of the Rio Grande, the settlements bore various names, such as La Habitacion, Rancho San Luis, and San Luisito. A ferry operated from Hidalgo to Reynosa on the Mexican side until it was replaced by an international bridge. It was the county seat of Hidalgo County for a short time. As the community grew, a section away from the river was called Edinburg and the county seat was moved there. The river community reverted to Hidalgo.[29]

Hidalgo probably never developed as a river port since Reynosa, just across the river, was a trading center. With a ferry to link the two cities, it was probably easier to trade across the river.

Notes

Red River

1. Walter Prescott Webb, ed., *The Handbook of Texas* (Austin: Texas State Historical Association, 1952), 2: 449, 450.

2. Henry Sinclair Drago, *The Steamboaters* (New York: Dodd, Mead & Company, 1967), 70, 73, 74, 76, 77, 79, 80, 81, 82, 84, 85, 86, 87.

4. Carl N. Tyson, *Red River in Southeastern History* (Norman: University of Oklahoma Press, 1981), 92, 93.

5. *Ibid.*, 94, 95, 97, 99, 100, 150.

6. *Ibid.*, 150, 152.

Grayson County

1. Walter Prescott Webb, ed., *The Handbook of Texas* (Austin: Texas State Historical Association, 1952), 1: 252, 369, 726, 2: 379, 410; Mattie Davis Lucas and Mita Holsapple Hall, *History of Grayson County* (Sherman: Scruggs Printing Co., 1936), 68.

2. Lucas and Hall, *Grayson County,* 64, 65.

3. *Ibid.*, 69.

4. Charles Deaton, *Texas Postal History Handbook* (Privately printed, 1991), 141; Harry M. Konwiser, *Texas Republic Postal System* (New York: Harry L. Lindquist, 1933), 21.

5. *Handbook of Texas,* 1: 726; Lucas and Hall, *Grayson County,* 90, 91, 146.

6. Deaton, *Texas Postal History Handbook,* 132; Lucas and Hall, *Grayson County,* 60, 68, 91.

7. Grayson County Frontier Village, *History of Grayson County,* Vol. 2 (Tulsa: Heritage Publishing Co.), 33, 34.

8. Lucas and Hall, *Grayson County,* 68, 90; *Handbook of Texas,* 2: 599.

9. Lucas and Hall, *Grayson County,* 91.

10. *Ibid.*, 146; *Handbook of Texas,* 1: 371.

11. Lucas and Hall, *Grayson County,* 146, 149.

12. *Handbook of Texas,* 1: 509; Jo Lou Spleth, "Ruddy Red of the North," *Texas Highways* (December 1991): 15, 16.

13. *Handbook of Texas,* 1: 341–342.
14. Lucas and Hall, *Grayson County,* 144.
15. *Handbook of Texas,* 2: 599.

Fannin County

1. Walter Prescott Webb, ed., *The Handbook of Texas* (Austin: Texas State Historical Association, 1952), 1: 583; Rex Wallace Strickland, "History of Fannin County, Texas, 1836–43," *Southwestern Historical Quarterly* 33: 262–273; Charles Deaton, *Texas Postal History Handbook* (Privately printed, 1991), 77.
2. *Handbook of Texas,* 1: 583, 2: 511; Strickland, "Fannin County," 262–273.
3. Strickland, "Fannin County," 262–273.
4. *Fannin County Folks and Facts* (Dallas: Taylor Publishers, 1977), 9.
5. *Ibid.*
6. *Ibid.,* 271.
7. *Ibid.,* 269, 271 fn32.
8. *Handbook of Texas,* 2: 864.
9. Gerald S. Pierce, *Texas Under Arms* (Austin: Encino Press, 1969), 176, 177.
10. Deaton, *Texas Postal History Handbook,* 151.
11. Pierce, *Texas Under Arms,* 77.
12. *Handbook of Texas,* 1: 369.
13. *Ibid.,* 2: 433.
14. *Fannin County Folks and Facts,* 78.
15. *Ibid.*
16. *Ibid.*

Lamar County

1. Walter Prescott Webb, ed., *The Handbook of Texas* (Austin: Texas State Historical Association, 1952) 2:15, 938.
2. *Ibid.,* 1: 641, 657.
3. A. W. Neville, *History of Lamar County* (Paris, TX: North Texas Publishing Co., 1937), 82.
4. *Ibid.,* 86.
5. *Ibid.,* 96.
6. *Ibid.*

Red River County

1. Walter Prescott Webb, ed., *The Handbook of Texas* (Austin: Texas State Historical Association, 1952), 2: 452.
2. William Ransom Hogan, *The Texas Republic* (Austin: University of Texas Press, 1990), 6, 7, 69, 79, 80; E. W. Bowers Papers, in possession of Anne Evetts of Clarksville, a granddaughter, 8, 9, 10, 11.
3. *Handbook of Texas,* 2: 937; *A History of Present Red River*

County, Texas, Area Through 1845, vertical file on Red River County, Clarksville Public Library, 31.

4. *Red River County,* 31-36.
5. Bowers Papers, 4.
6. *Ibid.*
7. *Ibid.,* 3.
8. *Red River County,* 36.
9. *Handbook of Texas,* 1: 928.
10. Bowers Papers, 4.
11. *Red River County,* 36.
12. Bowers Papers, 4, 5, 6, 7.
13. *Red River County,* 35.
14. *Handbook of Texas,* 1: 928; John Osburn, *Jonesboro: Its Historical Significance* (historical marker copy from the files of Texas Historical Commission).
15. Pat B. Clark, *History of Clarksville and Old Red River County* (Dallas: Mathis, Van Nort & Co., 1937), 7.
16. Bernice Lockhart, "Navigating Texas Rivers," master's thesis, St. Mary's University, 1946, 112.
17. Clark, *History of Clarksville,* 91; Bowers Papers, 9.
18. Interview with Mary Kate Hale of Clarksville, June 1, 1992.
19. Bowers Papers, 1; original instruments in possession of Mary Kate Hale.
20. Charles Deaton, *Texas Postal History Handbook* (Privately printed, 1991), 79.
21. Hale interview.
22. Bowers Papers, 10.
23. *Ibid.,* 18.
24. *Ibid.,* 15, 16.
25. *Ibid.,* 19.
26. *Ibid.,* 10.
27. *Handbook of Texas,* 1: 186, 357-358, 2: 939; A. W. Neville, *The History of Lamar County* (Paris, TX: North Texas Publishing Co., 1937), 10, 79, 80, 81, 82, 83, 84; Clark, *History of Clarksville,* 6-9, 88; *History of Red River County, Texas Through 1845,* 31-34; *Southwestern Historical Quarterly* 47: 216, 217; clippings on steamboats, vertical file, Clarksville Public Library; Rex Wallace Strickland, "History of Fannin County, Texas, 1836-1843," *Southwestern Historical Quarterly* 33: 262-273.
28. "The National Road of the Republic of Texas," *Southwestern Historical Quarterly* 47: 216, 216fn, 217.
29. Bowers Papers, 1; A. W. Neville, ed., *The Red River Valley Then and Now* (Paris, TX: North Texas Publishing, 1948).
30. Bowers Papers, 12, 13, 14.
31. *Ibid.,* 17.
32. *Dallas Times Herald,* September 5, 1957; *The National Observer,* December 7, 1970; unmarked clippings dated Saturday, September 2, 1967; *Dallas Morning News,* August 6, 1957, and May 7, 1958, all in vertical file, Clarksville Public Library.

Bowie County

1. Walter Prescott Webb, ed., *The Handbook of Texas* (Austin: Texas State Historical Association, 1952), 1: 198, 2: 191, 871.
2. *The Red River Planter,* 80; William Ransom Hogan, *The Texas Republic* (Austin: University of Texas Press, 1990), 80.
3. J. J. Scheffelin, *Bowie County, Texas, Basic Background Book* (Privately printed), 108.
4. Barbara Overton Chandler and J. Ed Howe, *History of Texarkana and Bowie and Miller Counties* (Texarkana: Texas-Arkansas, 1939), 97-106.
5. E. W. Bowers Papers, in possession of Anne Evetts of Clarksville, a granddaughter, 3 (case tried before Judge John T. Mills in Red River County).

Jefferson

1. Walter Prescott Webb, ed., *The Handbook of Texas* (Austin: Texas State Historical Association, 1952), 2: 450-451.
2. Fred Tarpley, *Jefferson: Riverport to the Southwest* (Austin: Eakin Press, 1983), 33.
3. *Louisiana Historical Quarterly* 25: 25, 396-525.
4. V. H. Hackney, *Port Caddo – A Vanished Village* and *Vignettes of Harrison County* (Marshall: The Marshall National Bank), 26.
5. Tarpley, *Jefferson,* 41.
6. *Ibid.,* 42, 43.
7. "Marion County," vertical file, Jefferson Carnegie Public Library, 1105.
8. Tarpley, *Jefferson,* 44, 45; Rebecca M. Cameron and Ruth Lester, *Jefferson on the Bayou* (Marshall: The Demmer Co., Inc., 1966), "Historic Homes," 10.
9. *Jefferson Jimplecute,* June 17, 1965.
10. Clarksville *Northern Standard,* April 17, 1844.
11. *Ibid.*
12. Tarpley, *Jefferson,* 50.
13. William Ransom Hogan, *The Texas Republic* (Austin: University of Texas Press, 1990), 7.
14. Tarpley, *Jefferson,* 51.
15. *Marshall News Messenger,* 1859.
16. *Ibid.,* 1866; Charles Deaton, *Texas Postal History Handbook* (Privately printed, 1991), 109.
17. *Handbook of Texas,* 2: 145.
18. "Marion County," 1104.
19. Judy Watson, "Jefferson, Texas, The Rise and Decline," master's thesis, Texas Christian University, January 1967, 14.
20. Mrs. Arch McKay and Mrs. H. A. Spellings, *A History of Jefferson* (Jefferson: Episcopal Church), 4.

21. Cameron and Lester, *Jefferson on the Bayou,* 10-16.

22. *Ibid.,* 21, 22.

23. Watson, "Jefferson, Texas," 20.

24. Winnie Mims Dean, *Jefferson, Queen of the Cypress* (Dallas: Mathis Van Nort & Co., 1953), 67, 68; Watson, "Jefferson, Texas," 21, 22.

25. *Handbook of Texas,* 1: 943, 944.

26. Dean, *Queen of the Cypress,* 68, 69; "Marion County," Jefferson Public Library, vertical file, 1106; Watson, "Jefferson, Texas," 74.

27. Watson, "Jefferson, Texas," 32, 33.

28. McKay and Spellings, *History of Jefferson,* 11, 12, 13, 14; Cameron and Lester, *Jefferson on the Bayou,* 19, 22. Other merchants were: Russell, Rainey and Co., Wholesale Grocers and Commission Merchants; Ellis Bagby and Co., Wholesale Grocers and Commission Merchants; Bateman & Bro., Wholesale Grocers and Commission Merchants; Bogel & Riddle, Wholesale Grocers and Commission Merchants; Norwood & Scott, Commission Merchants; S. Frankle, Commission Merchant; Bell & Robinson, Commission Merchants, and Real Estate Agents; Torrans & Rives, Commission Merchants and Cotton Buyers; B. J. Terry, Cotton Factor; Wayland & Whatley, Wholesale Grocers; J. G. Fellner, Jr., Wholesale Grocer; Collins, Epperson & Ezell, Wholesale Grocers; T. J. Rogers, Wholesale Grocer.

Barns & Ellington, Wholesale Grocers; F. Robinson, Wholesale Grocer; R. C. Baker, Wholesale Grocer; Jno. A. Fielder, Grocer and Importer of Fancy Goods; J. M. Murphy, Grocer and General Merchandise; O. C. Herrenkind, Retail Grocer; Nance & Modrall, Retail Grocers; E. Marx, General Merchandise, Wholesale; P. Eldridge & Bro., General Merchandise; Mooring & Lyon, General Merchandise; K. Meyer, General Merchandise, Birge, Nickols & Co., Dry Goods, Wholesale; James Hoban, Dry Goods; F. A. Schluter & Son, Dry Goods, Staple and Fancy; Sims & Norris, Dry Goods; S. W. Stone, Hardware Merchant; John C. Kolter & Co., Hardware Merchants; R. Ballauf and Co., Hardware; Boney & Brooks, Druggist, Wholesale and Retail.

E. W. Taylor, Druggist and Bookseller; W. J. Sedberry, Druggist and Bookseller; Bradford, Bridge & Co., Furniture and Carriages; J. Bruckmuller, Furniture Dealer; W. H. Wyman, Furniture Manufacturer and Dealer; Rufus Muse & Co., Wholesale Dealer in Liquors, Tobacco and Cigars; Taylor & Pinson, Agricultural Implements and Machinery; R. Man Waring, Real Estate Owner; Dopplemayer & Eberstadt, Real Estate Owners; Ney & Bro., Real Estate Owners; V. H. Clairborne, Real Estate Owner; Ward Taylor, Real Estate Owner; W. C. Baker, Real Estate Owner; L. Moody, Property Owner; R. Towers, Property Owner; T. G. Anderson, General Insurance Agent; Cotton Bros., General Insurance Agents; Frank O. Seth, General Agent, Universal Life Insurance Co.; Gilbert & Co., Agents for Capitalists and Manufacturers;

J. A. H. Hosack, Auctioneer and Real Estate Broker; W. H. Johnson, District Clerk and Notary Public; W. E. Kneeland, Notary Public; Edward Gutheridge, Deputy District Clerk and Notary Public; J. Oppenheimer, Recorder and Collector of City of Jefferson; S. A. Thompson, Boot and Shoe Manufacturer and Dealer; Lawrence & Reaton, Crockery, China and

Glassware; J. H. Carlin, Merchant Tailor; Hugo Fox, Manufacturer of Candies; J. B. Tullis, Surgeon Dentist; Adam Stroll, Butcher; G. A. Kelly, Proprietor Kelly's Foundry; Morris, McKeown & Co., Proprietors of Foundry and Machine Manufactory; E. W. Morten, Proprietor National Cotton Compress; Trice Stewart & Co., Proprietors of Jefferson Planing Mill; J. B. Ligon, Building Contractor; Crump & Hunsucker, Builders; C. F. L. Smity, Civil and Mechanical Engineer; J. M. Tucker, Alderman; Geo. W. Roberts, Supt. Jefferson Chamber of Commerce; Capt. W. H. Coit, Principal Coit's Military and Commercial Academy; Roots & Hynson, Railroad Contractors; *Jefferson Democrat,* Miller, McEachern and Alexander, Proprietors, J. B. McEachern, Editor; *Jefferson Times,* R. W. Loughery, Editor and Proprietor; J. C. Rogers & Co., Printers, Lithographers, Wholesale and Retail Books, Stationery, Blank Books, etc.

L. T. Gray, Mayor of Jefferson City; A. G. Clopton, M.D., President of Chamber of Commerce; Capt. J. M. DeWare, Chief of Police, Jefferson; Mason & Campbell, Lawyers; Moseley & Sparks, Attorneys and Land Agents; Crawford & Crawford, Attorneys at Law; Epperson & Maxey, Attorneys at Law; Penn & Todd, Lawyers; M. F. Moore, Attorney at Law; Reeves & Word, Attorneys at Law; Thomas J. Hudson, Attorney at Law; R. DeJernett, Physician and Surgeon; L. S. Rayfield, Physician and Surgeon; G. H. Wootten, Physician; S. Eason, Physician and Surgeon; A. P. Brown, Physician and Surgeon; A A. Terhune, Physician and Surgeon; National Bank, W. M. Harrison, President; Citizens Saving Bank, W. Q. Bateman, President and Jno. M. Lewis, Cashier; James Arbuckle and Co., Bankers; J. A. Norsworthy and Cox, Bankers; Earstus Jones, Banker.

29. Watson, "Jefferson, Texas," 80.

30. Cameron and Lester, *Jefferson on the Bayou,* 15, 21, 22.

31. McKay and Spellings, *History of Jefferson,* 15; Watson, "Jefferson, Texas," 37.

32. *Marshall News Messenger,* March 1883.

33. Cameron and Lester, *Jefferson on the Bayou,* 23.

34. "Diamond Bessie Case, One of Most Notorious in Texas History," newspaper clipping in Jefferson Carnegie Library, vertical file, undated.

35. Dean, *Jefferson,* 130, 131, 132, 133.

36. *Marshall News Messenger,* March 1877.

37. Watson, "Jefferson, Texas," 81.

38. List taken from Jefferson *Jimplecute* in vertical file of Jefferson Public Library.

39. Watson, "Jefferson, Texas," 81.

40. Cameron and Lester, *Jefferson on the Bayou,* 23, 24, 25.

CADDO LAKE

1. Mildred Mays McClung, *Caddo Lake: Mysterious Swampland* (Texarkana: Southwest Printers, 1974), 14.

2. Walter Prescott Webb, ed., *The Handbook of Texas* (Austin: Texas State Historical Association, 1952), 1: 267.

3. McClung, *Caddo Lake,* 14.

4. *Ibid.*, 13.
5. *Handbook of Texas,* 1: 264-266.
6. Marquis James, *The Raven*, 101.
7. V. H. Hackney, *Port Caddo — A Vanished Village* (Marshall: The Marshall National Bank), 24.
8. *Handbook of Texas,* 1: 780, 2: 452.
9. *Ibid.*, 1: 6.
10. Hackney, *Port Caddo,* 6, 7.
11. Caddo Facts and Figures, Legends and History, Harrison County; unidentified clippings in vertical file, Harrison County Historical Museum.
12. *Handbook of Texas,* 1: 450.
13. Hackney, *Port Caddo,* 6, 7.
14. Wyatt Moore, *Every Sun that Rises,* edited by Thad Sitton and James H. Conrad (Austin: University of Texas Press, 1985), 24, 25.
15. *Louisiana Historical Quarterly* 25: 396-535; Harrison County Historical Museum, Marshall, vertical file.
16. Lentz Papers, Harrison County Historical Museum.
17. Hackney, *Port Caddo,* 26, 27, 28.
18. Mildred McClung, *Caddo Lake: Mysterious Swampland* (Texarkana: Southwest Printers, 1974), 52.
19. Harry M. Konwiser, *Texas Republic Postal System* (New York: Harry L. Lindquist, 1933), 20.
20. Hackney, *Port Caddo,* 24.
21. *Ibid.*, 15.
22. Lentz papers.
23. Rev. Billy B. Bonner, booklet prepared by Lions Club in 1959.
24. Hackney, *Port Caddo,* 31, 32.
25. *Stagecoach Road,* pamphlet in Harrison County Museum, 15, 19; Hackney, *Port Caddo,* 2, 29.
26. Hackney, *Port Caddo,* 29.
27. Notes in vertical file, Harrison County Historical Museum.
28. Paper in Eudora Solomon and V. H. Hackney file, Harrison County Historical Museum.
29. Caddo Facts and Figures, Legends and History, Harrison County; unidentified clippings, vertical file, Harrison County Historical Museum.
30. "The Sinking of the *Mittie Stephens,*" files of Texas State Archives, Austin.
31. Hackney, *Port Caddo,* 15.
32. Joe Tom Davis, *Legendary Texians,* Vol. 3 (Austin: Eakin Press, 1986), 143-165.
33. Landing mentioned in Franklin Jones' tapes of interviews with Wyatt Moore.
34. Tapes by Franklin Jones, Sr.

MONTEREY

1. Daniel Horace Boon, "Monterey," paper submitted to East Texas State Teachers College, Commerce, summer term 1947 (Boon was county judge of Cass County and noted local historian); map of Caddo Parish, Louisiana, enlarged, showing part of Harrison and Marion counties dated 1871 (Marion County was formed out of Cass County in 1860) *Handbook of Texas,* 1: 306.
2. Boon, "Monterey," 12.
3. Charles Deaton, *Texas Postal History Handbook* (Privately printed, 1991), 121; Boon, "Monterey," 3.
4. Boon, "Monterey," 3.
5. *Ibid.,* 11.
6. Annual Report of Clinton or Van Zant Lodge No. 42 for year 1848. (This was the Monterey Masonic Lodge.)
7. Boon, "Monterey," 11.
8. *Ibid.,* 4, 5.
9. *Ibid.,* 13.
10. Joe Tom Davis, *Legendary Texians* Vol. 3 (Austin: Eakin Press, 1986), 122.

BRAZOS RIVER

1. *Los Brazos de Dios,* unidentified article entitled "Brazos de Dios" by Mrs. J. B. Fowler, vertical file, Richmond Museum; Fannie May Barbee Hughs, *Legends of Texas Rivers* (Callas: Mathis, Van Nort & Co., 1937), 97–109. *Legends of Texas Rivers,* 97–109; Julien Hyden, *Texas: The Land of Beginning Again* (Waco: Texian Press, 1990); J. Frank Dobie, *On the Open Range* (Dallas: The Southwest Press, 1940), 236, 237.
2. Walter Prescott Webb, ed., *The Handbook of Texas* (Austin: Texas State Historical Association, 1952), 1: 211, 212.
3. Waco *Weekly-Tribune,* June 3, 1905; *Galveston Daily News,* June 22, 1836.
4. D. E. E. Braman, *History of Texas* (Philadelphia: J. B. Lippincott & Co., 1857).
5. John Q. Anderson, *Tales of Frontier Texas 1830–1860* (Dallas: Southern Methodist University Press, 1966), 133.
6. *History of Waller County,* Waller County Survey Committee, 28–32.
7. "The Great Brazos River Levee," vertical file, Bryan Public Library.
8. *Handbook of Texas,* 3: 106, 107.

Surfside

1. James Maughn and Tim Johnson, "Surfside," in Brazoria County Historical Museum vertical file; *Texas Almanac,* 1990–91, 299.
2. "Fort Velasco Project still in limbo," *Brazosport Facts,* vertical file of Brazoria County Historical Museum.
3. "Fort Velasco project" and "Surfside," articles printed in *Brazosport Facts,* in vertical file of Brazoria County Historical Museum.

Quintana

1. R. S. Alcott, "Old Quintana," Brazoria County Historical Museum, Quintana file, 1.
2. Mattie Austin Hatcher, ed., *Letters of an Early American Traveler* (Dallas: Southwest Press, 1933), 72.
3. Walter Prescott Webb, ed., *The Handbook of Texas* (Austin: Texas State Historical Association, 1952), 2: 424; Alcott, "Old Quintana," 2.
4. Alcott, "Old Quintana," 7.
5. Marie Beth Jones, first of a series of articles written about Quintana in *Angleton Times,* January 31, 1960.
6. Pamela Ashworth Puryear and Nath Winfield, Jr., *Sandbars and Sternwheelers* (College Station: Texas A&M Press, 1989), 44.
7. James A. Creighton, *History of Brazoria County* (Waco: Texian Press, 1976), 191.
8. *Angleton Times,* February 10, 1960.
9. Marie Beth Jones, "Quintana Tale Revives Memories," *Angleton Times,* March 1960.
10. "Quintana Site of First Hospital," *Angleton Times,* Sunday, April 20, 1986.
11. *Angleton Times,* February 21, 1960.
12. *Ibid.,* February 24, 1960.
13. John C. Duval, *Early Times in Texas* (Lincoln: University of Nebraska Press, 1986), 21.
14. Alcott, "Old Quintana," 7.
15. *Ibid.,* 5.
16. Creighton, *History,* 150.
17. Marie Beth Jones, *Peach Point Plantation* (Austin: University of Texas Press, 1982), 97.
18. *Angleton Times,* second in series, February 3, 1960.
19. Creighton, *History,* 10.
20. *Angleton Times,* fifth in series, February 14, 1960.
21. *Ibid.*
22. Puryear and Winfield, *Sandbars,* 52.
23. Bernice Lockhart, "Navigating Texas Rivers," master's thesis, St. Mary's University, 1946, 128.
24. *Angleton Times,* February 17, 1960.
25. *Angleton Times,* February 14, 1960.
26. Creighton, *History,* 271.
27. Puryear and Winfield, *Sandbars,* 5, 6.
28. Creighton, *History,* 232; *Angleton Times,* sixth in series, February 17, 1960.
29. Creighton, *History,* 310.
30. *Handbook of Texas,* 3: 107.

Velasco

1. "The Destiny of Buffalo Bayou," *Southwestern Historical Quarterly* 58 (October 1943): 94.

2. Newspaper clipping in Brazoria County Historical Museum dated Thursday, January 15, 1942.

3. Mattie Austin Hatcher, ed., *Letters of an Early American Traveler* (Dallas: Southwest Press, 1933) 35, 36.

4. Marker copy in files of Texas Historical Commission submitted by the Brazoria County Historical Survey Committee in 1969. Mrs. John Caldwell is credited with the research.

5. Marker copy; Mary Delaney Boddie, *Thunder on the Brazos* (Dallas: Taylor Publishing, 1978), 15.

6. Marie Beth Jones, "Fort Velasco Skirmish Paves Way for Independence," *Angleton Times,* April 20, 1986.

7. "Velasco," article in vertical file of Brazoria County Historical Museum.

8. James A. Creighton, *History of Brazoria County* (Waco: Texian Press, 1976), 63, 65, 66.

9. Boddie, *Thunder on the Brazos,* 12.

10. *Angleton Times,* Sunday, April 20, 1986; Boddie, *Thunder on the Brazos,* 17, 18.

11. Boddie, *Thunder on the Brazos,* 30, 31, 33.

12. Creighton, *History,* 80, 86, 100, 114, 115, 150, 162, 165, 167; Mrs. Oscar Johnson, *Plymouth Rock of Texas,* vertical file, Brazoria Co. Historical Museum, 2.

13. Hatcher, ed., *Letters,* 73.

14. *Ibid.*

15. *Angleton Times,* Sunday, April 20, 1985, and February 7, 1960; William Ransom Hogan, *The Texas Republic* (Austin: University of Texas Press, 1990), 131.

16. Pamela Ashworth Puryear and Nath Winfield, Jr., *Sandbars and Sternwheelers* (College Station: Texas A&M Press, 1989), 44.

17. Creighton, *History,* 232, 235, 240.

18. Puryear and Winfield, *Sandbars,* 106, 113–114.

19. Donald F. Schofield, *The Story of W. M. D. Lee* (Austin: University of Texas Press, 1985), 92–110.

20. Marie Beth Jones, "Harbor Chronology," in Brazoria County Historical Museum, vertical file "Port."

Slave Ditch

1. "The Brazos Canal," vertical file, Brazoria County Historical Museum, Angleton, 3, 4; Abner J. Strobel, *Old Plantations and Their Owners,* (Houston: Union National Bank, 1930), 8, 23, 29.

2. Gammel, Hans Peter Nielson, *Laws of Texas, 1822–1897* (Austin: The Gammel Book Company, 1898), 3: 571–576.

3. "Early Surfside Landmarks," prepared by A. A. Callihan, vertical file, Brazoria County Historical Museum.

4. Pamel Ashworth Puryear and Nath Winfield, Jr., *Sandbars and Sternwheelers* (College Station: Texas A&M Press, 1989), 21.

5. Washington *Texas Ranger* and *Lone Star*, July 13, 1854, and August 3, 1854.

6. James A. Creighton, *History of Brazoria County* (Waco: Texian Press, 1976), 212.

Freeport

1. Marie Beth Jones, "Brazos River bridge recognized in 'Ripley's Believe It or Not'," *Brazosport Facts*, July 20, 1990.

Old Brazoria

1. Robert Edward Crane, Jr., "Customs Service of the Republic of Texas," master's thesis, University of Texas, June 1939.

2. Mrs. Dilue Harris, "Reminiscences," Texas State Historical Association *Quarterly* 4 (January 1901): 170.

3. Mary Nixon Rogers, *A History of Brazoria County* (1958), 8; Mrs. T. C. Mandrell, "Brazoria, Texas," Brazoria County Historical Museum, Angleton, vertical file, 7.

4. Walter Prescott Webb, ed., *The Handbook of Texas* (Austin: Texas State Historical Association, 1952), 1: 207.

5. Mattie Austin Hatcher, ed., *Letters of an Early American Traveler* (Dallas: Southwest Press, 1933), 51, 116.

6. Mandrell, "Brazoria," 1, 2; "Town of Brazoria" information file in Brazoria County Historical Museum, Angleton, 6.

7. James A. Creighton, *History of Brazoria County* (Waco: Texian Press, 1976), 165, 178.

8. Billy J. Doree, "History of Maritime Trade Prior to 1836," master's thesis, University of Houston, 1962, 182, 183, 184, 185, 186, 187.

9. William Ransom Hogan, *The Texas Republic* (Austin: University of Texas Press, 1990), 70, 71.

10. Bernice Lockhart, "Navigating Texas Rivers," master's thesis, St. Mary's University, 1949, 14.

11. Ben Stuart, *Brazos and Colorado*, original articles in Rosenberg Library, Galveston, 23, 24.

12. Col. Edward Stiff, *The Texas Emigrant* (Waco: Texian Press, 1968), 64.

13. Pamela Ashworth Puryear and Nath Winfield, Jr., *Sandbars and Sternwheelers* (College Station: Texas A&M University Press, 1989), 50.

14. Mandrell, "Brazoria," 1.

15. Hogan, *Texas Republic*, 68, 69.

16. Harry M. Konwiser, *Texas Republic Postal System* (New York: Harry L. Lindquist, 1933), 19, 21, 23. A U.S. post office was established in Brazoria in 1846.

17. Charles Deaton, *Texas Postal History Handbook* (Privately printed, 1991), 78.

18. *Handbook of Texas*, 2: 623.

19. Joe Tom Davis, *Legendary Texians,* Vol. 3 (Austin: Eakin Press, 1986), 1–14.
20. Mandrell, "Brazoria," 55.
21. *Handbook of Texas,* 1: 582.
22. Mandrell, "Brazoria."
23. *Handbook of Texas,* 2: 891–892; Davis, *Legendary Texians,* 76, 77.
24. *Handbook of Texas,* 1: 922.
25. *Ibid.,* 1: 63.
26. Crane, "Customs Service," 9.
27. Customs Records, Texas State Archives, 4-26/35.
28. Amelia Williams and Eugene C. Barker, eds., *The Writings of Sam Houston* (Austin: University of Texas Press, 1940), 3: 51.
29. Hogan, *Texas Republic,* 217; Marie Beth Jones, *Peach Point Plantation* (Austin: University of Texas Press, 1982), 53.
30. Hogan, *Texas Republic,* 228.
31. Jones, *Peach Point Plantation,* 34, 37.
32. Hogan, *Texas Republic,* 252.
33. *Ibid.,* 263.
34. "Journal of Ammon Underwood, 1834–1838," *Southwestern Historical Quarterly* 32: 128–129.
35. Texas State Historical Association *Quarterly* 9: 206.
36. Mandrell, "Brazoria," 54.
37. Rogers, *Brazoria County,* 7.
38. Creighton, *History,* 31, 37, 43, 44.
39. *Ibid.,* 48, 52.
40. *Ibid.,* 65, 70, 71.
41. *Brazoria County Facts,* July 11, 1971 (Brazoria County Historical Museum), 83, 85, 86.

Bell's Landing/Marion/Columbia/West Columbia

1. Walter Prescott Webb, ed., *The Handbook of Texas* (Austin: Texas State Historical Association, 1952), 1: 141.
2. James Creighton, *History of Brazoria County* (Waco: Texian Press, 1976), 31.
3. *Historical Notebook of West Columbia and Brazoria County,* 1977, vertical file, Brazoria County Historical Museum; "Columbia," vertical file.
4. Mattie Austin Hatcher, ed., *Letters of an Early American Traveler* (Dallas: Southwest Press, 1933), 76.
5. Creighton, *History,* 142.
6. *Ibid.,* 145.
7. *Historical Notebook,* Brazoria County Museum.
8 Creighton, *History,* 145, 150.
9. Pamela Ashworth Puryear and Nath Winfield, Jr., *Sandbars and Sternwheelers* (College Station: Texas A&M Press, 1989), 41, 42, 43.
10. Marie Beth Jones, *Peach Point Plantation* (Austin: University of Texas Press), 34, 37.

11. T. R. Fehrenbach, *Lone Star* (New York: American Legacy Press, 1983), 187; Creighton, *History,* 112.
12. *Handbook of Texas,* 1: 846.
13. Creighton, *History,* 163, 204, 205, 217.
14. Harry M. Konwiser, *Texas Republic Postal System* (New York: Harry L. Lindquist, 1933), 19-23.
15. Charles Deaton, *Texas Postal History Handbook* (Privately printed, 1991), 92, 152.
16. Creighton, *History,* 141, 169.
17. *Ibid.,* 142.
18. Puryear and Winfield, *Sandbars,* 94-101.
19. Josephine Polley Golson, *Bailey's Light* (San Antonio: Naylor Company, 1952), 126-128.

Richmond

1. Walter Prescott Webb, ed., *The Handbook of Texas* (Austin: Texas State Historical Association, 1952), 2: 67.
2. J. L. Boone, historical marker application, vertical file, Richmond Library, 1; Jack Moore, *History of Richmond,* vertical file, Richmond Library, 1, 2.
3. Moore, *Richmond,* 1.
4. A. J. Sowell, *History of Fort Bend County* (Houston: W. H. Coyle & Co., 1904), 89, 90, 91.
5. *Ibid.,* 95, 96.
6. *Ibid.,* 99.
7. *Ibid.,* 99, 100.
8. Map, Santa Anna's Operations in Fort Bend County, April 11-15, vertical file, Richmond Library.
9. Sowell, *History,* 103.
10. Richmond *Herald-Coaster,* Sunday, January 18, 1976.
11. *Galveston News,* December 1850, reprinted in *Democratic Telegraph and Texas Register,* Houston, January 3, 1851.
12. *Galveston Weekly News,* July 19, 1856.
13. The *Texas Ranger and Brazos Guard,* January 16, 1849.
14. "Reminiscences," *Southwestern Historical Quarterly* 4: 179.
15. Houston *Telescope,* April 4, 1840.
16. Jonnie Lockhart Wallis and Laurence L. Hill, eds., *Sixty Years on the Brazos* (New York: Argonaut Press, Ltd., 1966), 84, 85.
17. Houston *Telescope,* March 29, 1843.
18. William Ransom Hogan, *The Texas Republic* (Austin: University of Texas Press, 1990), 70, 71.
19. *Galveston Weekly News,* September 2, 1851.
20. Minutes of Fort Bend County Commissioners Court, Book A, 124, 125.
21. Fort Bend County License Record Book A, 1.
22. S. G. Reed, *A History of Texas Railroads* (Houston: St. Clair Publishing Co., 1941), 56-62.

23. Pamela Ashworth Puryear and Nath Winfield, Jr., *Sandbars and Sternwheelers* (College Station: Texas A&M Press, 1989), 18–29.

24. *Handbook of Texas,* 2: 239–240.

25. Clarence R. Wharton, *History of Fort Bend County* (San Antonio: Naylor Company, 1939), 126, 127; Boone, historical marker application, 3.

26. Harry M. Konwiser, *Texas Republic Postal System* (New York: Harry L. Lindquist, 1933), 19, 20, 21; Charles Deaton, *Texas Postal History Handbook* (Privately printed, 1991), 135.

27. Wharton, *History,* 126, 153.

28. *Houston Chronicle,* Sunday, June 20, 1937.

Washington-on-the-Brazos

1. Walter Prescott Webb, ed., *The Handbook of Texas* (Austin: Texas State Historical Association, 1952), 2: 865.

2. Jonnie Lockhart Wallis and Laurence L. Hill, eds., *Sixty Years on the Brazos* (New York: Argonaut Press, Ltd., 1966), 11, 12.

3. John Henry Brown, *History of Texas* (St. Louis: Becktold & Co., 1892), 74.

4. Jack Vincent Donoghue, "Washington-on-the-Brazos," master's thesis, University of Texas, 37, 39; *Handbook of Texas,* 1: 856.

5. *Handbook of Texas,* 2: 865.

6. "Documents Relating to the Organization of the Municipality of Washington, Texas," *Southwestern Historical Quarterly* 10: 96–99.

7. Wallis and Hill, eds., *Sixty Years on the Brazos,* 13.

8. *Handbook of Texas,* 2: 865.

9. James Creighton, *History of Brazoria County* (Waco: Texian Press, 1976), 150; *Handbook of Texas,* 2: 865; Archie P. McDonald, ed., *Hurrah for Texas! The Diary of Adolphus Sterne 1838–1851* (Waco: Texian Press, 1969), 76.

10. J. K. Holland, "Reminiscences of Austin and Old Washington," *Southwestern Historical Quarterly* 2: 93; *Handbook of Texas,* 2: 865.

11. Holland, "Reminiscences," 94.

12. Donoghue, "Washington-on-the-Brazos," 34, 36; Wallis and Hill, eds., *Sixty Years on the Brazos,* 13; Charles F. Schmidt, *History of Washington County, Texas* (San Antonio: Naylor Co., 1949), 59; Sue Winton Moss, "Where Texas Was Born," *Texas Parks and Wildlife* (March 1992): 13, 14; *Handbook of Texas,* 2: 237.

13. Donoghue, "Wasington-on-the-Brazos," 40, 41, 42, 50.

14. Wallis and Hill, eds., *Sixty Years on the Brazos,* 40, 41.

15. William Ransom Hogan, *The Texas Republic* (Austin: University of Texas Press, 1990), 68, 69, 70.

16. "Reminiscences of Mrs. Dilue Harris," *Southwestern Historical Quarterly* 4: 157.

17. A. J. Sowell, *History of Fort Bend County* (Houston: W. H. Coyle and Co., 1904), 110–111; "Reminiscences of Mrs. Dilue Harris," 158.

18. Wallis and Hill, eds., *Sixty Years on the Brazos,* 84, 85.

19. *Ibid.,* 86.

20. Pamela Ashworth Puryear and Nath Winfield, Jr., *Sandbars and Sternwheelers* (College Station: Texas A&M Press, 1989), 64, 65, 66; Wallis and Hill, eds., *Sixty Years on the Brazos,* 86.

21. Wallis and Hill, eds., *Sixty Years on the Brazos,* 86.

22. Puryear and Winfield, *Sandbars,* 13, 23, 25, 55, 57.

23. S. G. Reed, *History of Texas Railroads* (Houston: St. Clair Publishing Co., 1941), 73; "Birth Given on Brazos," undated, unidentified clipping, vertical file, Navasota Library.

24. U.S. Census roll, 1850.

Port Sullivan

1. Pamela Ashworth Puryear and Nath Winfield, Jr., *Sandbars and Sternwheelers* (College Station: Texas A&M University Press, 1989), 55.

2. John Martin Brockman, "Port Sullivan, Texas: Ghost Town," master's thesis, Texas A&M University, 1968, 15, 16.

3. *Ibid.,* 46, 47.

4. Norman L. McCarver and Norman L. McCarver, Jr., *Hearne on the Brazos* (Century Press, 1958), 99.

5. Brockman, "Port Sullivan," 18, 28, 34, 35.

6. Galveston *Weekly Journal,* November 5, 1852; Brockman, "Port Sullivan," 51, 52, 67.

7. Galveston *Weekly Journal,* May 20, 1853.

8. *Galveston Weekly News,* April 11, 1854.

9. *Columbia Democrat,* April 15, 1854.

10. *Washington Texas Ranger,* March 30, 1854.

11. *Texian and Brazos Farmer,* January 28, 1843.

12. Brockman, "Port Sullivan," 38, 39.

13. Puryear and Winfield, *Sandbars,* 69; Brockman, "Port Sullivan," 58.

14. Puryear and Winfield, *Sandbars,* 73, 74.

15. Brockman, "Port Sullivan," 49.

16. *Lone Star,* May 15, May 29, 1852.

17. *Texas Ranger,* February 1853; Galveston *Weekly Journal,* May 20, 1853.

18. Puryear and Winfield, *Sandbars,* 87.

19. Brockman, "Port Sullivan," 79.

20. *Ibid.,* 61, 62, 81.

21. *Ibid.,* 74, 143, 151, 161.

22. McCarver and McCarver, *Hearne on the Brazos,* 100, 101.

23. Census figures, notes from oral interviews in Hearne and Calvert, as well as newspapers; McCarver and McCarver, *Hearne on the Brazos,* 100, 101; Brockman, "Port Sullivan," 79, 80, 81, 84.

24. From oral interview with N. L. McCarver in 1991.

25. Brockman, "Port Sullivan," 63; *Handbook of Texas,* 1: 709.

Plantation Landings

1. Walter Prescott Webb, ed., *The Handbook of Texas* (Austin: Texas State Historical Association, 1952), 1: 67, 79; Mattie Austin Hatcher, *Letters of an Early American Traveler* (Dallas: Southwest Press, 1933), 42, 72, 80, 123.

2. *Ibid.*, 43.

3. Pamela Ashworth Puryear and Nath Winfield, Jr., *Sandbars and Sternwheelers* (College Station: Texas A&M University Press, 1989), 8.

4. Hatcher, ed., *Letters,* 37, 80.

5. James A. Creighton, *History of Brazoria County* (Waco: Texian Press, 1976), 462.

6. *Handbook of Texas,* 2: 318.

7. Harry M. Konwiser, *Texas Republic Postal System* (New York: Harry L. Lindquist, 1933), 23.

8. Charles Deaton, *Texas Postal History Handbook* (Privately printed, 1991), 127; *Handbook of Texas,* 318.

9. Hatcher, ed., *Letters,* 123; Creighton, *History,* 115, 139, 150, 175, 180-181, 470.

10. *Freeport Facts,* June 18, 1931, from vertical file of Brazoria County Historical Museum, Angleton.

11. Creighton, *History,* 465.

12. Puryear and Winfield, *Sandbars,* 10.

13. *Handbook of Texas,* 1: 739.

14. Donald Jackson, *Voyages of the Steamboat Yellow Stone* (Norman: University of Oklahoma Press, 1987), 121-131.

15. *Handbook of Texas,* 2: 550.

16. Puryear and Winfield, *Sandbars,* 42, 43.

17. J. W. Baker, *History of Robertson County* (Waco: Robertson Co. Historical Survey Committee, 1979), 241, 242.

18. *Ibid.,* 242, 243.

19. Puryear and Winfield, *Sandbars,* 11.

San Luis

1. Plat of City of San Luis on file in Brazoria County (pictured in this book).

2. *Brazosport Facts,* July 22, 1979.

3. James A. Creighton, *History of Brazoria County* (Waco: Texian Press, 1976), 158; *Brazoria Facts,* July 22, 1979.

4. *Dallas Morning News,* August 6, 1939.

5. *Ibid.*

6. Mattie Austin Hatcher, ed., *Letters of an Early American Traveler* (Dallas: Southwest Press, 1933), 79, 80.

7. Coldwell, "History of San Luis Pass," vertical file, Brazoria County Historical Museum, Angleton, 2, 3; *Dallas Morning News,* August 6, 1939.

8. *Dallas Morning News,* August 6, 1936.

9. *San Luis Advocate,* September 14, 1840.

10. Coldwell, "History of San Luis," 3; *Dallas Morning News,* August 6, 1939.
11. *Bay City Tribune,* July 12, 1956 ("Galveston to San Luis").
12. Coldwell, "History of San Luis."

HOUSTON

1. Walter Prescott Webb, ed., *The Handbook of Texas* (Austin: Texas State Historical Association, 1952), 1: 29, 30.
2. David G. McComb, *Houston: A History* (Austin: University of Texas Press, 1981), 9, 11.
3. Frances Lide, "The History of Navigation on Buffalo Bayou, 1836-1845," master's thesis, University of Texas, 1937, 14.
4. *Ibid.,* 20, 21.
5. William Ransom Hogan, *The Texas Republic* (Austin: University of Texas Press, 1990), 72.
6. Marilyn McAdams Sibley, *The Port of Houston: A History* (Austin: University of Texas Press, 1985), 37, 38; Francis Richard Lubbock, *Six Decades in Texas: Memoirs of Francis Richard Lubbock,* C. W. Raines, ed. (Austin: Ben C. Jones & Co., Printers, 1900), 45, 46.
7. *Telegraph and Texas Register,* May 2, 1837.
8. Sibley, *Port of Houston,* 39.
9. Jonnie L. Wallis and Laurence L. Hill, eds., *Sixty Years on the Brazos,* (New York: Argonaut Press, Ltd., 1966), 79, 80.
10. Ed Bartholomew, *The Houston Story* (Houston: The Frontier Press of Texas), 62, 63.
11. Z. N. Morrell, *Flowers and Fruits in the Wilderness* (New York: Griffin Graphic Arts, 1966), 66.
12. Adele B. Looscan, "Harris County, 1822-45," *Southwestern Historical Quarterly* 58 (October 1915): 52, 53, 55, 56.
13. Bartholomew, *Houston Story,* 66, 67, 69.
14. Looscan, "Harris County," 57, 58, 59.
15. *Ibid.,* 60, 61, 62, 65, 66.
16. *Ibid.,* 69.
17. Jesse A. Ziegler, *Wave of the Gulf* (San Antonio: The Naylor Company, 1938), 9, 10, 56, 14, 53, 54.
18. *Ibid.,* 56.
19. *Ibid.,* 41, 42.
20. McComb, *Houston: A History*, 32.
21. *Handbook of Texas,* 1: 843, 2: 467; McComb, *Houston,* 19, 20, 21.
22. McComb, *Houston,* 21, 22, 23, 24.
23. Sibley, *Port of Houston,* 74, 75.
24. *Ibid.,* 26, 27.
25. Ziegler, *Wave of the Gulf,* 92-96.
26. Sibley, *Port of Houston,* 21, 34, 35, 37, 40, 48, 49.
27. McComb, *Houston,* 34, 35.

BUFFALO BAYOU/TRINITY, GALVESTON BAY LANDINGS

1. Marilyn McAdams Sibley, *The Port of Houston: A History* (Austin: University of Texas Press, 1985), 17, 20, 21.

2. Walter Prescott Webb, ed., *The Handbook of Texas* (Austin: Texas State Historical Association, 1952), 2: 234.

3. Robert S. Gray, ed., *A Visit to Texas in 1831* (Houston: Cordovan Press, 1975), 50.

4. William Fairfax Gray, *From Virginia to Texas* . . . (Houston: Fletcher Young Publishing Co., 1965), 151.

5. *Handbook of Texas,* 2: 97; Charles Deaton, *Texas Postal History Handbook* (Privately printed, 1991), 116; Adele Looscan, "Harris County," *Southwestern Historical Quarterly* 58: 10.

6. Writings of Ben Stuart, reporter for *Galveston News* starting before 1900, from collection in Rosenberg Library, Galveston, 11, 12.

7. Deaton, *Texas Postal History Handbook,* 139.

8. Looscan, "Harris County," 11, 12, 13.

9. *Ibid.,* 9.

10. "Location of the town of San Jacinto, in the 1820s, through 1859," Grover Papers, Rosenberg Library, Galveston; *Handbook of Texas,* 1: 741.

Harrisburg

1. Adele B. Looscan, "Harris County, 1822–1845," *Southwestern Historical Quarterly* 58: 7 f9; Walter Prescott Webb, ed., *The Handbook of Texas* (Austin: Texas State Historical Association, 1952), 1: 739, 775.

2. *Handbook of Texas,* 1: 775.

3. *Ibid.,* 1: 774, 775.

4. Looscan, "Harris County," 9, 11, 12.

5. *Ibid.,* 9, 11, 12; *Handbook of Texas,* 774.

6. Looscan, "Harris County," 14.

7. *Handbook of Texas,* 1: 778.

8. *Texas Almanac,* 1861, 76, 77; Looscan, "Harris County," 26, 27, 32.

9. *Handbook of Texas,* 1: 775, 778.

10. *Ibid.,* 1: 217, 240, 778.

11. Charles Deaton, *Texas Postal History Handbook* (Privately printed, 1991), 103; Harry M. Konwiser, *Texas Republic Postal System* (New York: Harry L. Lindquist, 1933), 21.

12. *Handbook of Texas,* 1: 779.

Galveston

1. Virginia Eisenhour, *Galveston: A Different Place* (1983), 6; David G. McComb, *Galveston: A History* (Austin: University of Texas Press, 1986), 42. (It is obvious that writers have credited more than ten men as being on the Galveston City Company. No doubt some dropped out and

others were added.) Walter Prescott Webb, ed., *The Handbook of Texas* (Austin: Texas State Historical Association, 1952), 2: 170.

2. Michel Brindamour Menard file in Rosenberg Library at Galveston, 1, 2; *Handbook of Texas,* 2: 170.

3. Joe Tom Davis, *Legendary Texians,* Vol. 3 (Austin: Eakin Press, 1986), 6, 7.

4. *Galveston News,* February 27, 1910.

5. Eisenhour, *Galveston,* 40, 41.

6. *Ibid.,* 43.

7. Ben Stuart, "Texas Steamboat Days," unpublished work held in Rosenberg Library, Galveston, 9. (Stuart was a prolific writer for the *Galveston News* for many years about Galveston's early trade development.) Charles W. Hayes, *History of Galveston* (Cincinnati: 1879), 1: 276, 277, 279.

8. *Handbook of Texas,* 2: 809.

9. Stuart, "Steamboat Days," 10, 11, 12.

10. Eisenhour, *Galveston,* 45; Hayes, *Galveston,* 1: 293fn.

11. Hayes, *Galveston,* 1: 286–290.

12. Eisenhour, *Galveston,* 59.

13. *Galveston News,* August 1, 1909.

14. *Galveston Daily News,* November 8, 1908, 17.

15. "Waterfront Properties Have Developed From Modest Beginning," Galveston File, G-11, Rosenberg Library, Galveston.

16. Eugene Hollon and Ruth Lapham Butler, eds., *William Bollaert's Texas* (Norman: University of Oklahoma Press, 1980), 17, 18.

17. *Handbook of Texas,* 1: 224; *Galveston News,* November 8, 1908, 17.

18. *Handbook of Texas,* 2: 200; Hayes, *Galveston,* 314.

19. *Handbook of Texas,* 2: 586.

20. *Galveston News,* March 17, 1907.

21. Eisenhour, *Galveston,* 57.

22. *Ibid.,* 57, 58, 59, 60.

23. Ben Stuart, "The Morgan Steamship Line," unpublished material in Rosenberg Library, Galveston, 18, 21.

24. W. T. Block, *Cotton Bales, Keelboats, and Sternwheelers: A History of the Trinity River Trade, 1838–1893* (Privately printed), 17, 18, 22, 23.

25. *Ibid.,* 24, 25, 26, 27.

26. *Ibid.,* 29.

27. Ben Stuart, "Some Noted Marine Disasters," unpublished writings in Rosenberg Library of Galveston.

28. *Galveston News,* April 7, 1907, 20.

29. *Ibid.,* March 31, 1907, 24.

30. *Handbook of Texas,* 1: 662–663.

FREEBOOTERS/BUCCANEERS

1. *Galveston News,* March 3, 1907.
2. Walter Prescott Webb, ed., *The Handbook of Texas* (Austin: Texas State Historical Association, 1952), 1: 78, 79.
3. *Galveston News,* March 3, 1907.
4. *Ibid.*
5. *Handbook of Texas,* 2: 5, 6.
6. *Galveston News,* March 3, 1907.
7. Virginia Eisenhour, *Galveston: A Different Place* (1983), 5.
8. W. T. Block, *A Buccaneer Family in Spanish East Texas* (Privately printed, 1990), 3, 4.
9. *Ibid.,* 4, 5.
10. *Ibid.,* 5, 6.
11. *Ibid.,* 6, 7.
12. *Galveston News,* March 3, 1907.

RIO GRANDE RIVER

1. Walter Prescott Webb, ed., *The Handbook of Texas* (Austin: Texas State Historical Association, 1952), 2: 474-475, 1: 67.
2. Milo Kearney, ed., *Studies in Brownsville History* (Pan American University at Brownsville, 1986), 77, 78.
3. *Handbook of Texas,* 2: 475.
4. *Ibid.,* 1: 228-230.
5. Tom Lea, *The King Ranch* (Boston: Little, Brown and Co., 1957), 1: 36, 37.
6. *Ibid.,* 37, 38.
7. *Ibid.,* 39, 40, 45.
8. *Handbook of Texas,* 2: 185.
9. Kearney, *Studies,* 78, 141.
10. Lea, *King Ranch,* 1: 47, 48.
11. *Ibid.,* 50, 58, 59.
12. Milo Kearney and Anthony Knopp, *Boom and Bust* (Austin: Eakin Press, 1991), 67-73.
13. Milo Kearney, *More Studies in Brownsville History* (Brownsville: Pan American University, 1989), 194, 195.
14. *Ibid.,* 196; *Handbook of Texas,* 2: 475.
15. Lea, *King Ranch,* 1: 235; John Salmon Ford, *Rip Ford's Texas* (Austin: University of Texas Press, 1987), 370-372, 376-402.
16. Lea, *King Ranch,* 1: 239, 240, 242.
17. Kearney, *More Studies,* 143.
18. Lea, *King Ranch,* 1: 243, 244, 247.
19. *Ibid.,* 1: 252-255.
20. Kearney and Knopp, *Boom and Bust,* 159, 164.
21. *Ibid.,* 173, 174.

22. Charles Deaton, *Texas Postal History Handbook* (Privately printed, 1991), 135; Lea, *King Ranch,* 1: 25.

23. "Rio Grande City," (Starr County) Texas Historical Commission marker copy file, Austin, Texas.

24. Lea, *King Ranch,* 1: 25, 26, 37, 43, 221, 225, 226, Ford, *Rip Ford's Texas,* 361-362.

25. Ford, *Rip Ford's Texas,* 359.

26. Texas Historical Commission marker copy; Ford, *Rip Ford's Texas,* 361, 370.

27. *Handbook of Texas,* 2: 475.

28. *Ibid.,* 2: 394.

29. *Ibid.,* 1: 806.

Bibliography

Books

Anderson, John Q. *Tales of Frontier Texas 1830–1860.* Dallas: Southern Methodist University Press, 1966.

Baker, J. W. *History of Robertson County.* Waco: Robertson County Historical Survey Committee, 1979.

Bartholomew, Ed. *The Houston Story.* Houston: The Frontier Press of Texas, 1951.

Block, W. T. *Cotton Bales, Keelboats, and Sternwheelers: A History of the Trinity River Trade, 1838–1893.* Privately printed, 1978.

———. *A Buccaneer Family in Spanish East Texas.* Privately printed, 1990.

Boddie, Mary Delaney. *Thunder on the Brazos.* Dallas: Taylor Publishing, 1978.

Braman, D. E. E. *History of Texas.* Philadelphia: J. B. Lippincott & Co., 1857.

Brown, John Henry. *History of Texas.* St. Louis: Becktold & Co., 1892.

Cameron, Rebecca M., and Ruth Lester. *Jefferson on the Bayou.* "Historic Homes." Marshall: The Demmer Co., Inc., 1966.

Chandler, Barbara Overton, and J. Ed Howe. *History of Texarkana and Bowie and Miller Counties.* Texarkana: Texas-Arkansas, 1939.

Clark, Pat B. *History of Clarksville and Old Red River County.* Dallas: Mathis, Van Nort & Co., 1937.

Creighton, James A. *History of Brazoria County.* Waco: Texian Press, 1976.

Davis, Joe Tom. *Legendary Texians.* Vol. 3. Austin: Eakin Press, 1986.

Dean, Winnie Mims. *Jefferson, Queen of the Cypress.* Dallas: Mathis Van Nort & Co., 1953.

Deaton, Charles. *Texas Postal History Handbook.* Privately printed, 1991.

Dobie, J. Frank. *On the Open Range.* Dallas: The Southwest Press, 1940.

Drago, Henry Sinclair. *The Steamboaters.* New York: Dodd, Mead & Company, 1967.

Duval, John C. *Early Times in Texas.* Lincoln: University of Nebraska Press, 1986.

Eisenhour, Virginia. *Galveston: A Different Place.* 1983. Paperback in Galveston Library.

Fannin County Folks, Fannin County, Tex. Dallas: Taylor Publishing Co., 1977.

Ford, John Salmon. *Rip Ford's Texas.* Austin: University of Texas Press, 1987.

Gammel, Hans Peter Nielson. *Laws of Texas, 1822–1897.* Vol. 3. Austin: The Gammel Book Company, 1898.

Golson, Josephine Polley. *Bailey's Light.* San Antonio: Naylor Company, 1952.

Gray, Robert S., ed. *A Visit to Texas in 1831.* Houston: Cordovan Press, 1975.

Gray, William Fairfax. *From Virginia to Texas* . . . Houston: Fletcher Young Publishing Co., 1965.

Grayson Co. Frontier Village. *History of Grayson County,* Vol. 2. Tulsa: Heritage Publishing Co., 1981.

Hackney, V. H. *Port Caddo – A Vanished Village* and *Vignettes of Harrison County.* Marshall: The Marshall National Bank, 1965.

Hatcher, Mattie Austin, ed. *Letters of an Early American Traveler: Mary Austin Holley.* Dallas: Southwest Press, 1933.

Hogan, William Ransom. *The Texas Republic.* Austin: University of Texas Press, fifth paperback printing 1990.

Hollon, Eugene, and Ruth Lapham Butler, eds. *William Bollaert's Texas.* Norman: University of Oklahoma Press, 1980.

Hughes, Fannie May Barbee. *Legends of Texas Rivers.* Dallas: Mathis, Van Nort & Co., 1937.

Hyden, Julien Capers. *Texas: The Land of Beginning Again.* Waco: Texian Press, 1990.

Jackson, Donald. *Voyages of the Steamboat Yellow Stone.* Norman: University of Oklahoma Press, 1987.

James, Marquis. *The Raven.* Indianapolis, IN: The Bobbs-Merrill, Co., 1929.

Jones, Marie Beth. *Peach Point Plantation.* Austin: University of Texas Press, 1982.

Kearney, Milo, ed. *Studies in Brownsville History.* Brownsville: Pan American University, 1986.

———, ed. *More Studies in Brownsville History.* Brownsville: Pan American University, 1989.

Kearney, Milo, and Anthony Knopp. *Boom and Bust.* Austin: Eakin Press, 1991.

Konwiser, Harry M. *Texas Republic Postal System.* New York: Harry L. Lindquist, 1933.

Lea, Tom. *The King Ranch.* Vol. 1. Boston: Little, Brown and Co., 1957.

Lubbock, Francis Richard. *Six Decades in Texas: Memoirs of Francis Richard Lubbock.* C. W. Raines, ed. Austin: Ben C. Jones & Co., Printers, 1900.

Lucas, Mattie Davis, and Mita Holsapple Hall. *History of Grayson County.* Sherman: Scruggs Printing Co., 1936.

McCarver, Norman L., and Norman L. McCarver, Jr. *Hearne on the Brazos.* Century Press, 1958.

McComb, David G. *Galveston: A History.* Austin: University of Texas Press, 1986.

———. *Houston: A History.* Austin: University of Texas Press, 1981.
McClung, Mildred Mays. *Caddo Lake: Mysterious Swampland.* "Marquis James." Texarkana: Southwest Printers and Publishers, 1974.
McKay, Mrs. Arch, and Mrs. H. A. Spellings. *A History of Jefferson, Marion County.* Jefferson: Jimplecute Printing, 1936.
Moore, Wyatt. *Every Sun that Rises.* Thad Sitton and James H. Conrad, eds. Austin: University of Texas Press, 1985.
Morrell, Zachariah N. *Flowers and Fruits in the Wilderness.* New York: Griffin Graphic Arts, 1966.
Neville, A. W. *Red River Valley Then and Now.* Paris, TX: North Texas Publishing Co., 1948.
———. *History of Lamar County.* Paris, TX: North Texas Publishing Co., 1937.
Pierce, Gerald S. *Texas Under Arms.* Austin: Encino Press, 1969.
Puryear, Pamela Ashworth, and Nath Winfield, Jr., *Sandbars and Sternwheelers.* College Station: Texas A&M Press, 1989.
Reed, S. G. *A History of Texas Railroads.* Houston: St. Clair Publishing Co., 1941.
Rogers, Mary Nixon. *A History of Brazoria County, Tex., Old Plantations and Their Owners of Brazoria County, Tex.* Abner J. Strobel and Travis Smith (earlier writers), [S.1.: s.n.], 1958.
Scheffelin, J. J. *Bowie County, Texas, Basic Background Book.* Privately printed, n.d.
Schmidt, Charles F. *History of Washington County, Texas.* San Antonio: Naylor Co., 1949.
Schofield, Donald F. *The Story of W. M. D. Lee.* Austin: University of Texas Press, 1985.
Sibley, Marilyn McAdams. *The Port of Houston: A History.* Austin: University of Texas Press, 1985.
Sowell, A. J. *History of Fort Bend County.* Houston: W. H. Coyle & Co., 1904.
Stiff, Col. Edward. *The Texas Emigrant.* Waco: Texian Press, 1968.
Tarpley, Fred. *Jefferson: Riverport to the Southwest.* Austin: Eakin Press, 1983.
Tyson, Carl Newsom. *Red River in Southeastern History.* Norman: University of Oklahoma Press, 1981.
Waller County Survey Committee. *History of Waller County.* Waco: Texian Press, 1973.
Wallis, Jonnie, and Laurence L. Hill, eds. *Sixty Years on the Brazos: The Life and Letters of Dr. John Washington Lockhart..* New York: Argonaut Press, Ltd., 1966.
Webb, Walter Prescott, ed. *The Handbook of Texas.* 2 vols. Austin: Texas State Historical Association, 1952.
Wharton, Clarence R. *History of Fort Bend County.* San Antonio: Naylor Company, 1939.
Williams, Amelia, and Eugene C. Barker, eds. *The Writings of Sam Houston.* Austin: University of Texas Press, 1940.
Ziegler, Jesse A. *Wave of the Gulf.* San Antonio: The Naylor Company, 1938.

Unpublished

Bowers, E. W. Papers. In possession of granddaughters Anne Evetts and Dorothy Bonham, Clarksville, Texas.

A History of Present Red River County, Texas, Area Through 1845. Vertical file on Red River County, Clarksville Public Library.

Clippings on steamboats. Vertical file, Clarksville Public Library.

Moore, Jack. *History of Richmond.* Vertical file, Richmond Library.

Stagecoach Road. Pamphlet in Harrison County Museum, no date or publisher.

Public Records

Fort Bend County Commissioners Court. Minutes, Book A.

Fort Bend County License Record Book A.

Texas Historical Commission, Austin. Historical marker copy files.

U.S. Census roll, 1850.

Archival Materials

Brazoria County Historical Museum. Vertical file (covers all of Brazoria County as well as Brazos River).

Grove Papers. "Location of the town of San Jacinto, in the 1820s, through 1859." Rosenberg Library, Galveston.

Lentz Papers. Harrison County Historical Museum.

Plymouth Rock (Velasco, Texas). Vertical file, Brazoria County Historical Museum, Angleton.

Stuart, Ben. *Brazos and Colorado.* Original articles. Writings of Ben Stuart, reporter for *Galveston News* starting before 1900. Collection in Rosenberg Library, Galveston.

Newspapers

Angleton Times

Clarksville Northern Standard

Columbia Democrat

Dallas Times Herald

Galveston Daily News

Galveston Weekly News

Houston *Democratic Telegraph and Texas Register*

Houston Telegraph and Texas Register

Houston *Telescope*

Jefferson Jimplecute

Marshall News Messenger

National Observer, The

Richmond *Herald-Coaster*

Texas Ranger and Brazos Guard

Waco Weekly-Tribune

Washington *Texas Ranger* and *Lone Star*

Theses

Brockman, John Martin. "Port Sullivan, Texas: Ghost Town." Master's thesis, Texas A&M University, 1968.
Crane, Robert Edward, Jr. "Customs Service of the Republic of Texas." Master's thesis, University of Texas, June 1939.
Donoghue, Jack Vincent. "Washington-on-the-Brazos." Master's thesis, University of Texas.
Doree, Billy J. "History of Maritime Trade Prior to 1836." Master's thesis, University of Houston, 1962.
Lide, Frances. "The History of Navigation on Buffalo Bayou, 1836–1845." Master's thesis, University of Texas, 1937.
Lockhart, Bernice. "Navigating Texas Rivers (1821–1900)." Master's thesis, St. Mary's University, 1946.
Watson, Judy. "Jefferson, Texas, The Rise and Decline." Master's thesis, Texas Christian University, January 1967.

Pamphlets, Speeches, Interviews, Letters, Clippings

Hale, Mary Kate, of Clarksville. Interview on June 1, 1992.
"Diamond Bessie Case, One of Most Notorious in Texas History." Newspaper clipping in Jefferson Carnegie Library, vertical file, undated and unidentified.
Caddo Facts and Figures, Legends and History, Harrison County. Unidentified clippings in vertical file, Harrison County Historical Museum
Boon, Daniel Horace. "Monterey." Paper submitted to East Texas State Teachers College, Commerce, summer term 1947. (Boon was county judge of Cass County and noted local historian.)
"Marion County." Vertical file, Jefferson Carnegie Public Library.
Map of Caddo Parish, Louisiana, enlarged showing part of Harrison and Marion counties dated 1871. Harrison County Historical Commission.
Annual Report of Clinton or Van Zant Lodge No. 42 for year 1848 (the Monterey Masonic Lodge). Vertical file, Jefferson Carnegie Library.
Bonner, Rev. Billy B. Booklet prepared by Lions Club, 1959. Vertical file, Jefferson Carnegie Library.
Eudora, Solomon, and V. H. Hackney file. Harrison County Historical Museum.
Jones, Sr., Franklin, Marshall attorney and Marshall County historian. (Contains interviews of Wyatt Moore about Caddo Lake.)
Map of Santa Anna's Operations in Fort Bend County, April 11–15. Vertical file, Richmond Library.
Eisenhour, Virginia. "Galveston: A Different Place." Galveston Library, paperback booklet, 1983.
McCarver, N. L. Oral interview, 1991.
Jones, Mary Beth. *Brazosport Facts,* July 20, 1990. "Brazos River bridge recognized in 'Ripley's Believe It Or Not'." Brazoria County Historical Museum, vertical file.

Periodicals, Journals

Louisiana Historical Quarterly
Southwestern Historical Quarterly
Texas Highways
Texas Parks and Wildlife

Index